THE ST. KITTS
CONNECTION

ALAN TONKS

The St. Kitts Connection

This book is written to provide information and motivation to readers. Its purpose is not to render any type of psychological, legal, or professional advice of any kind. The content is the sole opinion and expression of the author, and not necessarily that of the publisher.

This book is a work of fiction, inspired in part by real events. Any events not clearly in the public domain are products of the author's imagination. Most names in this book have been changed to protect the privacy of those involved.

Copyright © 2024 by Alan Tonks.

All rights reserved. No part of this book may be reproduced, transmitted, or distributed in any form by any means, including, but not limited to, recording, photocopying, or taking screenshots of parts of the book, without prior written permission from the author or the publisher. Brief quotations for noncommercial purposes, such as book reviews, permitted by Fair Use of the U.S. Copyright Law, are allowed without written permissions, as long as such quotations do not cause damage to the book's commercial value. For permissions, write to the publisher, whose address is stated below.

Printed in the United States of America.

ISBN 979-8-9915908-7-7 (Paperback)
ISBN 979-8-9915908-9-1 (Hardback)
ISBN 979-8-9915908-8-4 (Digital)

Library of Congress Control Number: 2024926829

Lettra Press books may be ordered through booksellers or by contacting:

Published by Pinnacle Hybrid Publishing
14 2nd Street Budd Lake NJ 07828, USA
(860) 634-5535
info@pinnaclehybridpublishing.com

CHAPTER 1

Rajiv Ratma Gandhi, president of the Indian Congress Party, while campaigning for India's presidency in the upcoming general election, arrived at Meenambakkam Airport in Madras at 8:30 p.m. on May 21, 1991. He was on his way to an election rally, despite threats from Sikh extremists, Muslim fundamentalists, and the Liberation Tigers of Tamil Eelam. He was used to the threats. There had been a number of them over the past few years, including three assassination attempts.

At the airport, he addressed the media hordes, and by nine p.m., he was in a bulletproof car headed for Sriperumbudur, forty-eight kilometers southwest of Madras. His fifteen-vehicle motorcade included mostly Congress leaders, journalists, and police. Gandhi stopped to address the crowds wherever they gathered along the way, including a stop at the Indira Gandhi statue, where he placed a garland for his deceased mother. She had been assassinated seven years before by two of her Sikh bodyguards as she left her estate to attend a British television interview. Gandhi had been the seventh prime minister of India—from October 31, 1984, when his mother died, to December 2, 1989, when he resigned after a general election defeat. And now he was running on the promise of leading India into becoming a world economy with the first step being the installation of a multi billion dollar nationwide communication system.

Born in 1944, Rajiv was the eldest son of Indira and Feroze Gandhi. Rajiv was a pilot for Indian Airways and had always avoided politics. His brother, Sanjay Gandhi, was considered the heir apparent to their mother, but died in a plane crash in 1980. When Indira Gandhi was assassinated, Rajiv was nominated prime minister by the National Congress Party, and his fate was sealed.

Gandhi turned out to be a technocrat who sought to modernize India through investments in technology. However, he surrounded himself with buddies and cronies and did little to ease chronic poverty or the vast inequities within Indian society. Like his mother, he was not able to contain the political problems afflicting India and found refuge with international entanglements and commitments.

He committed the Indian Peace-Keeping Force (IPKF) to Sri Lanka to help its government stop the militants' pushing for a separate Tamil homeland. The five years he was in office were marred by scandals and allegations of corruption on such a huge scale that he lost the 1989 election.

Gandhi arrived in Sriperumbudur for the election rally. His bodyguards exited the car first, and immediately took protective positions. Then Gandhi appeared, smiling and waving to his cheering supporters. Police officials formed as he entered a barricaded pathway. He was soon covered in petals from different colored flowers thrown from the crowd. A special stage had been constructed with a crude makeshift podium where a number of dignitaries waited to receive him.

A young woman suddenly emerged from the crowd with a sandalwood garland fighting off police attempts to stop her. Gandhi noticed the incident and motioned police to let her approach him. He smiled and held his hands out to embrace her. She knelt at his feet.

A sudden deafening blast violently shook the ground as a huge cloud of dust and debris appeared over what was, a celebrating crowd of Gandhi supporters. Gandhi was dead along with twenty three others. Numerous supporters and police were wounded.

Dhanu, the nondescript twenty-five year old woman was a suicide bomber. The garland had helped conceal a highly sophisticated and powerful device with a foolproof triggering mechanism. The RDX plastic explosive, with the help of small metal pellets, achieved maximum impact.

Ten days later, on May 31, 1991, the Central Intelligence Bureau concluded that the terrorist act had likely been the work of the Liberation Tigers of Tamil Eslam, or at least that's what the narrative was supposed to be.

CHAPTER 2

Terry Downes was a vice president at the Bank of Wilmington in Wilmington Delaware where he managed a billion dollar real estate loan portfolio. He had an excellent record at the bank having financed numerous multi million dollar projects in Delaware and Pennsylvania. He was also active in the Delaware Bankers Association and therefore well known in the banking circles. He was 32 years old and the target of many management recruiters looking to fill 'lucrative opportunities' on behalf of their banking clients.

Downes had been contacted a number of times by head hunters to see if he would be 'interested in a move' but had never given them much thought, except for when he was passed up for a significant promotion.

The Bank of Wilmington was a very staid and conservative institution organized in 1907 by several family members of the St. Clair Paper Company, a huge multinational company based in Wilmington. Their influence and control had remained in the bank as evidenced by the fact that several family members remained on the bank's board of directors. In addition, there were many employees that were direct descendants of the founders which often created an uncomfortable environment at the bank.

Over the years, Downes had witnessed the role of politics being played in the movement of management personnel but wasn't personally affected, except for when he was passed over for an anticipated promotion. He thought that the fact that he was an 'outsider' was the reason.

So, when he received an inquiry from a management recruiter, he gave it a little more thought.

"Mr Downes, my name is Bud Gardner, management recruiter, Gardner and Associates. calling to see if you'd be interested in making a change?"

"What do you have?" replied Downes, who ordinarily would have simply responded - 'no thanks'.

"A client in the South East has retained us to search for a Vice Chairman and Chief Loan Officer. Would that be of interest to you?"

"I'd be interested in knowing who and where your client is," replied Downes with some trepidation.

Bud Gardner was a professional, forty year old management recruiter whose firm had gained the reputation of being one of the most reliable companies in the business. They were known to have successfully filled a number of top management positions in many large financial institutions in the country..

After signing a mutual non-disclosure agreement, protecting both Gardner's client and Terry Downes, Gardner disclosed the name and location of his client.

"The name of the bank is First Community Bank and Trust, (FCB)" announced Gardner, handing Downes a recent annual report of the bank.

First Community Bank and Trust was a two billion dollar bank located in Palm Beach, Florida. It had 10 branches, located in Palm Beach, Martin and Broward Counties, 500 employees and was the largest independent (non member of the federal reserve) bank in the South East. The banks' chairman, Bruce Stanier, age 56, had taken the bank from a new charter in 1974 with 10 employees, to a thriving regional bank heavily vested in real estate and land development. Jim North, Vice Chairman, had been with Stanier since its inception and had decided to retire, leaving an opening in their top management. Stanier was taking advantage of the massive population growth in South Florida and was available to assist land developers and construction companies in all aspects of financing.

"They're located in Palm Beach, Florida, about 50 miles North of Fort Lauderdale. The bank is the largest independent bank in Florida with assets of over two billion. The bank was founded in sixty four by Bruce Stanier, Chairman and a guy named Jim North who was the Vice Chairman. North recently retired. Stanier currently owns about 70 percent - not sure if North is still a shareholder. They have 12 branches in Palm Beach, Broward and Martin counties and are looking to expand further. The bank is heavily vested in real estate related loans and Stanier is looking for an experienced lender that can manage the lending functions and upgrade the 'backroom' operations of the bank. The job title is Vice Chairman and Chief Loan Officer. He will negotiate the employment package with you, but I can tell you that the pay will be in the six figures, stock options, insurance, moving expense reimbursement etc." explained Gardner. Can I send Stanier a copy of your resume?"

Downes, although a little skeptical, agreed and awaited a date and time for an interview with Stanier at his office in North Palm Beach, Florida.

Terry Downes arrived in Palm Beach feeling a little apprehensive since this was much more responsibility, albeit in a smaller bank. Despite management problems at The Wilmington Bank, he had been treated very well so he felt a little twinge of guilt. But he was convinced that this was the opportunity he had been looking for, and there couldn't be a better place to live than Palm Beach.

A driver met Downes at Palm Beach International Airport, driving a late-model Mercedes convertible with the top down. It was probably meant to impress Downes, even though the hot steamy summer weather didn't lend itself to riding in a convertible. So Downes was soggy and a little bit miserable by the time they arrived at the bank, about thirty minutes from the airport..

The "headquarters" of First Community was a two-story, stand-alone building on a busy road with a view of the Intracoastal Waterway at front and the Atlantic Ocean at back.. Very unusual and small for a bank this size, thought Downes, who was expecting a conventional main office building of sorts.

At the entrance, a huge American flag limped along in the humid air atop a twenty-foot flagpole. Underneath there was another flag with the logo "FCB" - the People's Bank." Inside the entrance to the left was a secretary and private waiting area, behind which was the chairman's suite.

A lobby that included five teller stations encompassed most of the first floor. The plush, dark green carpeting, dark mahogany wood, and brass fixtures created a very elegant décor. The lobby was filled with antiques and fine art. Crystal chandeliers hung from the ceiling and a silver coffee urn and cookies were set out for customers who could relax on two antique sofas. Remington statues nestled amid tropical foliage and fresh-cut flowers and an attractive young woman welcomed customers as they entered the bank. This looked like a bank that only catered to high-end customers - fitting for Palm Beach.

On the second floor was the commercial loan department, a very plush and spacious area with several private offices. It appeared that no expense was spared in creating an impressive decor for bank customers.

Downes followed the driver to the private waiting area, where they met Sheryl Mitchell, Stanier's secretary. "Mr. Stanier and Mr. North are expecting you," she said, as she dialed an extension to announce their arrival.

Without any wait, Stanier opened his office door, hand extended. "Welcome, Terry! Come in and have a seat."

Downes walked into a huge office filled with more exquisite antiques and artwork. What really caught his attention, though, was the biggest vase of fresh-cut flowers he had ever seen. How odd, he thought. It wasn't something he had expected to see in a bank executive's office.

"Terry, I'd like you to meet Jim North, our former vice chairman." Jim is stepping down after making a huge contribution to the bank's success.

North remained seated on a sofa across the room from Stanier's desk as Downes shook his hand and took a seat across from him. Sheryl Mitchell promptly appeared with coffee and cookies.

Jim North wore tacky white jeans, a red polka-dot shirt, red sports coat, white shoes, and no socks. Very tanned and in his early fifties, he had prematurely white hair, a white handlebar mustache, and did not appear to be the typical bank executive. Nor did he seem the least bit interested in meeting or speaking with Downes.

Stanier, by contrast, was immaculately dressed in a light tan suit with white shirt and tie and very verboise - the type that had to blurt everything out in one nonstop sentence, making it difficult to figure out what the question—or the point—might be.

When Downes did get to talk, he focused on the possible regulatory changes that would allow banks to branch outside their states and asked about the impact on First Community if they came to fruition. He emphasized the technological changes he thought would have an even bigger impact on banks and their ability to remain competitive.

North gruffly cut him off, "If it ain't real estate related, we ain't interested, no matter what changes are in store for banks."

Stanier backed him up, sort of: "Jim is right. We make all our money on real-estate deals. But we must be up-to-date in our back office," he said, with a little snicker, which Downes found immediately irritating.

"You mind if I ask why you're stepping down Jim?" asked Downes

North paused while he lit a huge cigar. "Personal reasons."

North then went on to talk about his relationship with Stanier, how they had gotten involved in banking in the sixties, and his desire to get more involved in real-estate deals on a personal basis. He felt good about the bank and he thought he'd done a good job in the operating areas.

"It's time for somebody else to take over, but don't worry: I'll still be around," North assured Downes. "I still have a bunch of shares in the bank."

When Downes asked about the overall management structure, Stanier attempted to draw an organizational chart on a notepad. After identifying the managers and supervisors, he checked off the names of those he thought were doing a good job and placed an X through the names of those who needed to be replaced.

"Do you have a long term plan for the bank?" asked Downes.

"We have a budget system, but we don't do any formal planning," said Stanier

"How can you plan, when we don't know when these deals will come up," interrupted North.

Really! Thought Downes

Stanier then spent some time talking about his branch network, how successful they had been in circumventing the regulations, and his desire to expand into counties where real-estate projects were taking off.

Neither asked about Downes's background or experience, and the whole meeting lasted no more than fifteen minutes. It ended when Stanier looked at his watch and abruptly stood up, saying that he had an important meeting scheduled. He told Downes how much of a pleasure it had been to meet him and looked forward to talking again.

Downes was flabbergasted. Totally unimpressed and thought it was a complete waste of his time.

"Jim will show you our 'operations facility' in Lake Worth, where his office used to be. "He'll introduce you to some of our people, then we'll discuss making you an offer to join us and let you know," Stanier said, as he shepherded them out the door.

North looked a little putout but Downes was too stunned to really notice. He was caught off-guard by the casual nature of the meeting, the lack of curiosity about his credentials, and by Stanier's abrupt brush-off.

Downes would rather have gone to the airport rather than Lake Worth. However, since there were no earlier flights out other than the one he'd already booked, he thought he might as well check it out.

Along the way, North pointed out projects that First Community had financed, who the developers were, and how much money had been or was being made on each project.

The Lake Worth operations center was also a branch where the original First Community Bank had been chartered in 1968. On the main floor, the branch had the same expensive décor as the North Lake location and roughly the same number of employees. Portraits of Stanier and North appeared in the vestibule.

Downes was taken to the 2nd floor to the Accounting and Finance Department, where Jim North introduced him to Frank Chadwick, the bank's CFO, a very timid thirty-year-old who had recently passed the CPA exam.

"This is Terry Downes. He may be joining us, so talk to him about what you do and answer any questions he has," North said. "Nice meeting you, Terry, and we'll be in touch."

With that, North was gone. A fitting end to an incredibly unprofessional interview, Downes thought.

Chadwick had the only individual office on the floor. Twenty five staff members worked at metal desks crammed in a space large enough for ten. The floor was bare of any carpeting and the office equipment looked outdated. Two noisy fans at the entrance helped circulate the air since the air-conditioning system wasn't working that well.

Downes couldn't help but make a mental note of the contrast in conditions between the first and second floors and, of course, the Palm Beach branch.

Chadwick, without question, had the most difficult job in the bank. His problems were compounded by a boss who had little interest in what he was doing and a chairman who dictated accounting and tax procedures that were often wrong if not outright illegal.

Chadwick was recruited from a small bank in Peru, Indiana, where he had been controller. He was wooed by a 'headhunter' to join a "fast-growing, multi billion-dollar commercial bank in one of the best places to live in the country." He jumped at the opportunity to become a CFO, moving his wife and three kids. He had regretted taking the job every day since then, and was actively looking for other opportunities.

Apparently, nobody had thought about making plans to get Downes back to the airport for his eight-p.m. flight, and nobody knew what to do with him for the rest of the day.

Downes was annoyed and frustrated. He couldn't believe the lack of professionalism and common courtesy displayed by Stanier and North. He was also a little pissed off in that his interview was supposed to be confidential but was being handed off to other employees in the bank. The last thing he needed was for anyone back in Wilmington to hear that he was looking at a possible change..

After inquiring about catching a cab to the airport, Chadwick offered to take him. which Downes gratefully accepted since it would give him a chance to ask more questions about the bank.

Chadwick was dumbfounded at the way Downes was treated and decided to reveal some startling information.

Mr. Downes," he said, "Did you know that Jim North just got released from federal prison?"

"What! No!"

"And he's not supposed to be associated with the bank in any capacity.

Downes caught his breath and swallowed, but maintained his composure. "How long was he in for?" he asked, keeping his voice steady.

"Six months," Chadwick replied. "He was serving a seven year sentence for bank fraud, racketeering, wire fraud, and conspiracy to defraud a bank. According to the newspapers, North was involved with some pretty bad characters, including some overseas business and illegal non banking activities, although that wasn't proven. How he got released after serving only six months, go figure."

"How come he's still associated with the bank?" Downes wanted to know.

"Because he thinks he can be, since he still owns stock in the bank and Stanier is extremely loyal to him."

"Unbelievable," Downes muttered, as his mind raced.

"And, get this. A couple of years ago, Stanier was handed down a twenty seven count indictment for basically the same charges. He went to trial and was found not guilty on all charges. I have the newspaper articles. I can send them to you if you wish."

"Of course. Remarkable!" responded Downes.

"Everything is a mystery here! I don't see the end results of each month. They are altered," said Chadwick. And, as you know, the bank is a public company regulated by the Securities and Exchange Commission and various other government agencies," Chadwick continued, "and is supposed to uphold sound fiduciary principles. Well, Stanier doesn't know what that means and thinks he can 'march to the beat of his own drummer'. But I think this leads to something more sinister. Why would the owner and CEO of a federally regulated commercial bank act this way?" Chadwick continued.

After hearing startling revelations, Downes expressed his thanks to Chadwick and wished him the best in his search for a better situation. He thanked him in advance for receiving the newspaper articles on Stanier and North and left himself available for any help he may need

First Community Bank and Trust originated in 1968 when Bruce Stanier and Jim North raised the 3 million dollars required capital through some community businessmen and began operations as an independent retail bank. The bank grew rapidly, acquiring additional capital, and developing a commercial lending function to fill the needs of the community.

Staniers first run-in with the federal regulators was when he ran into problems maintaining the required capital ratio as the bank increased its core deposits. He included in the capital the value of an antique Rolls Royce and jewelry worth 500,000.

Needless to say, the Feds were outraged and threatened to close the bank down.

Downes gladly left West Palm Beach and couldn't wait to put this bizarre day behind him.

Upon arrival at his office in Wilmington the following morning, he received a call from Bud Gardner.

"Terry, how did it go?" Gardner asked, sounding excited—even hopeful.

"You don't wanna know," Downes growled back.

"What happened?"

Downes told Gardner about his twenty minute meeting, the total lack of professionalism on the part of Stanier and North, and his being "dumped" at the Lake Worth branch with no arrangements for the rest of the day. "Bud, this guy Stanier is a clown, and Jim North is an ignorant dick who, I understand, just got out of prison. As Vice Chairman, he's probably responsible for their problems and he's being retained as a consultant! Give me a break! I had a conversation with one of their senior officers and he made it clear there are insurmountable problems brought about by Stanier and North. I'll pass," said Downes.

"Well, I'm sorry it didn't go well, but I still think you're missing a great opportunity."

"How do you figure that? Forget it. I have plenty of opportunities where I am."

Although it was clear to Gardner that Downes had really soured on First Community, Gardner wasn't one to give up. A couple of days later, he called again: "Terry, I heard from Stanier and he said the meeting went great and wants to know if he should send you a formal offer. He also said that he had to cut the meeting short because of a conflict in his schedule, for which he apologizes, and was sorry to hear that Jim North didn't spend much time with you."

Downes chuckled. "That's nice, but I'm not interested. The number-two guy just got out of prison. Are you kidding me?"

"Terry, look, you have witnessed firsthand the problem here. Everybody knows the kind of guy North is. He's still hanging around because of Staniers' loyalty. North helped him when he first formed the bank, and he's been with him since. Stanier is not a banker; he's a dealmaker. You can do whatever you want in this bank, and you'll have ownership. I know there are huge problems, but that means you can show progress quickly. Why don't you make one of your conditions of employment that Jim North be completely out of the bank?"

Gardner was doing a good job of pleading: "I know it's a different type of bank, but you can organize it the way you want. North's involvement will not be an issue and Stanier is looking for a successor"

Downes listened but was not persuaded.

Gardner plowed through: "How about if I can arrange a meeting with a couple of directors who wanted North replaced before he got into trouble and see how you feel?" he suggested. "You have nothing to lose."

Downes agreed, he had nothing to lose.

Gardner was a pro. He could be very persuasive and he struck Downes as being quite the stand-up guy. So, despite his misgivings, Downes figured he could give it another shot. He knew, however, that if they wanted him that bad, he would insist that he be given the freedom to make necessary changes.

Downes met with director Ben Gilbert, President of the Gilbert Companies, where he spent a couple of hours listening to all the reasons why he should accept the job. Then he met with Dr. Clem Samson, President of the local community college and close friend of Staniers.

Both directors agreed that the bank needed somebody with the background that Downes offers. In fact, both had gone on record that if Stanier didn't recruit someone, they would resign from the board. They both said the same thing about Jim North in that he should not be allowed in the building.

After considerable thought, Downes decided to take the chance and accept the position.

Wellington, Florida with ten thousand acres of land and twenty thousand residents, had always been a quiet community of ranches and farms, but in 1986 it was rapidly transforming into an exclusive hideaway for the jet-set. Anchored in the center of town was the Palm Beach Polo and Country Club, winter home to some of the world's wealthiest people.

Most of the land was owned by the Kalahari Corporation, a multinational cosmetics components firm, based in San Jose, California. Kalahari's chairman, Bill Grabowski, developed the

Country Club and brought world championship equestrian events to the community.

Wellington had been mostly swampland until a young developer took a chance in the 1960s and by 1986, had created one of the nicest 'bedroom communities' in South Florida.

On August 21st 1986, Terry Downes was ready for his first day on the job as Vice Chairman and Chief Lending Officer of First Community Bank. He had purchased a home in Wellington and his wife and two young kids were excited to start a new life.

He arrived at the office in his new Ford Granada, a cheap four-door sedan that was left for him at the airport. His employment package stipulated ' an upscale four door sedan' but what he got was about ten thousand dollars cheaper. He thought about making an issue of it, but he would have much bigger issues to address when arriving at his office. He did wander though, if he'd be short changed on any other 'guaranteed' perk.

Downes had a small temporary office with glass walls in the lobby of the Lake Worth facility. At Wilmington, he had gotten used to executive quarters with all the perks and privileges that were afforded top management.

He knew this was a step down in terms of the size of the bank, but it still struck him as strange that the president of a two billion dollar bank would have such a small, glass-enclosed office in the middle of the lobby of one of the bank branches. Again, he told himself he had bigger issues to address. Besides, he thought, in his mind, this had to be temporary.

Downes was responsible for all bank operations including commercial and retail lending. The only area he didn't have direct responsibility for was the bank's investment portfolio. Stanier needed to have the final say in how the bank invested its excess funds.

CHAPTER 3

A special board meeting of First Community Bank was held at another branch of the bank, in West Palm Beach, to officially welcome Downes on board. Stanier, as always, wore a business suit despite the sweltering summer heat. So did Clem Samson. But the rest of the board members looked as though they were ready for the beach. It was another far cry from Downes's old life at he The Wilmington Bank.

Stanier's secretary, Sheryl Mitchell, sat at the back of the conference room with a steno pad taking the minutes of the meeting.

Stanier called the meeting to order and formally introduced and welcomed Downes as the new President and Chief Lending Officer. He asked that each director introduce themselves and offer a brief overview of their background and affiliation.

Downes was dumbfounded to see Jim North sitting at the table. "We've been introduced," North announced when it was his turn. There were glares and snickers from various directors around the table. Downes wondered if anyone could see the heat rising under his collar. He couldn't believe that North was ignoring the consent decree that had barred him from any and all involvement in the bank. He had trouble figuring out what the hell Stanier was doing, since he had to have signed that decree.

As soon as the introductions were over, it was down to business—the business of a political campaign.

Doug Styles had been campaigning heavily for a seat in Congress and that's where the focus of the special board meeting turned.

He was putting up a good fight against Republican incumbent Tom Claiborne. Styles apparently had the support of the sitting President, who was scheduled to make a local campaign appearance on his behalf in the following week. Styles was a young, single guy, born and raised in Lake Worth, where he had worked in his parents' restaurant while furthering his education at South County Community College. He brimmed with self-confidence, especially since his campaign chest had risen to double that of his opponent. He was often referred to as Stanier's "friend," since there had been growing speculation that he was gay, as there had been with Stanier. The media were having a field day with the rampant rumors but Styles handled it well, managing to divert attention to the issues, which ended up helping him on his campaign efforts.

Claiborne had been fighting back with television spots slamming Styles for being a director at First Community, a bank whose vice chairman was a convicted felon and he being accused of accepting illegal campaign contributions.

Other than Clem Samson, the directors were all new-money people. They were arrogant and pompous and all were indebted to Stanier, since they all had healthy lines of credit with the bank. The business relationships between Stanier and the directors were not entirely transparent. The status of their loans were kept confidential, although they often talked about their 'projects' since most involved Stanier as Chairman and CEO of First Community or Stanier personally.

As Downes quickly learned, board meetings were simply get-togethers for the directors to provide Stanier with their project updates. Agendas were distributed but never followed and although minutes were taken they were seldom read or approved. Monthly earnings reports were distributed but seldom discussed unless it was a banner month..

These so-called board meetings, that lasted about two hours, took place during lunch, with sandwiches and soft drinks served, with each director being compensated five hundred dollars for their attendance.

Coming in, Downes suspected that the infrastructure, organization, and support systems at the bank would be in some state of disarray. The processes had not kept pace with the bank's growth or the technological changes within the industry.

While the shareholders were delighted with the financial success of the bank, the good results were going to be very temporary, unless significant changes were made. Not to mention the regulators response to Jim Norths' involvement if disclosed.

Downes's first regularly scheduled board meeting was tough. North was there again, although it had been mentioned beforehand that he was no longer a director. The FDIC had issued a Cease and Desist order that specifically stated that Jim North excommunicate himself from First Community Bank. The order was received and acknowledged by Stanier and the Board. At Downes' first regularly scheduled board meeting, North was in attendance and participated in the meeting as if nothing had happened.

"As long as we keep this quiet," announced Stanier, "and Jim's name is not mentioned in any minutes, we'll be fine. I'll arrange to pay Jim for his services from one of my companies."

Downes was astounded and looked directly at Gilbert, who simply shook his head.

At the end of rambling updates on each of their projects and requests for loans or payment extensions, Stanier turned the meeting over to Downes.

Downes was methodical as he laid everything out. He emphasized the growth that could be anticipated with updated technology and system improvements. He laid out the serious operational deficiencies that would have a significant negative impact on the bank if left uncorrected, and the need for a capital plan. Included in his recommendations was the hiring of a 'loan workout' person since he was concerned with the number of delinquent loans.

He made his recommendations, provided the breakdown in costs, and supplied the rationale. All he got in return were blank stares. He couldn't believe that anybody in the room would risk the monumental consequences of continuing to operate with unsafe and inefficient practices.

North was the first to speak up and it weirdly echoed what Stanier had said: "I thought we hired you to correct these problems."

What an asshole, Downes thought to himself. He was seething. To be spoken to, as he was, by a convicted felon fresh out of prison for bank fraud.... Hell, North wasn't supposed to be anywhere near the bank, never mind at a board meeting, and now he was questioning him.

Downes had never experienced anything so demeaning.

"That's exactly what I said, Jim," Stanier piped up. "Besides, if things are that bad, why haven't the bank examiners or the public accounting firm told us about the deficiencies?"

Ben Gilbert took this opportunity to confront North: "You've been in charge of the operating areas for a number of years, Jim. Why did you let it get out of hand?" he asked.

North didn't respond, so Gilbert pressed on. "These are operating and administrative issues that are the responsibility of middle management, so we can't expect Terry alone, or anybody else in his position, to solve them without the proper resources. It's imperative that we support his recommendations."

"I agree wholeheartedly," Samson said. "In fact, I would like to move that we approve Terry's recommendation as presented."

Gilbert quickly seconded the motion. The silence was deafening. Stanier was clearly fuming. He wasn't going to give up. "Do you realize the cost of hiring these people?" he asked.

"As I noted in my handout, three hundred and forty thousand dollars annually plus benefits," Downes replied. "We could probably reduce staff by one or two people, but I don't want this to be a condition."

The other twelve members of the board didn't say a word as the motion carried. Stanier abstained and North couldn't technically vote.

Downes thanked the board, collected his papers, and left the meeting. But he wasn't feeling terribly jubilant. He knew he was going to have a long fight ahead with Stanier, a man who had long grown accustomed to having his own way, but he was prepared to do whatever it took. Downes could hear some laughter from the meeting as he made his way down the empty hallway.

By the time four months had passed, Downes knew without a doubt that he had made a terrible mistake. There was no way Stanier was going to relinquish his control over the bank. In fact, if he weren't careful, Downes would end up being associated with a renegade bank, which would have a negative impact on finding another job.

His colleagues in Delaware had been right. They tried to warn him, but he hadn't listened. Downes was having a tough time coming to grips with the realization that there was no future at First Community and he had better start planning a move. He was trapped in an untenable situation and the strain was beginning to show.

Every conversation with Stanier became a battle. Employees soon recognized the friction between them and often joked about the senseless delays in getting things approved, since Stanier and Downes always had conflicting views.

Downes quickly learned that everything he said and did would get back to Stanier. He spent a lot of time in front of him defending himself over some of the most trivial issues. He was beginning to realize who his friends were within the organization and the community, and became very wary of whom to trust.

Downes was living with a constant knot in his stomach. He had heard rumors of payoffs being made to unsavory characters, real-estate brokers, lawyers, and politicians. It was difficult for him to witness the 'sideways' deals and the unusual relationships Stanier had with some of his employees, directors, and customers. One small comfort to Downes was that he quickly became persona non grata among Stanier's cadre of characters.

But the bottom line remained depressingly solid: First Community Bank was a joke, a piggy bank for Stanier, North and their minions.

And, unless half the workforce were fired and Stanier booted out of the bank, nothing was going to change.

Downes knew the house of cards was going to collapse and couldn't understand why Stanier or most of the board members didn't get it. He was aghast at North's continued involvement with the bank and couldn't understand the board's complacency. He had privately called Ben Gilbert and raised significant concern about North, and had been promised that it would be taken care of.

Clem Samson had already spoken to Stanier about it and been assured that North would not be attending future board meetings. However, after his conviction but prior to his sentencing, North had apparently approved a loan to Asiri Jayasinghe, a Sri Lankan and known supporter of an international terror group. This was brought to the attention of Downes by Frank Chadwick

Downes spoke to Bud Gardner, the recruiter who had done such a good job of convincing him to join the bank. Gardner was a straight-up guy and had a couple of conversations with Stanier, which only made things worse. Stanier was a force of nature. The more you pushed, the harder he pushed back.

On December 17, 1983, Downes's employment was terminated.

CHAPTER 4

Downes struggled with his short tenure with First Community. Things just didn't add up. It wasn't just the operational problems and lack of compliance with banking regulations, it was a case of not being able to reconcile the bank's earnings to the money being made by the deals handled. Further, he didn't understand why a local community bank was making loans to a foreign national guaranteed by a political group in Sri Lanka. Downes knew that Stanier was taking equity interests and profit participations on many deals and he also knew that many of the bank's directors had become millionaires from receiving illegal favors, but other issues were on his mind. The bank didn't have the capital structure to support the apparent loan growth. He surmised that loans were being funded from sources outside of the bank, off the books, but how could that be proved. He no longer worked at the bank.

It took some time for Downes to recover from the First Community debacle. He continually wondered if there had been anything he could have done differently, and the only mistake he thought he had made was not paying enough attention to the people who had advised him not to take the job in the first place.

While waiting for another banking opportunity to become available, Downes formed his own consulting business and joined the board of The Bank of Heywood, a small bank about 20 miles southeast of Wellington. The bank was owned by three local businessmen that he had met at various bank meetings. Downes was retained by the bank to find a buyer since neither of the owners had any interest in long term ownership. They had heard of small banks being acquired for large sums of money and they simply wanted to 'cash in'.

The adjustment of working from home, as opposed to working from an office, was difficult for Downes. He missed the traffic noise, the people, the lunches, and the elements of working in an office, but spent the days keeping busy on the phone and mailing to friends and former colleagues announcing his new business venture.

After returning home from a board meeting at the bank, Downes saw five messages on his phone. The first four were returned calls that he had made earlier but the fifth was unsolicited.

"Mr Downes, my name is Donovan Draper. I was referred to you by a mutual friend. I own several real estate related companies in and around Wellington and my partner and I are looking to organize or purchase a small bank. I was told that you could possibly assist in this matter. Could you give me a call when you get a chance."

Draper, and his partner Tim Ford, were Canadian investors and held majority ownership in land development, home and equestrian property construction and real estate sales companies. Downes called him back and a meeting was arranged at Monterey Realty in Wellington to discuss their specific needs and how Downes could help them.

Monterey Realty was a relatively small real estate office located in a strip shopping center between a hairdressing and a laundry business. It had the appearance of catering to the high end single family home buyers and sellers with pictures of listings in the millions of dollars hanging on the walls of the reception area. They also emphasized equestrian property sales and 'barnominiums', a combination of horse barns and condos. A large map of Wellington was pinned to a wall facing the entrance that showed Monterey properties available and under construction.

A well dressed middle aged man followed by a younger casually dressed guy with long hair introduced themselves to Downes and then led him to a conference room at the rear of the offices.

"I'm Don Draper and this is my partner Tim Ford, thanks for stopping over."

"You're welcome, how can I help you?" replied Downes

After reviewing, in some detail, the different entities owned and operated by the Canadians, Draper got to the reason he had contacted Downes.

"We heard about your background in banking and thought it would be good to meet and chat about what we're doing and the opportunities we have in our organization."

Draper talked generally about their companies and how difficult it was to manage them all especially since he and his partner were Canadian citizens and lived most of the time in Toronto.

Downes was a little taken back by the fact that two, relatively young guys, non US citizens, had amassed such a large enterprise that catered to wealthy clients.

"We are, what you would call, a 'one stop shopping' real estate company. We buy the land, develop into subdivisions, design and build the custom homes, and handle the sales through the realty company. The only thing we're missing is a financing outlet, like a bank. Our emphasis is on golf and equestrian properties as you can see," explained Draper pointing to the map on the wall.

Draper led them into a small conference room where refreshments had already been placed.

"We understand that you have quite a background in banking, Senior Vice President in a big bank up north, President of a bank in Minnesota and Vice Chairman of First Community, here in South Florida," said Draper

Downes nodded with a slight smile, wondering who gave them his 'resume'.

"We have also heard that, in your management positions, you have managed large real estate portfolios."

"Correct," replied Downes.

"Let me ask you this, are you looking to continue your career in banking or would you be open to using your experience in another field," asked Draper, cutting right to the chase.

"Right now, I'm just keeping my 'powder dry'. I'm not actively looking to get back into the 'corporate rat race'. I am assisting in the formation of a bank in Vero Beach along with six other investors. So I'm staying busy, for the most part."

"Good. Interesting. Then you might be interested in joining us."

"I thought you wanted assistance in forming or buying a small bank?" asked Downes.

"Well we do, but that's just one of the things that we'd like to get done. We believe that having a bank or savings and loan association would help us generate sales and we know you've had experience with First Community and de novo banks.

"You see Terry, we're not offering you a job per se, I guess you could say we're offering you a 'partnership.'"

Downes had established that Draper was the businessman, spokesman, and dealmaker of the two. At this time, he was unsure as to what Ford's role was in their business.

"Tim and I are involved in a number of companies, some of which we each own different interests, but together we own about eighty percent. Majority of our companies are real estate–related, especially in South Florida, where we own a land-development company, a real-estate brokerage, a commercial-construction company, and a residential home-building company. We own about five thousand acres in the southern part of Wellington where we plan to build equestrian-related projects. Our companies plan, develop, build, and broker high-end homes and equestrian facilities. We have just completed a bunch of large homes with stables on five-acre lots and we can't build them fast enough and sales are handled through our realty company

"Are you guys familiar with the process of acquiring more than a twenty-five-percent interest in a commercial bank?" asked Downes—Draper looking at him with a blank stare, waiting for him to explain. "It's pretty involved and will require you both to reveal a lot of personal data including all activities in Canada. Since you are non-U.S. citizens, you will come under tougher scrutiny than a U.S. citizen would," he added.

"Well, would you be interested in filing the necessary documents and negotiating, on our behalf, the acquisition of a bank?"

"Possibly," replied Downes. "Obviously, I would like to know more about you guys and the operations of your companies."

"No problem," Draper quickly responded. "Oh, I forgot to mention: we own an offshore bank in St. Kitts, in the West Indies. It's a restricted 'Class B' bank, so all of its business is off shore. We can't take deposits from or make loans to residents on the island. It's just an office; nothing like a regular bank."

"I understand," said Downes trying to hide his surprised look.

"Don't worry. The government granted us the charter, since we are planning on building a hotel on the island which will bring in tax revenues and jobs. There have been a few transactions, we have taken in some deposits from clients in Europe and India, and have some borrowers in Canada. As you may know, there are no reserve or liquidity requirements of the bank, no taxes and no usury laws, and strict privacy as to who our customers and directors are," explained Draper.

Downes knew this and his guard went up. St Kitts was a tax haven, and having access to an offshore bank in a country that upheld strict privacy laws lent itself to laundering money. He wasn't sure what the connection was between an offshore bank and the building of a hotel on the island.

After a great deal of discussion and emphasizing the need for him to see and verify before determining his interest, Downes agreed to travel with them to Toronto to meet their accountant. From there they would go to St. Kitts, then to Miami on their way back to Wellington.

The Bank of Heywood was a small commercial bank located about 60 miles south of Wellington. Organized in 1979 by three local business men, the bank remained the same community bank as it was when first organized. Downes was named a director shortly after leaving First Community after being asked by the owners to search for a buyer.

The asking price for the bank was way too high although maybe not in the eyes of the potential buyer.

None of the three owners of the bank had any experience in banking nor were they involved in the daily operations of the bank. Chairman of the Board, Gordon Tunney, received a salary of sixty thousand dollars a year but lacked any form of contribution to the bank's performance. Each shareholder had his own family business and all three were frustrated in that they had never been able to reap the returns on their investment. They were also clueless as to the value of the bank.

With local banks appraised at two-and-one-half to three times' their book value, they wanted six. In 1969, their investment in the bank had been a total of one million dollars; now they wanted twelve million.

The bank long had earnings problems because of poor management and no direction from the owners.

CHAPTER 5

After passing through customs and immigration, Draper, Ford and Downes were to be picked up at the Toronto International Airport by a driver and taken to Ford's home in Mississauga, where they would have their meeting. The following morning they were to fly to St. Kitts to visit with the board of trustees of First Investors Trust Company Limited, the bank, and then to Miami to meet with their U.S. law firm.

"We have made reservations on a British West Indies flight from Toronto to St. Kitts leaving at 8:30 am and arriving at 1 p.m. local time. So we'll pick you up at six a.m. We'll stay at the St. Kitts Hotel and Resort and leave the following morning for Miami.

"George McLoud, our manager at the bank," Draper continued, "lives in Toronto and St. Kitts part of the time and will meet us at Toronto Airport. Our chartered accountant, Steve Busby, will join us shortly and travel with us through to Miami, where we will be visiting with our lawyer, Bob Krieder.

"Now that we have that out of the way," Draper carried on with an enthusiastic tone to his voice, "let's talk some business before Steve gets here. Terry, have you thought any more about our last conversation concerning a bank?"

"Sure," replied Downes. "In fact, I had a conversation with Gordy. He's chairman of the bank, and he said they would love to sell the bank."

The bank was organized by Gordon "Gordy" Freland, an electrical contractor; Frank Turney, general contractor; and Johnny Watts Sr., who had since passed away and left his ownership to his son, Johnny Jr., who was in the trucking business.

They had formed the bank in 1969 after seeing some of their friends making lots of money from selling their ownership in a local bank to large financial institutions.

Freland, Turney, and Watts Sr. had been approached by an ex-bank president who had convinced them to open a commercial bank in the community. He provided the experience and know-how and was able to get their application approved by the state without any problem.

The bank had only been open for six months when their new president unexpectedly died of a heart attack, leaving the three owners in a quandary as to who would run their bank.

Over the next several years, they had hired and fired several bank presidents, none of which could manage the bank effectively. The contribution of the three owners was minimal since none of them had any banking knowledge or, for that matter, any interest in the bank.

They thought they were sitting on a gold mine and that, sooner or later, a big regional bank would offer them a huge amount of money for their 'wise investment'.

In the meantime, they needed to figure a way to get money out of the bank, since its earnings couldn't justify paying them a dividend and the regulators frowned upon directors fees.

The bank had one location; a stand-alone building owned by a company that belonged to the bank owners who leased it back to the bank.. It had thirty-two employees and assets of fifteen million dollars.

In January 1986, Gordie Freland had asked Downes to serve on the board and provide input as to how they could increase the earnings of the bank to the point where the regulators would allow a dividend to be paid to the shareholders.

"The book value is around two million dollars, so you're looking at a twelve-million-dollar purchase," said Downes.

"Wow, that's a lot! What do you think, Don?" asked Ford.

"Way too much," Downes answered for Draper. "But it's all about what you can do with the bank, whether you have the capital to make it grow and whether you can operate in accordance with the banking regulations. This is not like owning an ordinary business, and you being Canadian citizens will be put under more scrutiny and probably monitored more carefully. Six times book value is way too high for this bank, and I think they would take a lot less."

Draper listened intently while Downes went through the pros and cons of owning a commercial bank.

"Would they take a note back?" asked Ford.

"No, not if you plan to have the bank debt-service the loan. You could borrow money from another bank and use your shares as collateral, but you will be closely monitored by the FDIC. It would be better if you didn't leverage the purchase. They could also condition the approval on your infusing more capital in the bank, if they feel the bank is currently undercapitalized."

"Well," said Draper, "when could we meet with them?"

"They will obviously want to know who you are and obtain your financial statements to make sure you are qualified buyers. They would probably want a letter of intent and some form of cash deposit."

"Okay, so go ahead and arrange the meeting," said Ford rather impatiently.

"Look, my name is on the line here so I need to know more about you guys and your companies before I agree to represent you. So far, you've talked about your companies but I need to see physical assets, corporate docs and, of course, financials.

"Assuming that we get a 'clean bill of health' from you—and there's absolutely no reason why we shouldn't—we would like to know if you'd be interested in joining us on a full-time basis," asked Draper.

"To do what?" asked Downes.

"Manage and oversee all operations in South Florida, negotiate and file the application for the change in control of the bank, or form a bank and oversee the operations of our offshore bank. We would also like your input on the Canadian interests that we own, as well as some opportunities in Europe. We would provide you with an office in Wellington, a vehicle, and whatever benefits you think are fair and what salary it would take."

Downes was surprised that, in such a short period of time, they had seemingly built that much confidence in him. "I'm flattered that you think I could take on this job, but what makes you think that I could manage these ventures? I have no experience in real estate, land development, or construction," said Downes.

"You were in charge of a billion dollar loan portfolio at FCB ."

Draper paused and said, "In any event we want you here, we need a management-caliber person who can plan and organize our companies and control our finances."

"Well, let's see how the next couple of days go…but you have my interest."

With much curiosity, Downes flew to Toronto where he met a driver that took him to Tim Ford's home in Mississauga, about 40 miles from Toronto International

The unpretentious ranch style house, where he lived with his girlfriend Marcie, was in a quiet middle-class neighborhood. Both Draper and Ford were waiting for Downes as he stepped out of the black town car.

"Great to see you Terry, Good flight?" asked Draper.

The house was modestly furnished except for the unbelievable artwork. Ford had several authentic paintings by famous artists—such as Monet, Van Gogh, and Salvador Dalí—hanging in every room in the house and looking totally out of place. Downes asked Ford if he was a collector and was told that he didn't have much interest in them and that he had inherited the paintings from his father. He didn't say if they were original or not.

Shortly after Downes arrived, a car pulled up in the driveway. A young, unassuming accounting type carrying an over-packed briefcase and a bunch of loose papers exited.

"Steve, I would like you to meet Terry Downes. Terry flew up from Florida and will be joining us on our trip the next few days," said Draper. Downes acknowledged Busby shaking his rather limp hand while handing him a business card that read James & Foster Chartered Accountants—Steve Busby, CPA, Staff Accountant.

"Steve, please provide Terry with copies of any tax returns, financial reports and answer any questions he may have concerning the businesses. I'm sure he'll have many over the next few days," said Draper.

"No problem," said Busby, looking a little confused. "Could you tell me what you'll be needing?"

"A list of all the companies that Don and Tim have an equity interest in, their percentage ownership, and a brief description of the businesses? I would also like a copy of any recent financial statements and tax returns," requested Downes, knowing that they probably wouldn't release anything until they had a fully executed Non Disclosure Agreement.

"Sure," Busby said, with no hesitation. "May take me a little while but I should be ready for you by the time we see Krieder, the attorney in Miami. I'll call my office and have them faxed there."

Draper took Downes to the hotel and suggested that he and Ford pick him up for dinner later in the evening. As they were leaving the house, Downes said to Draper, "By the way, Don, how do you fund your operations in Florida? It seems as though you have quite a lot of non-earning assets down there."

"We'll discuss that when we get to Miami," replied Draper, leaving him with the feeling that he'd been blown off.

At dinner they talked more specifically about the ventures in Wellington, their concerns about managing and controlling each project, and how having their own bank could help them.

Downes explained to them that he thought the best thing to do with the bank, in their application for change in control, would be to plan on infusing more capital and have a specific business model as to what they intended to do with the bank, such as marketing and capital planning.

They agreed and said that they had initially budgeted twelve million dollars for an acquisition, and if they could form a bank for less, they would put the difference into capital. It made sense to Downes.

At the Toronto International airport the next morning, they met up with George McLoud, manager of First Investors Trust Co.Ltd. He was one the most disgusting-looking characters Downes had ever met, standing around five-foot-five inches and weighing at least three hundred pounds. He looked as though he had three chins. His non-ironed shirt had a combination of egg, or mustard, stains and ash that fell from his cigarette drooping from the corner of his mouth.

"George McLoud, shake hands with Terry Downes. Terry, George is the manager and a director of our bank in Basseterre; and Terry is a financial consultant who we've asked to join us at our meetings," introduced Draper.

McLoud never took his cigarette out of his mouth as he said, "Pleased to meet you."

"I need to pick up a couple of things and will be right back," said Draper, as McLoud shook hands with Ford and Busby. Draper disappeared into the crowds carrying his carry-on bag but leaving his garment bag with Busby.

Steve Busby and Terry Downes talked about sports while Ford and McLoud talked about a pending transaction at the bank. McLoud knew Ford, of course, but Downes was surprised that he had never met Busby. Downes still couldn't get over this dirty-looking guy and the fact that he was manager of a bank, and wondered what the bank and the other employees looked like. Draper, Busby, and Downes were dressed in business suits; Ford in his usual trendy casual wear; and then there was McLoud. Unbelievable, thought Downes.

Check-in was a nightmare. It appeared that most passengers were expatriates carrying everything along but their 'kitchen sinks'. In addition to suitcases, most fastened with tape or string, passengers were carrying boxes of all shapes and sizes, some barely holding in the contents.

At the final boarding call, Draper showed up. He had his travel and garment bags but, in his other hand, he was carrying a large duffle bag which Downes knew he hadn't brought along when he left to "pick up a couple of things."

"Here, let me carry that for you," offered Downes, extending his hand toward the case.

Draper immediately rejected his offer and gave Downes his garment bag.

Downes wondered if the case had in fact been handed to him before he left, since nobody else seemed to notice the extra piece of luggage.

British West Indies Airways flight 402 took off from Toronto International to St. Kitts, West Indies, on time. Downes was not only surprised that there was a nonstop flight from Toronto but also that it was a packed wide-body DC-10. They had first-class tickets, which made for a very comfortable and relaxing trip scheduled to take four hours.

Draper had an aisle seat and sat next to Ford; Downes sat in the middle two seats with Busby; McLoud was by himself one row ahead. Throughout the entire flight, Draper kept the case by his feet, even after the flight attendant had strongly suggested that he place it in the overhead compartment.

The flight was smooth, food and service very good, and the liquor free flowing. Busby and Downes chatted a little, but didn't get into any of the questions that he had raised earlier. Downes did find out that Busby's firm had been the accounting and income-tax preparer for Draper and Ford's companies for a number of years, but that Busby personally had only known them for two years.

They talked about the bank in St. Kitts and that this was Downes's first visit, and Busby agreed with him on his initial impression of George McLoud. He also said that their holdings were very complex and was happy to hear that they were searching for someone like Downes to assist them.

Apparently Draper had already told Busby about Downes, so during the trip to St. Kitts, Busby thought he needed to determine how much Downes really knew about finance and accounting. Thus, the majority of their conversation centered on Downes's background.

CHAPTER 6

The Federation of St. Kitts and Nevis is located in the Leeward Islands in the West Indies. It is a small sovereign nation in the Americas, in both area—about one-and-a-half times the size of Washington, D.C.—and population—forty thousand inhabitants. The capital and government headquarters is Basseterre.

The country is magnificent. Both islands are both volcanic and their highest peak sits on the main island, rising to around 3,500 feet surrounded by lush, fertile ground. In the nineteen-eighties, their main industry was tourism and sugarcane growth, although rising production costs and low world markets at the time had caused losses that vastly contributed to the country's deficit. The people are delightful and unassuming.

The country had a democratic form of government and operated under the British parliamentary system. Offshore banks were allowed in the country, although there was only one, and were considered tax havens with strict corporate privacy laws.

It appeared as though the DC-10 was ready to land in a field. There was no semblance of an airport or terminal as the big jet banked on its final approach and landed safely on the only runway. The plane turned around and taxied back to, what appeared to be, the world's smallest international terminal. Downes had visions of chaos, trying to process four hundred people through customs and immigration, a task that the local people handled three times a week during the summer months.

But traveling first class meant that they were first off the plane, exiting down the mechanical stairs toward the terminal. Upon entering immigration, they were asked for their passports and immigration forms and directed to customs, where they were waived through without any delay.

Again, Downes offered to carry Draper's case and again was denied.

Outside of customs, they were greeted by an important-looking gentleman who immediately embraced and shook hands with Draper, then Ford, followed by McLoud. Draper, then, took the gentleman's arm and said, "Dennis, I would like you to meet Terry Downes and Steve Busby. Terry is a financial consultant and Steve our accountant."

"Pleased to meet you and welcome to St. Kitts," said Dennis Fisk.

"Terry and Steve, this is Dennis Fisk, Deputy Prime Minister of St. Kitts and Minister of Tourism."

Downes was impressed. No wonder everybody knew this guy.

Dennis Fisk was one of the founding members of PDM (People's Discretion Movement), the political party in power, and extremely popular in the community that he served. He was a very fit-looking forty-year-old man, well-dressed and with a very outgoing personality.

The climate was fantastic: temperature around eighty degrees Fahrenheit, with trade winds of around fifteen to twenty miles per hour.

Basseterre, the capital of St. Kitts, is just a couple of miles from the airport and located on the southwest side of the island. It is a tiny town, and one of the oldest in the Eastern Caribbean—founded in 1650. Basseterre is the main commercial and industrial center of St. Kitts and the country's main port of entry for both sea and air travel. It houses the federal government's administrative buildings and the headquarters of the Eastern Caribbean Central Bank.

St. Kitts was a member of Caricom, an organization of Caribbean Communities whose main purpose was to generate trade with other nations.

First Investors Trust Company Limited was a restricted, Class B, offshore bank. It had been chartered in 1985 and had a board of trustees composed of Draper (Chairman), Ford, McLoud, Henry Blackstone, and Dennis Fisk. Henry Blackstone was a prominent lawyer on the island and a savvy political arm of the PDM Party.

The bank was restricted from doing business on the island in so far as taking deposits and making loans, but could issue CDs, offer numbered accounts, and make loans to foreign corporations domiciled in St. Kitts. The advantages of the offshore bank were that there were no liquidity or reserve requirements for the bank, no usury laws as far as interest rates were concerned, no income taxes, and strict privacy laws.

St. Kitts maintained a high level of confidentiality for offshore entities as outlined in the Confidential Relationships Act of 1984. The Act safeguarded investors by prohibiting disclosure of any information obtained in the course of business and purportedly provided the most rigid secrecy in the Caribbean region as it applied to banks and professionals as well as government officials.

First Investors Trust was located on the Circus, in Basseterre, the center of town, on the ground floor of a two-story wood-structured building. The office looked relatively conservative when considering the neighboring cluster of pink-, yellow-, and orange-painted buildings.

Upon arriving at the bank, they were greeted by three ladies: Sophie Albrightson, originally from Norway; a student named Jazzi; and the third, a middle-aged lady named Doreen, who was in charge. All three were very nervous and in awe of their presence, especially Dennis Fisk's.

The office was quite small, with two metal desks at the front and a meeting room that could seat six at the back. Nothing in the office resembled a conventional bank since there were no tellers' windows, waiting areas, or bank marketing nor advertising material. There were two computer monitors, calculators, typewriters, and all the usual office fixtures, including an extra large safe that one would expect in a business office.

While Busby, Ford, and Downes chatted with the ladies, Draper, Fisk, and McLoud went into the meeting room, with the case, and closed the door. Tacky curtains covered the two windows of the room and Downes positioned himself to take advantage of a slight opening in the curtains, allowing him to see what was going on. And what he saw kind of took him by surprise—but then not really.

The case was emptied out of bundles of one-hundred-dollar bills, and he thought that it had to total several hundred thousand dollars. The three guys laughed and joked as the money was bundle-counted and placed in an old safe in the private room..

"There's a lot more to follow," he heard Ford saying.

By now, of course, Downes had more questions, and he planned to confront both Draper and Ford as soon as he could get them alone.

They left the bank shortly after six p.m. and decided to check in at the hotel and get freshened up for dinner. The red-carpet treatment was afforded them at the hotel, with fresh-cut flowers in the room and a bar full of beer and wine as well as fresh fruit and cheese. The rooms were air-conditioned—most hotels in St. Kitts were not—but the breeze from the ocean was perfect for Downes so he left all the windows open.

They met in the lobby of the hotel and Fisk announced that he had made arrangements to have dinner at the Wharf, a great outdoor seafood restaurant on the dock where the fish, shrimp, and lobster were cooked to order on a charcoal grill.

Everybody acknowledged Dennis Fisk as they ordered their dinner at the grill, shaking hands and stopping to chat with many patrons.

The Wharf was not conducive to private conversation since it was outdoors buffet style, where the seats were picnic tables and customers sat wherever there was an open seat. The fish and lobster were caught right in the bay, every day, and the veggies were locally grown.

The smell of the food being cooked on a charcoal grill, the local Caribbean music, and the steady ocean breeze made for a very pleasant evening, except for the constant interruption from the continual flow of people wanting to talk to Dennis Fisk.

A bank board meeting was scheduled at 10:00 am the next morning after a breakfast meeting with the deputy PM.

Dennis Fisk was a very powerful and influential member of the PDM Party and held a seat in parliament, as was the custom. Dr. Kendall Rudolph, the prime minister, considered Fisk a bit radical and a person known to line his pockets beyond acceptable limits when dealing with the promotion of tourism on the island. "Beyond acceptable limits" simply meant that, while government officials were encouraged to accept partnerships and, in some cases, take majority interests in ventures that involved foreign nationals, it was unacceptable to take bribes or accept personal favors for getting things approved by the government.

That ruling was a farce. Most government officials were on the take, including the prime minister. It's just that some were more flagrant and indiscreet than others, and Dennis Fisk was considered the worst. He lived very comfortably in his big home and enjoyed a lifestyle that not many Kittitians knew. He drove a brand-new Range Rover that, by his own admission, had been provided to him by the local dealer for his having gotten its permits approved and provided it with a hassle-free importation process. New cars cost up to three times more than they did in the U.S. due to taxes, and Dennis Fisk's salary was twenty-five-thousand dollars per year.

Fisk had a string of girlfriends "servicing" him pretty much on a daily basis, in addition to a beautiful wife who turned a blind eye to his philandering.

It was at the hotel coffee shop the next morning, before the Bank Board meeting, when Downes decided to confront Draper and Ford on the one thing that caused him great concern.

"I couldn't help noticing the cash dumped on the table yesterday. I could hear the dialogue and I could see the cash through a crack in the curtain. Is this a bank transaction, customer deposit, a typical deal, or what?" asked Downes.

Draper sipped his coffee, nonchalantly sat back, motioned to Ford not to respond, and said, "Terry, we brought with us three hundred thousand in cash, which is for a deposit for a friend. He wanted to give us cash, I guess to hide it from paying taxes. We don't care, we'll put fifty thousand in the operating account for the bank, out of which thirty thousand is a payoff to Fisk—which we gave him yesterday for pulling some strings in the government—and Henry Blackstone gets twenty thousand off that for his work."

"Okay, but as I told you, the purpose of me being here is to understand and get comfortable with your businesses so that I can decide whether or not to accept your offer. When I see things like that, it obviously gives me some concern, especially since I hadn't noticed the case when we left Tim's house or when we got to the airport. So if I'm out of bounds with these questions, please tell me."

"We had it with us all the time," said Ford.

The cash was in a lock box, a drop off that was often used for cash transactions coming out of Canada.

"Look, Terry," said Draper, sounding a little agitated, "Wait 'til you've seen the total picture and had the benefit of meeting everybody and getting to know our lawyers before you make any judgment. In Miami, you will be able to raise any questions you want and by then you should know if we're legitimate enough to work with."

Downes didn't respond.

Steve Busby arrived, then McLoud with the usual cigarette drooping from his mouth. McLoud had changed his shirt but not his pants and probably nothing else. Shortly thereafter, Fisk joined them, shaking hands with people on his way into the restaurant, as they ordered a quick breakfast and talked about a new cultural arts center that Fisk was developing in Basseterre.

They arrived at the bank at ten a.m. and gathered in the meeting room. Waiting for them was Henry Blackstone.

Blackstone was in his late thirties, early forties and was considered one of the best business lawyers on the island. He was married with two children and had two other kids whom he supported from two different girlfriends he still maintained relationships with, one of them being Doreen, who worked at the bank. It appeared that this was common in St. Kitts, even though the laws were very strict when it came to parents' obligations to support kids born out of wedlock. If a support payment was missed, it surely meant jail time for the irresponsible parent, and time spent in Her Majesty's prison was not very pleasant.

Sophie Albrightson was in the office to answer phones, serve them soft drinks, and arrange sandwiches for lunch.

Busby and Downes were introduced to Henry Blackstone and the board of trustees' meeting of First Investors Trust Corporation Ltd. was called to order by Don Draper. "First of all, and I trust everybody has met each other, thanks for coming. I would like to have a casual meeting with everybody today and take the time to establish some plans for the bank and each of our roles in achieving them. I think the most expedient thing to do is for me to discuss my items—and I apologize for not having a formal agenda—and then we can discuss anything that you may have. I've asked George to take the minutes, which he will have on hand for your review at our next meeting," said Draper.

Downes had the feeling that this was a bit of a show for his benefit and he was careful not to ask any questions that might be a little embarrassing to answer.

Like most office space in Bassatere, there was no air-conditioning. The front door was left open and two noisy-running ceiling fans helped circulate the air, but it was still humid and uncomfortable. McLoud sat with his usual cigarette drooping from his mouth, looking totally miserable and barely able to reach his notepad due to his huge belly being in the way. He labored under the heat and his frequent gasps of breath were heard around the table. He was a walking coronary.

"As you all know, our bylaws stipulate that we have five members of the board of trustees—Tim, Dennis, Henry, George, and me as chairman. Henry, we may want to increase that to six. I have asked Terry to serve on the board, which is why he's with us, and while he hasn't yet decided, I want us to have the paperwork done so we don't have to wait for another meeting. Tim and I have asked Terry to help us with the operations of our Florida companies and, given his banking and finance background, I thought it would make sense to have him involved with the bank. Terry, could you give the group a brief overview of your banking and business experience?" asked Draper.

He did, and there were no questions.

"Terry, I hope, will give us an answer in a few days, but in the interim I think it's fair to say that you need to feel comfortable that we are not operating against any laws of St. Kitts, the U.S., or Canada," Draper emphasized, with a slight glance toward Downes.

"So, Henry, I want you to review current transactions with Terry and allow him to see any and all documents, corporate or otherwise."

Henry nodded with a smile, with no reaction from the others except the beginning of an uncontrollable coughing spell from McLoud.

Downes had never bought up Draper's concerns with openly disclosing and addressing the money-laundering issue, but it was now on the table and he was anxious to hear how they were going to convince him that everything was kosher, for they knew it was on his mind. And he still thought Draper and Ford had lied about the briefcase.

"I would now like to discuss our roles in the company. At this time, Tim and I will be responsible for business development, both deposits and loans, and we will use brokers to bring us business as well. Commissions are negotiable and determined on a case-by-case basis. Dennis will act as ambassador for the bank while dealing with foreign investors in matters relating to tourism. Of course, we will pay you a commission on deposit business. Henry will handle all legal matters through his law firm, such as drafting contracts and numbered-account agreements. George is the manager of the office. Doreen, our bookkeeper, is the signer on checks, and George will reconcile the bank statements. I will approve all expenses."

This told Downes something: they didn't trust McLoud with the checkbook; they trusted Doreen, Henry's girlfriend.

"As far as employees are concerned, George is being paid twenty thousand dollars per year plus commissions. He is required to work fifty percent of normal hours until full time is required. George is free, of course, to seek other ventures on the island. We have agreed to reimburse George's air fare to Toronto four times per year. The three ladies are also part-time. Doreen is paid four US Dollars per hour and the two girls, three dollars. George will determine the number of hours to be worked," explained Draper.

There was no income tax on the island and the cost of living was relatively low. The local currency was the EC (Eastern Caribbean) dollar, but people would much prefer the U.S. dollar, since it was worth more and the local currency was fixed at $1.50.

Employment laws were typical of other Caribbean countries. Employees could not be fired, unless they committed a punishable crime, and had to be paid for thirteen months for twelve months' service so as to compensate for vacation, whether they took it or not.

Draper brought up some minor issues and then suggested that they break for lunch.

Sophie Albrightson delivered a tray of small sandwiches, prepared by a local restaurant, and soft drinks. Before eating, they took a stretch outside to get some fresh air and noticed the local hustle and bustle of locals trying to make a buck from the tourists.

Downes couldn't get over the warm breeze, the great climate, the colorful attire of the local people, and the architecture, which was Old West Indies. Many buildings were in disrepair but they were clean and manageable and added to the unique landscape of the capital. The roads were in terrible shape, and a rain gutter collecting trash and garbage flowed from the higher terrain through the town and down to the harbor. It wasn't particularly pleasant to see, but somehow it seemed to blend in with the ambiance of Basseterre.

The town had a traffic problem, and parking was definitely an issue. There were cabbies in their own reserved spaces on the Circus in Basseterre, the center of town marked by a huge stand-alone clock which chimed every hour on the hour..

The meeting resumed and Draper suggested that they all take a ride to Frigate Bay after the meeting, to visit a piece of property where the government had issued one of six casino licenses.

"So, the next item that I have is the transaction that Tim and I have brought into the bank. Friends of ours in Toronto have opened an account and made a deposit of three hundred thousand dollars. The cash is here in the safe, we brought the money with us, so George, please do the paper work before we leave and make sure that the money is deposited in our account at Carib Bank," said Draper, looking straight at Downes.

"We will be making arrangements for other deposits, either CDs or account deposits, from the same source over the next several months. The funds, for the most part, come from a company and its owners in Toronto. We will also be canvassing companies that we know of in the U.K. and which have expressed interest in doing business with us. As far as placing the money, that's easy, right, Tim?"

Ford wasn't paying any attention.

"We have a string of potential borrowers," Draper continued, "who are prepared to pay high interest rates and fees, especially in the real-estate and land-development businesses. The next and final item I have is the financial statement. George, will you pass around the profit-and-loss statement?"

McLoud removed the cigarette from his mouth and with ash falling all over his shirt, coughed, grunted, and finally said, "I'll have it before you leave. It's done but it needs to be typed."

"Okay. Please, don't forget."

"We have brought with us some cash for working capital, as part of our agreement. I understand we are a little behind in paying our bills and we need to make payroll for the month."

Still no comments from the group; they were just anxious to get out of the office.

"Does anyone have any other business to discuss?" asked Draper.

"Yes, I do," said Dennis Fisk. "I would like to discuss the hotel deal. As you know, I have told the cabinet that I would have a buyer for the property within weeks and architectural drawings presented to them within sixty days. It is absolutely imperative that we get this done, since the government has made an announcement about the development of the property and the number of jobs it will create. All PDM members are relying on this project getting completed in time for the elections next year. That's twenty months from now."

Ford wanted to say something, but once again Draper interrupted: "Okay, we need to secure an option to buy the property, first and foremost. All we have is a verbal deal with the owners and you know how much that's worth. So, Dennis, can you negotiate a ninety-day option and try to get away with as little as you can?" he asked.

"We also need a letter of confirmation from the government," Draper continued, "guaranteeing us a casino license on the property and under what conditions. Of course, this deal can't be done through the bank. We can lend money to a developer abroad, but I would rather not do that. I think I can get construction financing but I need to get the logistical things done. Dennis, can you get the letter?"

"Yes, of course," said Fisk. He had already negotiated a deal with the seller as the broker of record.

Several years prior, the government had issued six casino licenses to certain properties. They were non-transferable and could only be issued to predetermined properties. The government had issued a license to the Bailey's Hotel and Casino in Frigate Bay, hitherto the only operating license on island. It was known that Dennis Fisk and other government officials had made a ton of money from the licenses and fees paid by the owner in the development and construction of the property.

"Now," said Draper, "what is the deal that you've made with George, Dennis?"

McLoud shuffled in his seat. Fisk started to stutter: "Well, as you know, we heard from the owners of their desire to sell the property, so I asked George if he had any contacts that would be interested in developing the property, and he said he did. I told him that I needed fifty thousand dollars to secure the deal. He said he could get the money, but so far, nothing. Therefore, based on his telling me that he could get the money, I advised the cabinet that we could get it done."

"That's when I called you, Don, because my sources had let me down," said McLoud.

"So, Dennis, 'I'm assuming that the fifty thousand is for you and your colleagues' favorite charities, in order to get this letter, correct?"

"Yes, sir, that would be correct," replied Fisk, with a smile on his face.

"And I'm assuming that there will be more to follow, right, Dennis?" continued Draper, laughing out loud.

"Only when government is asked for favors, Mr. Draper," Fisk responded.

"Of course," said Draper.

The meeting was concluded. They got into Fisk's Range Rover and made their way over to Frigate Bay to visit the property.

Located directly across the road from Bailey's Hotel and Casino, the property was twenty acres between the road and the beach. It had five hundred feet of beachfront on the Atlantic Ocean side of the island and it was covered with small dunes and sea grapes.

Ford had a site plat with him as they walked the perimeter of the property. Draper had already run some numbers several months prior, when he had heard that the property was for sale. He had also estimated construction costs per foot, occupancy rates, and yield to break even. Further, he had contacted a casino-management company and had received estimated costs based on head counts. He had factored in all of his soft costs—such as architectural, mechanical, and electrical drawings—and had a list of items for the government to review, like sewage and power supply. This was critical, since the property would have to have its own power and sewage treatment plants. He figured that Fisk and his cronies would want upwards of three hundred thousand dollars in kickbacks by the time it was all said and done.

The asking price for the property was two million dollars. Draper had no clue on what the government (Fisk and his lackeys) would want for the gaming license, alcoholic-beverage license, and any ongoing fees. Draper did realize, however, that Fisk was the key to making this work. He also knew that it would cost him.

Even though he had calculated rough construction costs of building the hotel, Draper needed some assurance from Dennis Fisk that the government of St. Kitts would aggressively promote the property in their tourism plans. Now he needed to firm up the numbers, put together a budget, and hire an architect and construction manager. Henry Blackstone had already suggested using Doreen on a full-time basis to manage the finances. It was also important that Draper secured construction and permanent financing for the project—and it wasn't because he couldn't fund it himself.

Before leaving the property, Draper asked Fisk if he could get some numbers on the Bailey's Hotel, like occupancy rates, casino revenues, food and beverage profits, etc., and asked McLoud to make sure he had that P&L done before they left on the following morning. McLoud just nodded, hoping that he would forget.

Fisk dropped them off at the hotel, since he had another engagement, and Blackstone needed to get back to his office. Draper told McLoud to let them meet alone.

CHAPTER 7

They met for dinner at the hotel—Draper, Ford, Busby, and Downes. Downes was glad that Busby had been asked to join them. It was comforting to at least have someone who had ethical and legal standards to uphold.

The setting, again, was fantastic. The outdoor restaurant had the most beautiful foliage, overlooked the Atlantic, and had the usual ocean breeze. This was a place for a romantic dinner, not a business meeting.

After ordering a bottle of reasonably priced Chardonnay and some cracked conch for an appetizer, Draper started the conversation: "You know, I'm a little pissed off that McLoud didn't originally contact us on this hotel deal. He must have called his buddy Ernie to get the deal done, and when Fisk put the pressure on him for the fifty thousand, McLoud couldn't convince Ernie that it was a legitimate deal.

"I can imagine George trying to explain to Ernie," Draper proceeded, "that he needed fifty thousand dollars to pay off government officials in order to get a casino license for a piece of property that he didn't have. Ernie would have had too many questions and George would have too many nebulous answers. Or maybe he didn't ask him, but thought he could get it done himself."

"Who is Ernie?" asked Downes, casually.

"We would like to say that he's a friend of ours, but he ain't," said Ford, looking at Draper.

Once again, Draper took over the conversation: "Ernie Mueller is an asshole, but a very wealthy and influential asshole. He could be compared to Donald Trump in Canada, except that he's probably worth a lot more. George helped him get things done when he, George, worked for the City of Toronto and soon after became Ernie's PR guy."

Jacques "Ernie" Mueller was, indeed, a very wealthy guy, probably the wealthiest guy in Canada. He had major interests in a bunch of public and private companies, including the largest battery manufacturing business in the world. He did most of his business in India and had many ties to the Indian government. He was very influential in Canadian politics and forever in the news whenever major international financial deals were made and which affected India. Mueller had purportedly financed the Iran-Contra deal with help from his good friend and international arms dealer, Omar Khallehki.

"So Terry, what do we have to do to convince you that our businesses are legitimate?" asked Draper, quite seriously.

Just as serious Downes replies, "Tell me about the sources of cash that flows into First Trust."

"What about it?"

"For instance, who is your friend that opened the account?"

"Now, you know I can't disclose that Terry," replied Draper

"Would you disclose the names of sources after I've accepted your deal and become a board member?"

"The government has stipulated that, under the covenants of organizing a Class B bank, knowledge of depositors names and domiciles shall be restricted to approved individuals and in our case, it is Doreen and myself," replied Draper authoritatively.

"We hear a lot about unsavory characters in South Florida. After all, we are known as the cocaine-smuggling world epicenter. You have offered me a very lucrative opportunity that, quite frankly, is very attractive. I'm tired of banking; I don't like where the U.S. banking system is going, with bank holding companies being allowed to own various non-banking subsidiaries and the fact that it seems inevitable that we will have out-of-state banking. I'm looking for a change, but I need to assure myself that this opportunity is right for me," said Downes.

"We do not deal cocaine and you will see that all of our operations are legitimate," said Draper, very sternly. "You will have access to all records, but as you know we need your decision quickly—hopefully, by the end of this trip."

"Could you tell me how you fund your operations in South Florida?" asked Downes.

"Yes. We move money from some of our Canadian companies, and you'll see on the books of those companies the investments in these operations. There are times when we move cash and that's simply to avoid taxes in both Canada and the U.S.," replied Draper.

"How do you get cash into the U.S.?" Downes probed.

"We have a Canadian company called Monterey International Investments Ltd. This company owns a Dutch Antilles company called Monterey NV. MII has a number of investors, and I am the managing partner. We have our accounts in a bank in Jersey, an island off the coast of England, which we use periodically to deposit cash. We do this because the investors, which include Tim and me for the most part, choose complete privacy from the Canadian government. It's not a lot of money, but with the corporate tax rates in Canada being so high and the fact that we pay taxes in the U.S. as well, we need to shelter some income. When our bookkeeper, in Wellington, needs cash, she calls me and I arrange for funds to be wired from Jersey," explained Draper.

"And how will you fund the hotel project?"

"We can fund the initial soft costs and possibly half of the land cost ourselves. We hope that the seller will take a note back for the balance. I think we could get construction financing from Carib Bank, where we do a lot of business, and also permanent financing with a little help from Fisk and his colleagues."

"Who owns First Investors Trust Limited? I know who the directors are, but are they the shareholders?"

"Yes, they are."

"Well, can you tell me who owns what?" asked Downes.

"No, I can't disclose that until we have a deal."

"Okay, that's fair enough. What about tax returns and financial statements?"

"No problem. We'll have a non-disclosure for you to sign in Miami."

They ate dinner, during which the conversation centered on the hotel project. Downes could tell they were really excited about the project.

"We need to find a good construction manager," Draper remarked.

"Dennis should know somebody," suggested Ford.

"Forget it. He would want a cut of that, too, not to mention the control he would have on the guy. We will need to keep him at arm's length. I would prefer that we recruited somebody from another island, or Canada or the U.S."

They batted around a number of options and peoples' names and finally Draper said, "See how much we've got going on, Terry, and why we need somebody to oversee all this stuff? Tim is not qualified—he's a salesman—and I've got my hands full with the Canadian stuff."

"What's the story with George McLoud?" asked Downes, with a slight smile on his face. Draper knew, sooner or later, that McLoud's name would come up.

"He's been in and around Toronto Government for years. He worked in various public relations capacities for the City of Toronto. Believe it or not, he was once an aide to the city mayor, right, Tim?"

Ford nodded and laughed.

"George is a pig, as you can tell, and he's gotten worse over the past few years. We knew of him in Toronto but didn't get to know him personally until a couple of years ago, when we started coming down here. He's had a place down here for quite some time—I'm not sure if it's his—and everybody knows him as 'Fat George.' He knows everybody here, in government, and that's why we asked him to look after the bank for us," said Draper.

Draper would have loved to find somebody else, but McLoud knew too much. That's why he needed somebody like Downes to keep McLoud "honest."

Alone, Draper and Ford discussed whether or not they made a mistake in offering Downes a job. They concluded that he knew too much to stop now and decided to continue to convince him that they had a legitimate business enterprise.

They spent three hours over dinner, Steve Busby not saying a word but listening intently and making a few notes on a small notepad that he carried with him.

They left very early the next morning for the airport, on the way to the much anticipated meeting in Miami with Cohen, Gray, Stone & Krieder.

CHAPTER 8

George McLoud had lived all his life in Toronto. He had menial clerical jobs with the city, usually in marketing or public relations, but always seen at important city functions. Although a social outcast, McLoud had managed to become an aide to the mayor of Toronto.

McLoud was in the perfect position to do favors, usually big favors, for money or markers. He knew who was on the take, who was vulnerable, and was the perfect politician's lackey who prided himself in his ability to "put people and deals together."

He had always been obese but generally had gotten away with it because nobody knew him to be any different. Nobody would eat with him because of his eating habits and his personal hygiene. The fact that he was a chain-smoker was one thing, but always having a cigarette hanging from the corner of his mouth, with ashes falling on his clothes and smoke drifting in his eyes, was another. George only surrounded himself with sympathizers, those who really felt sorry for him.

McLoud had met "Ernie" Mueller early in his career. Mueller was having problems getting a liquor license for one of his strip clubs and McLoud got it pushed through for him. Whether he had actually done it was questionable but Mueller thought he had and McLoud wasn't about to tell him any different. That was the beginning of a relationship that added a special meaning to the word "bagman."

As Mueller grew in his sleazy but much more powerful business deals, McLoud became more of his sidekick and was becoming Mueller's "beard" in many deals where he didn't want the publicity.

Mueller had told McLoud of his interest in St. Kitts and his needs for an offshore facility to handle some business transactions. McLoud visited the country, carrying along a substantial amount of Mueller's cash, and immediately hit it off with certain influential people, despite his crude demeanor and socially unacceptable habits. They seemed to be more acceptable in St.Kitts than in Toronto, though, especially since McLoud had a lot of cash.

With a little encouragement, McLoud convinced Henry Blackstone to file an application for an offshore bank. Blackstone, in turn, convinced Sir Brian Ashe, the Governor General of St. Kitts, that this would be good for trade. Blackstone had written the law for the establishing of offshore banks and had gotten the Confidential Relationships Act passed in parliament. First Investors Trust would be the first charter granted under the new law.

Regardless of the privacy laws, Mueller hadn't wanted his name involved so he asked his lawyer, Donovan Draper, to work it out, as long as McLoud managed the bank. Mueller needed someone to be constantly aligned to the government officials and McLoud had shown that he could get almost anything accomplished with a little cash. Draper saw an opportunity for himself and assumed ownership for he and his partner, Tim Ford.

The People's Discretion Movement (PDM), under the leadership of Dr. Kendall Rudolph, was the party in power. But on this sleepy island of forty thousand people, politics were fierce and at times extremely violent. In addition to the PDM, the major political parties were the Labor Party, and the CPM (Concerned Peoples Movement),

Violence had always been a significant strategic tool used by the Labour Party and they, unlike the other parties, had never hesitated to violently eliminate those who, they considered, stood in the way of their political objectives.

In 1967, a number of PDM supporters were arrested on trumped-up charges, detained at Her Majesty's prison, and charged with attempting to overthrow the "lawfully" elected government. Mr. Robert Crawford, a prominent local lawyer, defended those charged, including Dennis Fisk and a prominent citizen and founder of the PDM Party, Dr. Cedric Flowers.

Midway through the trial of those accused and the public realizing that the government would lose all the trumped-up cases, Crawford suddenly and mysteriously took ill and died.

Then and now, many are convinced that Crawford's death was part of a conspiracy, contrived as part of Labour's strategy to win the case against the accused PDM leaders, and thereby put PDM to rest as a political force.

PDM was the obstacle between the Labour Party's proposed "One-Party State" and the people's freedom.

In 1979, C.A. Paul Southwell, then Prime Minister of St. Kitts, openly cried on local television, pleading with loyal Labour supporters to re-elect him as party leader and warned viewers about the consequences, should he not be re-elected Labour Party leader in the upcoming election.

Unbeknownst to Kittitians at the time, there had been an attempted coup taking place in the Labour Party. A group of young political upstarts, led by Charles Bison, was attempting to oust the popular prime minister and control the affairs of the nation.

Bison was a thug, a small-time drug peddler with great ambitions who always carried a lot of cash and who had a following of young, impressionable kids looking for a lifestyle that resembled what they saw on U.S. television. They wanted fancy cars, fashionable gear, and the ladies.

Bison saw how easy it was to make money and soon realized how being a politician would be the easiest way to fulfill his ambitions. The country was asleep, and he and his contacts saw an opportunity for a wake-up call by trying to kick out the prime minister and his cronies.

The coup failed and Southwell was re-elected, but shortly after re-election he died mysteriously in St. Lucia. Everybody knew who was behind his death, but it worked since it paved the way for a new faction of Labour. Gone was the old guard.

People grieved for a while and many Labour supporters were concerned with the savage process to remove Southwell, but if killing could solve a problem in the nineteen-seventies, likewise it would have to be used regularly to solve the numerous problems about to confront Labour in the nineteen-eighties.

They arrived in Miami around noon and, waiting for them at the airport, was a driver who took them to the offices of Cohen, Gray, Stone & Krieder, a law firm specializing in real estate and corporate law.

Jim Cohen had built, in ten years, a highly respected law practice with his partner, Craig Gray. Their offices, with twenty-three lawyers and total staff of around fifty, were located on the thirty-fifth floor of the Conseco Towers Building in downtown Miami. The offices were somewhat conservative, with a small lobby, a receptionist, four chairs, and a couch around a large coffee table.

"Ah, Mr. Draper, Mr. Ford, how are you? Mr. Krieder is waiting for you. He will meet you in the large conference room. You can go ahead there. Mr. Perry is also there," said the receptionist.

Roland Perry was their lawyer in Toronto. Downes was surprised that he was a sole practitioner and would have thought they would be represented by a firm at least the size of their Miami firm, with all the different companies and interests they had.

The introductions were made, and Krieder hugged both Draper and Ford. Sandwiches and soft drinks were ready for them, so each helped themselves and took a seat. Krieder handed out an agenda of items to discuss as his assistant, a beautiful Latino lady, interrupted their lunch to open two large wooden doors on the wall which revealed a dry erase board and a paper-flip chart. There was a blank sheet covering some charts that Krieder didn't want them to review ahead of his presentation.

Bob Krieder was a talented young lawyer who had been with the firm for six years or so. He had risen to the position of a lettered partner not necessarily because of his talent but because he had many wealthy German clients accounting for twenty percent of the firm's billings. Most of them were real-estate investors and had been referred to the firm through his wife's family and their friends in Munich. Krieder spoke fluent German, as well as Spanish, and was highly thought of and respected by the other partners in the firm.

Just after Krieder began his introduction, he was interrupted by Jim Cohen, the firm's managing partner. Cohen shook hands with everybody and offered any assistance, but was quick to point out that they were in good hands with Bob. Cohen was a well-known attorney, having represented a number of large international companies.

"First, let me just say, 'Welcome, everybody.' As you all know, we represent Don and Tim and their U.S. holdings, and since there are issues that may impact their Canadian holdings, we thought it appropriate to invite Roland to the meeting. We have a lot to cover this afternoon so let's begin," said Krieder.

"The first thing I would like to do is get some paperwork out of the way. Terry, would you mind taking a look at this non-disclosure agreement and executing it, if you will? Sorry for forcing this on you, but since you're not yet formally a part of the group, I think it necessary for both parties to be covered," Krieder continued.

"No problem," Downes replied.

"Good, and while you're doing that, maybe I can give the guys an overview of your background and possible role in the companies. As I understand it, Don, you've made an offer to Terry and he is doing his due diligence before accepting the offer."

"Correct," said Draper.

"As you know, I've been after Don for some time to get him to recruit somebody like Terry due to the complexity of operating and controlling the different entities. Later we'll discuss the merits of having a holding company own the different companies. Terry definitely has the background that we're looking for, especially in banking and real estate, and with the increase in business in St. Kitts it's even more relevant. Terry has twenty-plus years in banking and is currently a director of the Bank of Heywood. He has the management experience we need, and I for one hope that he comes with us. Hopefully, by the end of the day, we can answer all of his questions to his satisfaction."

Downes reviewed the mutual NDA. He signed it, requested a copy, and passed it to Krieder.

"Okay. Thanks, Terry. Now we can begin."

"Could you go over some of the things you need?" asked Krieder, looking toward Downes.

"Well, I was hoping that I could see some financial statements, especially cash flow for the Florida operations. I was particularly interested in how the operations in Wellington are being funded. Also, I had asked for financials for the bank in St. Kitts and thought I would get them before I left, but I understand the privacy issue and the fact that we didn't have an NDA executed. I would also like to know who owns First Trust and some idea as to what types of business will be transacted," Downes spoke firmly.

"Okay, let's address First Investors, the offshore bank. Don owns thirty percent and Tim nineteen percent; fifty-one percent is split between certain officials of the St. Kitts government, including Dennis Fisk whom, I understand, you had the pleasure of meeting. Since Don and Tim put up the money and organized the bank, they receive seventy percent of the cash flow after the first twelve months of operation. Its charter is pretty straightforward, Class B, offshore bank, and as such, is restricted from conducting banking within the country. This means that deposits cannot come from local businesses or individuals. Under some conditions, loans can be made to those St. Kitts companies that have foreign charters.

"An offshore bank," Krieder kept on, "is a bank located outside the country of residence of the depositor, typically in a low-tax jurisdiction (tax haven) that provides financial and legal advantages and includes greater privacy. Depositors are provided numbered accounts so as to protect their names from being known."

Offshore banking has often been associated with organized crime, tax evasion, and money laundering.

"As to the types of business," continued Krieder, "Don and Tim want to be able to shelter some of their income, legally of course, and also be able to have a vehicle for financing some of their deals. The bank will also offer trademark and ship registrations. I have a file of all the legal docs, which I will have copied and forwarded to you if you decide to join us."

Downes wasn't totally convinced that it was all kosher, but certainly Krieder and Cohen added credibility to their operation and, in the interests of time, he thought they should move on.

"The funding for the projects in Wellington is provided for from them personally or from certain ventures in Canada. Both Don and Tim have accounts in an offshore facility in Jersey, where some of the funds are dispersed," explained Krieder.

"As to financial statements, again I think it best that we wait until a decision is made before we distribute them. But we'll try to answer any questions that you have," continued Krieder.

"Well, I'm sure that you understand my concern," said Downes.

"Of course, but let me say this: we cannot concern ourselves with the origin of funds deposited in the bank. We don't do that in the U.S. nor do they do it in Canada. The IRS tries, though, by having banks record and report to them all cash deposits over ten thousand dollars. I would say that most of our deposits are cash, either from clients buying a CD or making a deposit to a numbered account. In St. Kitts, as in other tax-haven countries, we take advantage of its strict privacy laws and the fact that there is no income tax," Krieder elaborated.

Even though Krieder was eloquently addressing his concerns, Downes just couldn't determine, from the answers he was getting, whether there was anything wrong with what they were doing—and if there was, Krieder didn't know it—or, God forbid, that he was a party to any wrongdoing.

"Terry, Don may have told you, we anticipate more activity in First Investors and, as you probably noticed, we don't have anyone who can manage it. George McLoud is not the person, obviously, and quite frankly it has become an embarrassing situation for Don and Tim," said Krieder. "Right, Don?"

"Right," Draper confirmed.

Downes was very relieved to hear that, since he would have a problem with McLoud being involved with the bank in any position.

"If it's okay with you, I would like now to move on to the possible bank acquisition. Terry, Don tells me that, for the right price, the owners of the Bank of Heywood would sell their shares and that their price is six times the book value, which would be around twelve million dollars. I understand that you are currently a director of the bank."

"That's right."

"Why did you join their board?" asked Krieder.

"I have known Gordie Freland for a number of years and he asked me to advise how he could improve the earnings of the bank. After I told him where the problems were, he asked me to join the board because my recommendations would have a better chance of being implemented. And besides, he thought it was cheaper than hiring me as a consultant."

"Okay...so, how much do you think it's worth paying?" asked Krieder, getting right to the point.

"It's definitely not worth the six times' book value they're asking. There have been plenty of bank sales of late where the multiple has been three and their earnings performance a lot better than this bank," Downes replied.

"How much do you think we should offer them?" asked Krieder.

"I'm not sure why you would want it. The capital requirements are high, seven percent at least. It seems to me that the reason you need a financial institution is to facilitate your real-estate deals, in which case a savings and loan would make more sense. Capital requirements are only three percent and they are a lot less complex than a commercial bank. And don't forget: as I told Don and Tim, they will be scrutinized a lot closer if they are the controlling shareholders, since they are Canadian citizens.

"Having said that, if I were you, I'd offer them three times the adjusted book value, after an audit of the bank, and see what they say. I would also make sure that they realize that the book value could be adjusted based on what is disclosed in an audit."

"Interesting," said Krieder, looking directly at Draper.

What Downes found interesting however, was that nobody up to this point had said a word. He thought that he was giving everybody a lot to think about.

"Do you know of an S&L that's for sale?" Ford asked, as if he were looking for a used car.

"No, I'm afraid I don't, Tim. I'm not a broker. The only reason I know about this bank is because I'm a director and I know the owners," replied Downes.

"Well, I think we should go ahead and meet with these guys. What do you think, Don?" suggested Krieder.

"Sure, it can't hurt. It would probably take a lot longer to find or form a savings and loan."

Gordie Freland answered his phone from his office at East Coast Electric in Heywood. When Downes told him that he was calling from the law office of the Canadian investors about whom he had spoken about, he almost fell off his chair. He offered to gather Frank Turney and Johnny Watts right away and drive down to Miami.

Downes confirmed the availability of the group and they thought it would be good to meet while they were all there. He then asked Freland if they could possibly make it on such short notice.

"Be there in a couple of hours. Just give me directions," Freland said, excitedly.

"Gentlemen, the next item on the agenda is a discussion involving the review of all operating entities in Canada, in the U.S., and offshore. Roland, I'm going to need some help from you on this," said Krieder.

Bob Krieder passed two pages of an organizational chart that, even with some explanation, would leave Downes completely confused. Krieder walked over to the flip chart where he had drawn the boxes and inserted the names of the companies. As he talked about each one, he wrote a brief description and the owners' names.

The first page showed no fewer than thirty companies in boxes connected by vertical, horizontal, diagonal, and dotted lines. It was titled 'Legal Structure—Canada & USA, as of October 24, 1986' and looked more like an electrical circuitry design chart.

Written in each box was the name of the company, where the company was located, and in most cases the percent ownership and the type of business. At the top center of the first page were Draper and

Ford's names, and underneath Draper's name, a box with the names "Myrtos Inc., Ont., 100 %."

Underneath Ford's name, a box with the inscription: "630154 Ontario Inc., Ont., 100 %." Clearly, these were meant to be holding companies.

"Myrtos owns 'Blair House Inc., Fla.,' 'Sandy Lane Investments Ltd.,' and 'Ontario. 100 %'; Myrtos also owns a fifty-percent interest in 'Erintree Inc., Ont.,' which owns 'Pitroyal Ltd.' and 'Paradox Investments Ltd.' Both are offshore companies. The other fifty percent of 'Erintree Inc.' is owned by Tim Ford," explained Krieder, writing on the board.

"'Erintree Inc.' owns an eighty-percent interest in '633365 Ontario Inc., Ont.,' a real-estate company; one-hundred percent of 'Erintree Development Ltd. Ont.'; fifty-percent interest in '664564 Ontario Inc. Ont.,' a home-building company; one-hundred-percent interest in 'Erintree Financial Corp. Ont.,' a mortgage broker; a fifty-percent interest in 'Erintree Building Systems Ont.'; a fifty-percent interest in 'Excel Realty Associates, Fla.'; and one-hundred-percent interest in 'Erintree Management Services, Fla.,'" he continued.

"Tim's holding company, '630154 Ontario Inc.,' holds interests in similar companies, including a fifty-percent interest in 'New Southfields Farms Inc.,' a Florida Corp. that owns 'CS&W Construction Company.' The other fifty percent is owned by Ed Devine, the manager of 'CS&W.'"

Downes was totally bewildered.

There were a number of other companies owned in whole or in part by other companies owned by Erintree Inc. They included fitness centers, restaurants, a water-bottling company, and a box with dotted lines pointing to Proposed Bank Holding Company and The Bank of Heywood.

The chart had been recently drawn up, since they had only known about the bank a few days before the meeting.

The second page of the chart was less confusing but nonetheless intriguing. It showed "Greentree International Investments Ltd.," an offshore Dutch Antilles company owning "Monerey Homes, Inc.," a Florida Corporation; "Monerey NV," a Dutch Antilles holding company, owning forty-nine percent of "First Investors Trust Corporation Limited (St. Kitts)."

"'Monterey NV' owns a twenty-five-percent interest in 'High Tech Homes Inc.,' a Delaware Corp.," Krieder continued, "and one-hundred percent of 'Monterey Farms Partnership (Fla.),' which owns seventy-five percent of 'Monterey Equestrian Centers Inc. (Fla.).' The other twenty-five percent is owned by Ed Devine...correct, Don?"

"Correct," said Draper.

Although most of them were real estate–related, it was beyond comprehension to Downes how this myriad of companies, all of which he was told were operating entities, could be kept track of by one person. Ford, in Downes's short time of knowing him, did not impress him as being a manager of anything, and Draper was a lawyer. What did he know about managing companies? Downes mused.

He asked who the other investors were and was told that the main person was a Canadian multimillionaire whose name was confidential. Of course, Downes guessed, it had to be Ernie Mueller.

It was also interesting to note that the organizational chart showed the fifty-one-percent interest in First Investors Trust as "George McLoud and friends," not Dennis Fisk and his cronies.

CHAPTER 9

Busby and Perry left for the airport while Ford called his limo buddy to pick up the other three and take them to Wellington, about seventy miles north of Miami.

The limo was actually waiting for them outside the lobby of the building, a comfortable stretch town car equipped with beer and snacks.

It wasn't long before Draper started the conversation about Downes' deal: "Terry, do you have more of a comfort level now?" he asked.

"Sure. I think meeting with Busby and Krieder left me with the feeling that, if there are any wrongdoings, either your lawyers and accountants are involved or you have managed to cover it up pretty well."

"Right," said Draper, with a chuckle.

"But I still need to get the financial statements and follow up on the status of tax returns," said Downes.

"Okay, then, let's see: Tim and I have been discussing this and we would like you to take over all Florida operations. We would give you a list of things that we need and you do whatever you need to better control the companies and make them more efficient. You can hire and fire whoever you need to, but I would like you to call me first. We need to put together an operating budget for each company with cash-flow projections and, of course, complete the review of the bank. We want you to be Chairman of the new bank as well as oversee the St. Kitts operation and, after we've reorganized, we'll talk about you having a piece of the holding company. There's an office in Monterey that you can use and if you let me know of any expense reimbursement, I will authorize payment.

"We have a pretty good administrative assistant in Janice Radico," Draper went on, "she handles the books and is a signer on all bank accounts. We would prefer that this stay as is until you get settled, then if you want to sign checks, no problem. One of us is usually here every other week but you can reach us anytime," said Draper.

"Okay. Sounds good!"

"How about if we start you off at a two fifty base and a sign up bonus of a hundred. Do you know if we have insurance, Tim?"

Ford was asleep.

"Well, see what suits you. Let us know, and we'll get it. And let us know what type of vehicle you would like. How about starting Monday, then?" Draper wasn't one to waste time.

"Does anybody know about this yet?" asked Downes.

"Not yet, unless Tim has said something, but if it's okay with you, maybe I'll tell everybody tomorrow."

They shook hands on the deal.

Downes still had some apprehension but felt it was worth taking a chance. Maybe they were trying to legitimize the business or hiring him to cover their tracks, he thought. After all, he knew he could quit anytime if he found any hanky-panky going on. The thing that gave him the most comfort was their willingness to be put through some added scrutiny in the change-of-control application. If they were involved in drug trafficking and money laundering, they would be stupid to put themselves on a stage, he thought. He was also pleased that they had retained a well-known law firm such as Jim Cohen's.

The ride to Wellington was all smiles. Downes had agreed to the terms that were discussed and asked that they be put in the form of a letter confirming what they had agreed to

Terry Downes arrived at his new office, quite unlike the offices he'd been used to over the years. He still had a number of questions after he tried to come to grips with the unusual events of the past several days.. He was convinced that the story they had told about the case full of cash having been with them before they had gotten to the airport was bullshit. Was it drug money? What was the relationship between Draper and Ernie Mueller? After all, Draper was Ernies' lawyer and confidant although, at the meeting in St. Kitts, he had referred to Mueller as an asshole. How much money had been transferred from Canada to Jersey, and from which company? How much was being transferred to the Florida companies from Jersey? It must have been substantial to keep the companies running. The offer for the bank had been made without much thought at all. Do they really intend to go through with the purchase?

Downes knew that a number of his concerns would be addressed as soon as he got his arms around the businesses He was anxious to get started.

While driving around Wellington over the weekend he had noticed a subdivision with 'For Sale - Monterey Realty Partners' signs on new homes. This, he thought, was an indication that they were building spec homes and they either had sufficient cash flow to finance construction or they had a healthy bank line of credit.

Downes was greeted by Janice Radico, the administrative assistant and apparent manager of the cash flow for the companies. She welcomed Downes and offered her assistance in getting settled.

A number of people had gathered around to introduce themselves and welcome him to the company, including two people of particular interest, Ed Devine and Tony Sprano. Devine was a fifty-percent owner in New Southfield Farms, which owned CS&W Construction. Tony Sprano was the S in CS&W and an owner until Devine convinced Ford to buy them out. Sprano held the general contractor's license for the companies.

Draper and Ford showed up a little later and made sure that Downes had been introduced to everybody. Draper announced that both he and Ford were leaving later in the day to go back to Toronto and, before they left, he wanted to show Downes the properties that they owned and the status of each.

Those in the office appeared to be a friendly group of people and willing to help in getting him organized. The offices were in a strip shopping center with a bold green sign that read "Monterey Realty Associates" and a logo that resembled a splash of green ink. It was a typical real-estate office, with agents coming and going, and which also served as a construction office for CS&W and the other construction companies.

They had an office reserved for him with a new desk and all the accouterments—a computer, phone, filing cabinets, even a picture on the wall. Radico had done a good job of rearranging all the offices to make room for Downes, and he showed his appreciation. It was practical and he had gotten used to a small office with limited privacy.

Radico was an attractive forty-year-old, although her facial expressions revealed a great deal of sadness. She had been in real estate for some fifteen years and had seen Wellington grow from swampland into one of the fastest-growing, multifaceted bedroom communities in South Florida. She was married to a drunk and had recently lost a teenage son to suicide. Downes couldn't wait to sit and chat with her.

Draper interrupted and gave a briefing on the status of certain projects, as other employees were arriving. Downes met Scott Neeley, the office manager; "Dutch Cramer," a salesman for the equestrian center, also Canadian and obviously a friend of Tim Ford's; and a couple of job superintendents. Then a number of workers showed up.

Downes was starting to feel pretty impressed with the reception he was getting, until he heard Devine say, "Don't worry. Payroll is here. Give me a minute, everybody."

There was a sigh of relief on everyone's part. Payroll was supposed to have been made the previous Friday but the funds hadn't been available. Some guys were panicking, since this was not the first time this had happened. Most of them lived from hand to mouth and needed their paychecks the very day they were supposed to be paid.

Draper was a little embarrassed, especially since this was Downes's first day, but he smiled it off and told everybody that he was there to make sure this didn't happen again. Tim Ford was on the phone in Downes's new office with the door closed.

After the cash was being given out, in lieu of payroll checks, he noticed that Ed Devine had interrupted Ford while he was on the phone, and said that he had to leave. He needed to make sure he got reimbursed for the payroll. Radico, who had heard him, walked over and said, "Ed, I thought we agreed that you weren't going to do that again."

"You try telling construction workers that we can't make payroll because funds ain't available," laughed Devine.

"That's fine, but when you pay them in cash, I have to reconcile the amount you give them to what they earned. I have to record withholding taxes and other deductions and pay the IRS, Ed," said Radico, sternly.

"Ah, don't worry about it. This is the last time. Uncle Sam won't notice and the guys were happy," said Devine, as if it was much ado about nothing.

"Ed, please, I have to keep the records straight."

"Okay, okay, okay," replied Devine, and turned to Ford.

Ford held his hand over the phone and said, "How much?"

"Twelve," replied Devine.

Ed Devine had cashed a personal check earlier for ten thousand dollars and requested one-hundred-, twenty-, and ten-dollar bills at the bank. He had time sheets available and quickly calculated hours worked for those who needed their pay, rounded out the gross amount, and gave them the cash. In the eyes of the workers, he was "the man." The total given out was Ten Thousand, Four Hundred and Eighty Dollars .

Trying to hide her frustration, Radico simply walked over to Downes and said, "We have to talk."

Draper grabbed his briefcase and motioned to Downes to follow him. "Let's go. We've got a lot to cover."

Both men walked toward Devine's pickup truck. Their first stop was a subdivision called Greenview Shores, a gated community with about one hundred homes occupied and twenty under construction.

"We built all these homes. Fifteen that you see under construction have been sold; the others are spec. homes. They range in price from one hundred eighty thousand to three hundred thousand dollars, and we have about seventy-five lots remaining."

"Which company owns the property and builds the houses?" asked Downes.

"Erintree Inc. in Canada owns the property, Monterey Homes is contracted to build the homes, and Monterey sells them," replied Draper.

The homes were beautifully landscaped and all built on one-third-of-an-acre lots.

Their next stop was the property that had the CS&W trailer and the hole in the ground. The dredging equipment was in operation. Huge dirt-moving tractors and bulldozers were busy moving and leveling dirt.

"We have about a thousand acres here. The land is being developed by CS&W, which Tim and Ed Devine own, and will be divided into two-five-acre lots and an equestrian center. Devine has the plans and we've sold twenty lots already. Monterey NV owns the land and High Tech Homes will build the homes and horse barns. The equestrian center will be separate and owned by Monterey Farms Partnership.

"We have another project called Rainbow Farms," Draper continued, "over on the other side of the canal, where we have two hundred acres, and we're building custom barns on one-acre lots. Next to that, we have two polo fields with training and dressage facilities. Actually, we have a project a little south of here where your old boss, Bruce Stanier, and his gay friend, Senator Dougie Styles, are partners with Tim and Ed Devine."

"Really, Bruce Stanier and Doug Styles? asked Downes, visibly taken by surprise.

"Yes, they both highly recommended you."

Downes was very impressed and anxious to look at the financial status of each project.

Draper mentioned that he'd be back the following week but didn't know if Ford could make it. He assured that he would have a chance to spend some time with Downes and go over any questions or concerns that he would have. They got back to the office, where Ford was ready with his luggage, and his friend, the limo man, waiting to take them to the airport.

Soon after "the guys"—as everybody referred to them—left, Janice asked if she and Downes could talk. She was obviously upset.

"You look like you have mountains on your shoulders," Downes commented.

She broke down into tears and it took several minutes before she was able to talk.

"Take it easy," he tried to appease her. "There's nothing here we can't correct."

"Don't be so sure," she sobbed. "I hope you know what you got yourself into."

"Tell me, what's the problem?"

"I wish I knew where to start. First of all, that 'little incident' this morning: Ed does it all the time. He takes it upon himself to pay these guys out of his pocket. He tells Tim, and Tim reimburses him. I never hear how much, and I can never get any information out of Ed. And of course, the employees think he walks on water and that I'm the company bitch. You know he owns fifty percent of CS&W with Tim, so I can't go complaining to Don."

"Does this happen with the other companies?" he asked.

"No, just New Southfield and CS&W," she replied, still sobbing.

"What does Devine do when he's here?"

"I don't really know. He seems to have an interest in everything that's going on and he's always having private meetings in his office. Whenever he's on the phone his door is closed. There have been times when he's asked me for confidential information such as how much money we've received from Don and wanted to see copies of wires," she said nervously.

"You ever give it to him," asked Downes.

"No, I always tell him to ask Don or Tim."

He promised Janice that there would no longer be payroll problems, at least as long as he was there, since he knew the IRS implications and the fact that they would come after them sooner or later.

"Why can't you make payroll on time? This morning, you said that the funds weren't available. What's the problem?"

"We never have the cash. None of these properties generate cash except Monterey Homes, and I never see that. It goes into another account."

"Well, where do you get the operating cash from?" Downes probed.

"The way it works is this: I calculate how much money I need for payroll and operating expenses for the next two weeks. I call Don and he wires me the money."

"Where does the money come from?"

"It comes from a bank in Jersey, from an account called Monterey NV. You know where Jersey is, right? Off the coast of England."

"Yeah, I know, how long have you been here, or working with Draper and Ford?"

"Two years," she sniffed. "Look, I know there's nothing wrong here, but it's a nightmare trying to get things accounted for. I've tried a number of times to establish a set of books for each company; I know how to do it. I have bookkeeping experience, but I don't get cooperation from anybody except Tony Sprano. I'm really worried that, if we get audited by the IRS, we will not be able to substantiate a thing. Seldom does anybody submit receipts, except Tony, and when I don't do the tax-withholding from these guys, my neck is on the line because I'm a signer on the accounts," she said.

"There is no track of costs on the homes they build and nobody seems to care," Radico kept on. "I seldom get invoices for materials or subcontractors; I just get a call from Tim asking me to send a check to so and so."

Downes just shook his head in disbelief. "How do these guys know if they're making money or not?"

"They don't, unless somebody else is keeping track. Nobody knows what's going on. Terry, you wouldn't believe the amount of cash that floats around here, but it's never predictable like 'feast or famine.'"

This was beginning to scare the crap out of Downes. "Okay, let's just calm down here and tackle one thing at a time," he proposed, as though he really knew where to begin. "I asked Don about the corporate tax returns. He said that extensions had been filed and to see you about their status."

"You've got me. I have no clue about tax returns. I only know about payroll taxes, and you saw what I have to put up with. We don't even have a CPA firm to do the returns."

"Why don't you let me stay here for a couple of hours? I need to review the files and get a feel for what these companies are about, then we'll talk later in the afternoon, how's that?" suggested Downes.

"Good luck," she said, in a tone which insinuated that he was about to get an eye opener.

CHAPTER 10

Ed Devine was from the East Side of Chicago and had moved to Wellington after being given an assignment by his employer, the Federal Bureau of Investigation.

He had worked under cover for the FBI for a number of years and was considered one of the best in the business. He was generally given the most difficult and dangerous undercover assignments with the objective of becoming part of an illicit operation and accumulating as much evidence as possible. He was given different identities for each situation and had a knack for blending into the operations of any suspected criminal organization, which, over the years, had led to numerous arrests, convictions, and the elimination of many illegal entities.

Devine was a fun guy to be around and enjoyed the game of polo, although limited to that of a spectator. He was a young, fifty-year-old single guy and had been divorced four times. His dynamic personality enabled him to meet and, at times, become very friendly with the movers and shakers in the land-development business. Devine was very social and enjoyed the nightlife. Upon arriving in Wellington,. Devine became a part of the polo scene and the related social activities. He met Tim Ford at a polo function and they soon became buddies. Ford talked about his businesses and how he and his partner were buying tracts of land in Wellington to develop and build equestrian-designed facilities and their need for a general contractor's license. Devine told Ford about his background in construction management and his desire to get involved with a local company. Ford was in need of a general contractor's license in order to have his company build as planned.

Devine had heard of a small construction company in the area which, he thought, could be purchased and would provide Ford with the GC's license and a book of business in the community.

Devine was asked if he would make the introduction and within a couple of weeks, Ford had closed the deal with Tony Sprano, owner of CS&W Construction, paying him more than what he had asked for his company and also offering him a multiyear employment contract.

Ford, then, asked Devine to oversee the company with Sprano handling the day-to-day operations and offered him a good salary plus fifty percent of the company. Devine accepted the offer without hesitation, but not because of money or the ownership. His motivation was much different.

Downes's thinking that his first day on the job had been troubling, the next day would prove much worse.

As soon as he got to the office, Downes received a call from George McLoud saying how pleased he was to hear that he was on board and apologizing for not getting the financial statements together for him. He invited him down to St. Kitts and suggested that they spend more time talking about the opportunities on the island. Downes expressed his appreciation for the call but cut him short; he had lots to do.

Janice Radico came into his office, offered him a cup of coffee, and asked if there was anything he needed.

"I chatted with Tony Sprano yesterday, and he told me about his role in CS&W and how glad he was that he wasn't involved in the big deals," Downes told her.

"Tony is a really good guy and so are the guys working with him. He keeps to himself, does his job, makes money for the company, you know," she said.

"I talked to him about Ed's handing out cash for payroll and he told me that was not the only problem. He wouldn't elaborate. Do you know what he was talking about?"

"Sure, but is now the right time to talk about it?" she asked, nervously.

"I've got my coffee, so I'm all ears."

"First of all, Terry, I need my job and I wouldn't want this to get back to Don or Tim. I need to make sure that what I tell you stays between us, okay?"

"Okay," he said. "But I'll find out sooner or later, and remember: I can only fix the problems I know about."

"Don and Tim are great guys and they treat me really well. They both have a lot of money, but Tim flaunts his while Don is very conservative. You can tell, right? Tim is the playboy and Don the businessman. You can't get Tim to talk business."

"How did they get their money?" he asked.

"From what I understand, Tim inherited a huge amount of money from his dad when the old man died. Part of his will stipulated that fifty percent of the cash left him be invested in properties in South Florida. He was an only child and his mother passed away several years earlier. Don is a lawyer, or solicitor, as they call them in Canada. They have been friends since childhood and when Tim inherited this money, he needed some help so he asked Don to give up his law practice and form a partnership, which they share fifty-fifty. Can you imagine? From what I understand, Don really didn't have anything except some business sense, when they formed their company," replied Radico.

"That's why Don doesn't say much when Tim gets crazy," she said.

"The problem really is the guys that hang around here and who are in business with them," continued Radico.

"Like who?" he asked.

"Well, look at Ed Devine. He's a drunk. True, he works hard when he's here but sometimes he's gone for days at a time. Nobody knows where he is or how to get a hold of him. He owns fifty percent of New Southfield Farms with Tim, who owns CS&W. To my knowledge, it's all Tim's money and Ed has yet to put a dime into the deal. Now, you tell me, how are you going to control that?"

Downes just let her vent out the dismay.

"And, look at this guy Neeley: what a waste of time!" Radico kept on. "He's a friend of Tim's and gets paid a bunch of money for doing nothing. Same with Dutch Cramer."

"What about the construction of the big houses and horse barns that Don showed me yesterday morning?" Downes asked.

"Well, they do build them, but I have no clue as to the construction schedules or costs."

"And the land-development projects?" he probed.

"They just move dirt out there; they've been moving dirt for months. They dig a hole, then fill it in, dig a hole and fill it in. There's no development or construction schedule."

"Don told me that they've already sold a bunch of lots," he said.

"Really? Well, I haven't seen any deposit money and I haven't seen any closing schedule. Isn't that strange?"

"So, what do you think is going on, Jane?" Downes sounded really inquisitive.

"I think that Tim has surrounded himself with idiots and Don has way too much on his plate. Ed Devine is telling everybody about the huge home he's building for himself in Rainbow Farms and—get this—is planning on building a hotel on property one mile down on South Shore. Believe me: Divine doesn't have a pot to piss in. He's owed me five hundred dollars for two months."

"He cashed a check for the payroll on Friday," said Downes.

"That wasn't his money; that was his girlfriends'. She controls the money and besides, he usually screws Tim out of a few grand when he does it, and you can bet she gets some vig on the deal. I think they're doing their damndest to avoid paying taxes and so they work in cash. I've seen suitcases full of cash right here in the office," Radico raised her voice.

"Do you think there are drugs involved?" he asked, cautiously.

"Well, if there are, I haven't seen any. None of these guys are into drugs. Booze, yes, but not drugs."

"I didn't mean using them."

"No, I wouldn't think so. Now, it wouldn't surprise me if the buyers of houses or lots were into peddling drugs. A lot of them pay in cash."

Unbelievable, thought Downes. "Ever heard the names Bruce Stanier and Doug Styles?" he asked.

"You mean the banker and the senator?"

"Yes."

"I've never met either one, but I understand they have business deals with Tim."

"What kind of business deals?"

"Well, they are in a partnership with Tim that involves a large tract of land, but I can tell you that Stanier finances all the deals in Wellington that our companies sell. And Styles is involved somehow because they're both rumored to get payoffs from Tim and the buyers."

"Payoffs for what?" asked Downes.

"Well, rumor has it that whenever changes in zoning or permits are needed, cash is collected from the buyer and given to Dutch, who makes sure it gets to Styles. I've heard that he and Stanier are involved in a number of shady deals and have an arrangement with most commercial builders and contractors in Wellington."

Downes wasn't surprised.

Later in the day, Downes arranged to visit with Gordie Freland at the bank, to start the due-diligence review. At the same time, he gave Freland a list of things that he needed.

"So what do you think, Terry? Do you think these guys are serious?" asked Freland.

"Sure they're serious. Otherwise, I don't think they would lay down a hundred grand. Plus, they're paying me to do this review."

CHAPTER 11

Terry Downes had been on the job two weeks and spending a lot of time at the Bank of Heywood finishing off the due diligence. Freland couldn't stop talking about his pending financial windfall and wanted to make sure all the bases were covered. He asked Downes numerous times about his review and wanted to make sure there was nothing disclosed that could stop the deal from closing.

On a Friday morning, Downes was in his office compiling a list of issues to discuss with Draper, who was scheduled to arrive shortly after lunch. He either would get from Draper plausible explanations for some of the things he had witnessed or heard of, or he was prepared to tell him that he couldn't be involved. It was that simple.

He just couldn't believe what he had been seeing. He wanted to purge the office, disallow certain unsavory characters from entering it, and fire all the people who weren't doing their jobs, whether they were friends of "the guys" or not. He needed the straight scoop on the cash transactions in the office, on whether they were serious about buying the bank or was this just a decoy to lure him into a highly lucrative but illegal business.

Downes also intended to ask Draper about the lack of financial records and the non-filing of tax returns. Things were just not adding up. He had completed his review of the bank and had concluded that the book value should be adjusted for an increase in the loan-loss reserve, as a result of charge-offs outlined in a recent FDIC examination.

He had compiled a lengthy report for Draper, which addressed asset quality, different financial ratios compared with peer-group averages, and his thoughts relative to the bank's management and capital needs.

It was around ten a.m. Janice Radico was in her office with three or four realtors mulling over their listings. Tony Sprano was at his desk reviewing some site plans. Overall, it was a quiet Friday morning.

Downes happened to be staring out of the window when he noticed two large, plain white vans pull up in front of the office. The side door opened and five guys and a woman in plain clothes exited from the vehicles wearing bulletproof vests and carrying weapons. All had ID tags hanging from chains around their necks, revealing the obvious. Soon after, sheriff's deputies arrived in green-and-white squad cars and the strip shopping center came alive with onlookers wondering if a shootout was about to happen.

Downes' heart began to race as they entered the office—the lead guy carrying papers and three of them walking directly to the rear of the building, where they opened the back door and let the fifth guy in.

"Terry Downes?" asked an agent.

"Yes," he answered, nervously.

"Mr. Downes, I'm Special Agent Tony Lopez, FBI. This is Special Agent Judy Dunlop and the other guys are with the IRS, DEA, and the Palm Beach County Sheriff's Office."

"Yes," Downes said, literally shaking in his shoes. "What's going on?" he asked in a quiet but alarming way.

They showed their IDs and Lopez handed him an official-looking document titled United States Treasury Department, Search and Seizure Warrant.

Downes looked at it but couldn't read it. His hands were shaking and his eyes refused to focus. "What's going on?" he asked again, only this time in a more demanding tone.

Dunlop left and walked into Radico's office, where she sat in a state of shock. The other three guys had positioned themselves in such a way that none of the other employees could touch or remove a thing. They were asked to stand away from their desks.

"Mr. Downes, I would like to talk to you. My partner will speak with Miss Radico and then we would like to talk to Mr. Sprano. Will Mr. Devine be coming to the office?" Agent Lopez asked, knowing the names of all the players.

"I would assume so, but I don't know when."

"Okay, we have agents at the trailer."

"Holy shit, please tell me what's going on," Downes pleaded.

"Sure, but first of all I want you to know that we're shutting down the entire operation. We are seizing and removing all files, computer hard drives, and any other records we feel we need. That document that I gave you gives us the authority to do this, understand?"

"Yes, but I'm not an officer of these companies," he said, hoping to be excused.

"We don't care," said Lopez.

"Mr. Draper was arrested yesterday by Scotland Yard in London. He's been charged with conspiracy to traffic narcotics, money laundering, bank fraud, wire fraud, and conspiracy charges."

"Fuuuuuck!"

"Mr. Ford was arrested early this morning in Montreal, by the Royal Canadian Mounted Police, on similar charges," Lopez continued.

"Un-fuckin'-believable!"

"We will be making other arrests as we continue our investigation," he said.

"Could you tell me what has been going on?" repeated Downes.

Draper and Ford had been getting shipments of marijuana from a Mexican drug cartel in Guadalajara—the same cartel responsible for the much-publicized torture and murder of Enrique "Kiki" Camarena, a DEA agent who had infiltrated a drug-trafficking group before being kidnapped, tortured, and murdered.

The authorities knew every move that Draper and Ford had been making, mostly due to Ed Devines constant surveillance, so when the DEA and the RCMP made up their minds to make an arrest, it had to be simultaneous and take effect in several countries. When the RCMP decided to execute the warrants, Draper was on an airplane bound for Jersey, via London; Ford was on his way to Montreal to close another drug deal.

As they were talking on the phone, the Palm Beach County Sheriff's Office came through the front door and started removing file cabinets, hard drives, and anything left on the desks, even trash cans.

Lopez answered a call from an agent, who confirmed that the CS&W trailer had been secured. Shortly thereafter, he received another call confirming that Ed Devine had been arrested at his home. They were looking for Dutch Cramer, Jim Neeley, and two or three others whose names Downes was not familiar with.

"We have had this operation under investigation for two years, ever since the day they moved some of their companies to Florida. It started several years ago in Toronto and we have been working closely with the RCMP, DEA, Scotland Yard, and Interpol. The search-and-seizure warrant was issued by the criminal division of the IRS," said Lopez.

Downes's cell phone rang and he placed it on 'busy'. It rang again, and again he placed it on 'busy'. On the third try, Lopez said that it was okay, he didn't mind, but asked to listen to the conversation. He moved closer to the phone with notebook in hand.

"Hi Terry, this is Sol Perlin. I'm an attorney representing Donovan Draper."

"Yes," Downes replied.

"Have the authorities arrived yet?"

"Yes, they have."

"Have they questioned you?"

"Not really, not yet."

"Good. How about Janice?" asked Perlin.

"I don't know," replied Downes.

"Do you have a lawyer?"

"Yes."

"Well, my advice is to say nothing and call your lawyer. The same with Janice. I will be there later in the day and I need to talk to both of you. I'm in Miami so it may take a little while. I'll call you when I get close to your office," said Perlin, unaware that Lopez was listening.

Lopez had heard of Sol Perlin and said that the first thing the shrewd lawyer would do would be to secure his huge retainer.

Still in a state of shock, Downes walked past Radico's office, where Special Agent Dunlop was grilling her.

Lopez followed him back to his office and said, "Mr. Downes, you may as well tell everybody to leave now. We just need Sprano, Ms. Radico, and you to remain behind. When we've completed removing the things we need, they can return."

Downes decided not to call his attorney right away, unless he felt that he was incriminating himself in answering any questions. After all, he thought, he'd done nothing illegal.

"Mr. Downes, could you talk to me about your role in First Investors Trust Corporation Ltd. the offshore bank in St Kitts?" Lopez asked.

"Yeah, I was there a couple of weeks ago for the first and only time. I was asked to be a director and oversee the operations of the bank," he replied.

"What about the cash that was deposited in the bank while you were there?"

"I was surprised to see that. I asked Draper about it and he kinda blew me off. He said it came from a friend of his who wanted to open an account."

He was asked a ton of questions about St. Kitts and was stunned again when Lopez told him that there had been an agent on the island, while they were there, and that every move they made had been recorded. He was asked about George McLoud, Dennis Fisk, and others whose names he was not familiar with. Before they left the subject of St. Kitts, Lopez asked, "Oh, by the way, was Ernie Mueller's name ever brought up while you were there?"

"I think Draper may have mentioned his name in conjunction with a hotel that he was planning on building."

"You know, Mr. Downes, I just don't understand why a guy with your background, experience, and stature would get involved with guys like these…unless of course, you were partners with them," said Lopez.

A lump was forming in Downes's throat and stared at the agent until he could find the right words, and then said, "Special Agent Lopez, I have done nothing wrong here except to commit a huge error in judgment. I agreed to work with these guys after I went to St. Kitts, met with government officials, went to Miami, and met with their attorneys and spent considerable time mulling over whether or not I should do it. Quite frankly, I was expecting Draper to be here this afternoon and I was going to confront him with a number of concerns that I've had in the two weeks that I've been here. And if I didn't get the right answers, I was prepared to quit."

"What were your concerns?" the agent asked.

"Here's my list," Downes handed his list of questions and concerns.

Lopez just shook his head.

"We know who most of the players are, and we're not talking about your local drug dealers here. We're talking about a major international conspiracy of which Draper and Ford are the lieutenants but not the captain. We've been building our case for the past two years. It involves a number of different countries. We didn't want to arrest them when we did, but the RCMP were the lead investigators and we are assisting them while, at the same time, charging them with crimes in the U.S.," Lopez tried to sound reasonable.

"Okay, we need to get going here. Could you come down to our office tomorrow? We need to take a statement from you—on the record," asked Lopez.

"No problem. What time?"

"Is ten okay? Here's my card."

"Sure."

At that, Lopez folded his notepad, motioned to his partner, and left the building. The others had already left. Downes collapsed in his chair and put his hands to his head. What a day!

Radico walked into his office, as white as a sheet. "Terry, what's happening here?" she asked, eyes bloodshot and still trembling.

Tony Sprano came back and said, "Well, surprised? I'm not, Terry! Could I call you tonight? I'm going home."

"Terry, this lady tells me that I'm in a whole heap of trouble," Radico sobbed and wailed.

"You need to call your lawyer," Downes advised.

"The problem is that I am a signer on the accounts."

"I know," said Downes.

CHAPTER 12

Several hours earlier at his Downtown Toronto townhouse, Don Draper had finished packing clothes for his trip to Jersey, via London, to straighten out some issues with his partners and plan for another infusion of cash into the Florida companies. From there, he was to travel to Miami and then Wellington for his planned week with Tim Ford and Terry Downes.

Don Draper's pad, in the old section of Toronto, was convenient and practical since it was only twenty minutes from the airport. His completely restored townhouse was on the Canadian Historical Registry and he had spent a ton of money refurbishing a block of homes where he lived. The condo was cluttered with books, magazines, papers, and charts that covered the expensive pieces of antique furniture. Several law books were scattered around his living room and classical music played constantly in the background, which he found soothing to his soul.

In the larger of the two bedrooms was a walk-in closet packed with expensive suits, shirts, sweaters, and footwear. On the right side, a large safe containing numerous bundles of Swiss francs, British pounds, German marks, and Dutch guilders. In the other bedroom there were more clothes, a foldaway bed, and another safe containing hundreds of thousands of American dollars.

His den was a place for him to relax. He had several chess sets, one of which was hand-carved from ivory and ebony, two televisions, and a floor-to-ceiling bookshelf. Several original oils were hung on the walls, most of which had been given to him by Tim Ford.

One painting in particular was a Monet, but it wasn't the painting that interested Draper as much as what was behind it. The diamonds, watches, bracelets, and the spectacular stones packed the vault behind the painting, all of which he had purchased with the excess cash he had difficulty in hiding or spending.

Draper had been a scholar in high school, before attending the University of Toronto, where he obtained a law degree and from whence he went on to being admitted to the Canadian Bar. As a lawyer he did okay, but it wasn't until he met George McLoud, while being retained by the City of Toronto, that he started to make some decent money. He was a single guy and had one friend: Tim Ford.

McLoud introduced him to a local businessman, Jacques "Ernie" Mueller, who was in need of a lawyer that was not afraid of shady deals and who could give him priority on all his work. Draper accepted Mueller's offer and before long, Mueller had become his only client.

Draper always enjoyed the transatlantic flights. He activated his elaborate alarm system and climbed into a waiting taxicab, which took him to the international terminal at Toronto Airport, where he checked in and made his way to the first-class lounge.

Tim Ford grabbed a clean shirt and a down-feather jacket, jumped into his Jeep Cherokee, and headed to the highway en route to Old Montreal, where he had a meeting with a couple of guys at La Orange Restaurant.

The RCMP visited Ford's home shortly after he left, arrested his girlfriend on drug-trafficking charges, and learned of Ford's meeting in Old Montreal.

As Ford exited his car at the restaurant, he was arrested and taken into the Royal Canadian Mounted Police custody, and charged with mail fraud, wire fraud, drug trafficking, and conspiracy.

Draper was pampered on his evening flight to London: a seven-course meal, expensive wine, a movie, a long nap, hot towels, and a great breakfast. It was seven a.m. local time, the sun was breaking through the horizon, and the Air Canada 747 was on its final approach into London's Heathrow Airport.

Draper felt great. He had planned to get a shower at the first-class lounge and make his way over to terminal two, where he would board a flight to Jersey.

The plane pulled up to the gate and the first-class passengers were allowed to exit. After thanking the flight attendants and wishing them a good day, Draper walked toward the door of the plane. He was met by two well-dressed gentlemen: "Mr. Donovan Draper, you are under arrest for charges filed against you by the government of Canada."

Draper was stunned. He was placed in handcuffs and taken off the ramp, using the side door and outside into the frigid air.

Janice Radico and Terry Downes chatted for some time. She shared with him certain things that, in retrospect, would have confirmed the suspicions that he had had from the outset, such as Ford's handing out cash to employees, including to Radico herself, whenever he announced he had "closed another deal."

Sol Perlin had called and was expected anytime.

Downes tried to assure her that, as long as she hadn't benefited in any way from these wacky deals and that she had exercised good judgment in what she did, she would be okay. Her meeting with the FBI was scheduled for two p.m.

Soon after, Sol Perlin arrived. Perlin was over six-feet tall and weighed two hundred eighty to three hundred pounds. He wore a business suit and carried an attaché case. He was a man of few words, except for when he was making money from talking: "Hi, I'm Sol Perlin," he said, with a strong handshake.

"Hi, I'm Terry Downes, and this is Janice Radico."

"Well, we have a lot of excitement here in Wellington, huh?"

That was an understatement.

"As you know, I represent Donovan Draper," said Perlin.

"Where is Don, Sol?" asked Radico.

"Don is fine. He's in a London prison awaiting extradition to Toronto, where he will be charged with conspiracy to traffic narcotics and other charges, and then the U.S. is charging him with the same in San Diego."

"What about Tim?" she asked.

"All I know is that he was arrested in Montreal and faces similar charges, but I don't represent him. Could you tell me where Rainbow Farms is?" Perlin asked. "When talking with Don last night, I negotiated a piece of property with some stables as partial payment for my fee. I need to get some pictures before it gets dark and submit them to the DA for approval. Then, I can prepare my pitch for the arraignment and possible bail. He should be out in a couple of days."

Radico couldn't believe how cold and callas Perlin was. He wasn't going to lift a finger until he had gotten at least double of what he thought his fee would be.

Defending drug traffickers was different than any other case, Downes learned. First, the defendant is almost always found guilty and second, they never have money for their lawyers.

Perlin related the obvious, that his client was innocent of all charges and the only thing he needed right then was the list of things taken from the office. Radico had it, gave him a copy, and he left in search of his fee.

Sol Perlin had been referred to Draper by one of his buddies months before, in case something like this happened. Perlin had represented a number of high-profile drug dealers and, although most of his clients were behind bars, he had gained a reputation of getting reduced sentences.

Tony Sprano called to chat about the day's activity. "I'm not surprised at all about what happened," he said. "You would never believe what went on in that office, with all the cash floating around. I knew that sooner or later something like this would happen. They didn't really care about the businesses' making money; it was all a big joke to them. They had run out of places to hide the cash. Anyway, the FBI wants to talk to me, so I'll call you and let you know how that went," Sprano assured Downes.

The next day, Downes met with Lopez and went on record with the answers that he'd already given him. Nothing was new there. Lopez asked more questions about St. Kitts and dwelled more on the cash that Draper had carried there.

Lopez knew that the money had been taken out of a lockbox at Toronto Airport and said that the RCMP had Marcie Travers in custody, as well as warrants for the arrest of certain other people who had been providing Draper and Ford with cash. The six hundred thousand dollars that had been transported to St. Kitts was the proceeds of a drug deal in Toronto. The cash had been placed in a lockbox at the airport and retrieved by Draper.

Lopez also asked Downes about certain transactions in their operating accounts and Downes simply told him that he had not had the time to review bank statements. He would have to talk to Radico about the flow of funds.

Downes asked him why the IRS was involved and told that the IRS knew each time Ed Devine had paid cash to his employees. And the real kicker: they had never filed corporate-tax returns or extensions for any of their companies in the U.S. Further, the IRS had interest in money laundering and the loss of tax revenue.

"Okay, great, Mr. Downes!" Lopez got up. "We will be in touch. We may ask you to testify in front of a federal grand jury. You okay with that?" he asked.

"I guess so," replied Downes.

When Downes got back, he called his lawyer, Art Lavelle, who proceeded to chew him a new ass to the point where he even told him to get another lawyer to represent him. Apparently, he had committed a cardinal sin by meeting and going on record with the FBI without counsel present. Lavelle finally softened up and said, "Get your ass down here and don't talk to anybody, understand?"

"Okay," Downes said and hung up, completely frustrated, thinking why he should call his lawyer when he knew he hadn't done anything wrong.

Lopez met with Janice Radico together with another agent who was a CPA. The agents had collected all bank statements, canceled checks, deposit slips, etc. What they were doing was finishing the connecting of dots that formed a paper trail—from the source money, obtained illicitly, to its final destination, usually a company either in Canada or South Florida.

It was staggering how much information the FBI had accumulated over the previous two years as a result, in part, of the cooperation between agencies in the U.S. and those of foreign governments. Very impressive, indeed, but in order to complete their case for the grand jury, they needed witnesses that could confirm transactions, conversations, actions, etc. Those witnesses would be Janice Radico, Tony Sprano, Terry Downes, and a lady by the name of Arma Lozo.

Over the next few days, Downes chatted with Radico, but Tony Sprano didn't call. He was concerned that Downes may be involved in some way. Repetto brought Downes up-to-date with what the FBI was doing and still couldn't believe what had happened.

Sol Perlin had secured his fee and was preparing to go to Toronto to meet his client, who had already been extradited from London, and Draper's Canadian counsel.

Properties were confiscated by the government under the RICO (Racketeer Influenced and Corrupt Organizations Act), including the homes and stables.

Downes spent considerable time pining over his immediate future, but his main priority came after his lawyer called to tell him that his life and the lives of his family could be in danger as a result of his willingness to testify in front of a federal grand jury.

A meeting was arranged with Agent Lopez and a detective from the Palm Beach County Sheriff's Office to give him some advice on how to prevent him and his family from being put in compromising situations. They agreed to have his home watched and recommended that he not have any fixed schedules when leaving the house. His wife and kids were not to leave the house alone and a sheriff's deputy would be positioned at the end of their road.

Very, very reassuring! thought Downes. For the next several weeks, his life would be completely screwed up.

Downes received a call from a Sergeant Pete Sankowitz with the Royal Canadian Mounted Police in Toronto and requested that they meet at a hotel in West Palm Beach the following day. Sankowitz had called Repetto and asked the same of her, later in the day.

Sergeant Sankowitz had just checked into his room at the Omni Hotel in West Palm Beach when Downes tapped on his door.

"Mr. Downes," he said, opening the door to his room.

"Yes. Sergeant Sankowitz?" Downes extended his hand.

"Come in, and please call me Pete. I really appreciate you taking the time to meet with me."

"No problem. Is this your first time in West Palm?"

"First time in Florida, and I'm just here for the day. I have a return flight late tonight."

"Oh, so you came down here just to meet with me?" asked Downes.

"Well, you and Janice Radico. I tried to get Tony Sprano but he declined. Do you know Arma Lozo?"

"No, never heard of her before."

"Mr. Downes, you understand why I'm here, right?"

"I do."

"I have a whole bunch of questions to ask you in regards to this case. I have read a copy of the transcript of your statement to the FBI and I'll be asking some of the same. The reason, of course, is that we are prosecuting these people in Toronto and we need to have our own statements from witnesses. As you know, the U.S. Attorney's Office in San Diego, California, is presenting the case to the federal grand jury in a couple of weeks, but we will prosecute and try them first."

Sankowitz was a very polite guy and genuinely appreciative of Downes's agreeing to meet with him. He had been involved in the case from the outset and had developed an obsession with getting these guys behind bars. "Do you mind if I turn on the recorder?" he asked.

"No, not at all."

Sankowitz asked Downes the normal stuff: home state, full name, age, home address, etc. Then how long had Downes known Mr. Draper and Mr. Ford, where had they first met, and so on.

He was particularly interested in St. Kitts "How often have you been to St. Kitts?" he asked.

"Just the one time—a couple of months ago."

"Did you meet with any government officials?"

"Dennis Fisk, the deputy prime minister."

"Were you introduced to anyone else in government?"

"I don't recall anyone else. I was introduced to Walter Jones, who, I understand, founded the PDM Party but is not a politician."

"Yes, we know Mr Jones."

"How about the name Ernie Mueller?" Sankowitz asked.

"I think his name was mentioned by Draper, something to do with George McLoud and the hotel they were attempting to build."

"Ever seen Mueller's name on any documents or invoices?"

"No."

"What about McLoud? What was his role, and did you see his name on anything?"

"Well, I can't tell you what his role was. He was involved in all the conversations. If you want my opinion, I think the guy is a real dirtbag and I wouldn't trust him as far as I could throw him. He appeared sneaky, not to mention his appearance and general demeanor. I understood him to be a director and an owner of the bank, but I think Draper needed to have somebody there who he knew and who could deal with the government people. I didn't see his name on anything, but then again...they didn't show me much."

"Any reference to any Indian people? Asian India?"

"No," replied Downes, somewhat surprised.

At this point, Sankowitz turned off the recorder while he changed a tape. This gave Downes an opportunity to engage him in conversation off the record.

"Pete, is this a big deal, as far as drug trafficking goes?" he asked.

"It's huge, probably one of the largest marijuana-smuggling deals on record. I don't know how much the FBI has disclosed, but the properties that they had in Florida were just a fraction of what they held in total."

"Could you elaborate?"

"Sure, but only in general terms. They had numerous interests in Canadian companies, much more than they had revealed. They had property in London—prime property on the Thames; property in France and Germany; owned a gold mine in South Africa; and owned a company that had a large interest in the Sports Dome in Toronto and many other companies that they organized as a front for laundering drug money.

"We have secured tens of millions in cash from bank accounts that they had around the world," Sankowitz went on, "and I'm sure there's a lot more that we have yet to identify. We think that this is just the tip of the iceberg."

"Really!"

"Yes, we have evidence that Draper and Ford, although the kingpins of the drug-trafficking business, either answered to, or were partners with, other more influential players. This is a very complex case and these guys knew how to cover their tracks. We've spent a lot of time and effort trying to get the evidence to prosecute them, and it ain't been easy," Sankowitz shook his head in dismay.

"Tim Ford told me that he had inherited money and expensive oil paintings from his father, who died several years ago. True?" asked Downes.

"His mother and stepfather live in Calgary. His biological father nobody knows," Sankowitz replied. "But they never had any money."

"Unbelievable!" said Downes.

Sankowitz replaced the tape and continued with the more mundane questions. He was happy with what he had gotten so far and asked if Downes would appear as a witness in a Toronto court.

Janice Radico was scheduled in thirty minutes, so they shook hands and Downes agreed to testify.

Art Lavelle called Downes to tell him that he would be accompanied by U.S. marshals on his trip to San Diego and that his ticket and hotel reservations would be given to him at the airport.

A few days before leaving for California, he returned a call to a friend of his, Judy Smythe, a newspaper reporter for the Palm Beach Journal. Smythe had been working on an article involving Bruce Stanier and First Community Bank and needed to get some information from him.

They met for lunch and talked about Stanier, the bank, and his buddy, Senator Styles, both of whom, interestingly enough, were involved with Draper and Ford in a partnership purchase of some property in Wellington.

Smythe was shocked to hear about Downes's involvement in the drug conspiracy and would anxiously await the outcome of his testimony in front of the federal grand jury.

Terry Downes and Janice Radico arrived in San Diego accompanied by a U.S. marshal and joined by the lady named Arma Lozo who, according to Janice, was Draper's girlfriend while he was in Florida. Apparently, she had been offered a deal with the FBI that afforded her immunity from prosecution for her testimony in front of the grand jury. She declined and was prepared to "plead the fifth" at the hearing.

Arma Lozo was a very confident woman. She had met Draper at Shakey's Restaurant in Wellington and they had been dating for the previous two years. Radico had heard about the woman but had never met her. Nobody knew the extent, if any, of her knowledge or involvement in any illegal activities.

She was a strikingly attractive woman, dressed in an outfit suited for a nightclub date and wearing some pretty expensive jewelry. Both Radico and Downes were hoping that she would be dressed a lot more business-like for her testimony the next day.

Downes's meeting with the assistant U.S. attorney was scheduled at eight a.m. and his testimony with the grand jury was to begin at ten a.m.

He was so shaken-up that morning that he couldn't eat, but he must have consumed a gallon of coffee prior to meeting Horatio Caicedo, Assistant U.S. Attorney, at Caicedo's office in the federal building. "Hi, good morning. I'm Terry Downes," he said, nervously.

"Hi, Horatio Caicedo. Pleasure!" the attorney replied, in the middle of shuffling papers in preparation for the meeting. "Ever attended a federal-grand-jury hearing before?" he asked.

"No, I haven't."

"Well, it's pretty straightforward and kinda informal. I will ask you basic questions for the record, and then the jury members are free to ask anything they want. Just be factual, to the point, and don't answer any questions that you're not sure of. Remember: they have seen your previous testimony," said Caicedo. "Are you represented by counsel?" he asked.

"No, I'm not," replied Downes.

"Good...because your lawyer is not allowed in the room."

Downes didn't know.

"Usually, when witnesses bring their lawyers. They sit outside the courtroom and they can delay answering a question until they've consulted with their lawyer, after getting permission from the foreman of the jury. It's a pain in the ass and can delay the process for hours," Caicedo informed.

"Anyway," he continued, "this will be pretty straightforward, I hope. We've kinda fast-tracked this case, done a lot of work, and to me it's a slam dunk, but you never know. Your testimony and that of Ms. Radico are key. Would you like some coffee?" he asked.

Like Downes needed more coffee...! "Yes, please. Black," he accepted, anyway.

Caicedo called out to whoever heard him, "Can we get two black coffees in here, please?"

The offices were buzzing with activity. Caicedo's tiny office was cluttered with law books, and his monitor left on with an incomplete brief on the screen. It looked like organized chaos.

Radico's meeting was scheduled for two p.m., Arma Lozo's for four, and they were all advised to remain flexible regarding their return flight.

Sipping his coffee, Caicedo said, "Are you aware of the background of this case and why it means so much to the DEA's office?"

"'I'm aware of the 'Kiki' Camarena murder and that some agents here worked on that case," replied Downes.

"Right. Well, these guys are chomping at the bit to build a case against anybody doing business with these assholes," said Caicedo, still arranging papers for the meeting.

"I guess that's understandable," said Downes.

"Yeah, but they don't understand what the law requires before we can prosecute anybody. That's why your testimony is key to this case," Caicedo emphasized.

Downes thought that if his testimony was the difference between their eventually being set down for trial or not, then they must have a pretty slim case against those guys. After all, he had only known Draper and Ford for a couple of months..

At ten a.m., he was escorted to the grand-jury room by Caicedo. The room was quiet where twenty-one expressionless people were seated. Downes stood in the witness box and Caicedo approached the podium.

"Ladies and gentlemen, members of the grand jury: today we are to present witnesses in the case of the United States versus Donovan Draper, a Canadian citizen, and Timothy Ford, also a Canadian citizen. The U.S. is claiming that Messrs. Draper and Ford have conspired to traffic narcotics, perpetrated mail fraud, perpetrated bank fraud, traveled unlawfully to avoid prosecution, evaded federal taxes, and engaged in conspiracy from January 1984 through December 1986," Caicedo enunciated his words carefully.

"In this regard, our first witness is Terry Downes, a resident of Wellington, Palm Beach County, Florida, and former employee of Monterey Inc., a U.S. company owned by Draper and Ford. You have been provided the personal profile of Mr. Downes and his affiliation with the defendants and also a copy of the transcript of his testimony, which he gave the FBI on January 23, 1987.

"Bailiff, would you please swear in the witness?" Caicedo asked.

"Raise your right hand, please," said the bailiff. "Do you promise to tell the truth, the whole truth, and nothing but the truth, so help you God?"

"I do."

"Thank you. Please, be seated."

Without any delay, the first question from Assistant U.S. Attorney Horatio Caicedo was, "Would you state your name and spelling, please?"

"Terence Downes," he answered, spelling out his name.

"And could you state your address?"

"12265 Victoria Lane, Wellington, Florida, 33414."

Caicedo spent forty-five minutes asking Downes questions about his relationship with Draper and Ford, their companies, the money trail, the offshore bank, and his affiliation with certain individuals before he asked the members of the jury if they would like to ask any questions.

"Yes, I have a question," said a juror from the back of the room. "What were you thinking when you agreed to work for these guys?"

"Jesus Christ," Downes mumbled to himself, thinking that the questions would be easy.

"Sir, I was at the stage in my career where I thought a change from banking would be good. I thought meeting with Draper and Ford's accountant and lawyers offered reasonable explanations to some irregular transactions and the fact that they were willing to file a change-of-control application for the purchase of a commercial bank added some credibility," he replied nervously.

"They had no intention of going ahead with the bank purchase," the juror stated.

He couldn't get over how informal this was. Horatio Caicedo stood at the podium the whole time, shuffling papers and taking notes.

"That they were from Canada and they would periodically bring cash with them when coming to the U.S. because they wanted to avoid paying the IRS in Canada. They said that they used cash because of the loss in the exchange rate," Downes elaborated.

"Did you have any clue about what was going on?" was a question from the back.

"After the first week of working there, I had a number of issues to discuss with Draper, not the least of which was the lack of records and bookkeeping substantiating the infusion of cash to support the different companies."

The questions kept coming, generally from the same four or five members of the panel.

"Mr. Downes, we're trying to account for and locate tens of millions of dollars. We understand that their biggest challenge was laundering this money, or at least placing it somewhere for future use. Were you not flush with cash in the Florida companies?" asked a juror.

"To my knowledge, it was quite the contrary. They didn't have money available for the Friday payroll before I started working there and on the following Monday, my first day, there were twenty or so workers waiting to get paid," Downes replied.

"And how did they get paid?" he was asked by another juror.

"Ed Devine paid them in cash," replied Downes.

"How much was that?"

"Around ten thousand dollars."

"Did Devine always carry that much cash?" asked the same juror.

"I don't know, but I was told that although he lived from hand to mouth, on occasion he would have as much as fifty thousand cash in his desk."

"If you, God forbid, were forced to conceal millions in cash, how would you do it? You're a banker?" asked another juror.

Everybody got a chuckle and then Downes responded, "With all due respect, sir, it's not the job of a banker to hide or conceal money."

The juror apologized.

"However, if I had to conceal money," Downes went on, "I would deposit it in an offshore bank, in a numbered account, where privacy laws are very strict—like in Switzerland."

"Or St. Kitts," said another juror.

"I would invest in art, gold, restaurants, casinos," Downes added.

"Any evidence of them doing that?"

"Well, yes. They were getting ready to purchase property in St. Kitts and build a hotel. I know that Tim Ford had a collection of oil paintings that seemed to be worth a lot of money."

"Did he ever say where he got it?"

"Yes, he said that he had inherited the paintings from his father."

They obviously knew that this had not been the case.

As Downes sat there answering question after question, he got the distinct impression that they already had all the answers, even without referencing his testimony. They broke for lunch and Downes was asked to reconvene at 1:30 p.m.

A DEA agent who happened to be a close, personal friend of the late "Kiki" Camarena was assigned the task of taking Downes to lunch. It was a great lunch, great place, good food, and totally interesting conversation, and the government picked up the tab.

Agent Harry Daniels had been with the DEA for fifteen years and was very passionate about his work. They talked a lot about his friend Kiki, what a great guy he was, how their families got together for picnics, and how much he was missed. They also talked about the 'sadistic motherfuckers' who killed him and the role that Daniels had played in kidnapping Velasko, the doctor who had kept Camarena alive while he was being tortured, and putting him away for three life terms.

Harry Daniels was a Navy Seal, a guy who loved his country and who had developed pure hatred for those who dealt in drugs. He talked about Draper and Ford, his familiarity with the case, and the amount of marijuana that was shipped from Guadalajara destined for places like Detroit, New York, and Chicago. In his estimation, eighty to ninety percent passed successfully through customs as a result of officials being paid off.

Daniels further told Downes that the number of people arrested in this case had already been forty-two and was climbing; that they had customs people on their payroll; and that they were taking shipments by the tractor-trailer load. Ford had paid as much as fifty thousand dollars to a crooked U.S. customs officer for each truckload let through the border station.

Daniels thought that this case was much bigger than Draper and Ford. Downes asked him to elaborate, but that's where he drew the line.

Downes arrived back at the courtroom as the jurors were taking their seats.

"Mr. Downes, have you ever traveled to India?"

Wow! he thought. He was beginning to wish he had Art Lavelle outside. "No, I haven't," he replied.

"We understand that you were born and raised in England, correct?"

"Correct."

"When was the last time that you were there?" asked the same juror.

"A couple of years ago."

"Ever met a guy by the name of Ernie Mueller? Jacques 'Ernie' Mueller?"

"No, never have."

Downes didn't want to tell them that his name had been mentioned by Draper while in St. Kitts. They didn't ask if he'd heard of him but if he'd met him.

"Chandrasastari. Indian, Hindu?"

"No."

"How about Bill Grabowski?" asked one juror in the front row—his first question.

"Who?" Downes asked.

"Bill Grabowski. He's the CEO of the Kalahari Corporation, the developer of Wellington and Palm Beach Polo."

"Why should I know him?" Downes asked, shrugging his shoulders.

Big mistake.

"Mr. Downes, we ask the questions here. Besides, the juror simply asked if you knew the man, not that you should know him," the foreman barked.

"Sorry," he said, looking down at the desk.

"Did that name ring a bell while you were at the Bank?"

"No, sir."

"First Community Bank had a branch in Wellington, correct, Mr. Downes?"

"Correct."

"Do you recall attending a customer appreciation event at the Wellington branch of First Community Bank in December 1981?"

"Yes, I do."

"Who was in attendance from the bank?"

"Bruce Stanier, the bank's chairman; a few loan officers; and the branch manager, if I recall correctly."

"How about customers?"

"Yes, there were many."

"How about executives from the Kalahari Corporation?"

"Yes, there were one or two, if I recall. The chairman and a Russian guy," replied Downes.

"Then you must have met Grabowski."

"No, I don't think so, but there was a guy who spent the entire evening talking to Stanier."

"Did he have a Russian accent?"

"Don't recall."

"How about Senator Douglas Styles? Was he there?"

"Yes, sir, he was."

"Thank you, Mr. Downes. We have no further questions," said the foreman.

"Thank you, Mr. Downes. You may leave now," said Caicedo.

Downes walked outside the grand-jury room with his legs shaking and a bad case of cottonmouth. He needed a drink of water and somebody to talk to. Were the last few questions a part of the iceberg that Pete Sankowitz had been talking about? he wondered.

The U.S. Attorney's Office had made a reservation for Downes on a ten-p.m. flight from San Diego, stopping in Los Angeles and arriving in Fort Lauderdale at seven a.m. local time. He left the courthouse at four and saw agent Harry Daniels before he left to thank him again for his hospitality. Downes, then, found a place to relax—a small restaurant close to the airport which the cab driver had recommended. He pulled a notepad out of his briefcase and after calling his wife to see if everything was okay at home, he started to make some notes of the events leading to all this, including the day's hearing.

He called Lavelle to keep him apprised of the hearing and left a message. He then called Judy Smythe, his newspaper-reporter friend. "Hey Judy, this is Terry. I'm in San Diego. I've just finished my testimony with the grand jury."

"How did it go?" she perked up.

"Judy, I need to talk to you. This is a much bigger deal than I thought—not that I hadn't thought it was a big deal before. I get into Fort Lauderdale at seven in the morning. Can you pick me up, my car is parked in Palm Beach International?"

"I'll be glad to pick you up. You can buy me breakfast."

"Good. I'll see you then. Delta flight 122 from L.A."

The flight was miserable. Downes had a middle seat with some fat guy taking his armrest on one side and a woman with a screaming kid on the other. To top it off, there was, what seemed to be, a seven-foot guy sitting directly behind him with his knees firmly embedded in the back of his seat. So, by the time he landed, he was fit to be tied. No sleep, no change of clothes, no food to speak of, and a thundering headache.

Judy Smythe was waiting at the gate and greeted him with a big hug and an unexpected and surprising kiss on the cheek. He'd always liked her—a young, attractive, and very smart and ambitious woman. She was divorced but never talked much about her ex-husband. Downes needed to vent in the worst way and needed her to help him try to unravel this web of intrigue.

"You look like crap," Smythe said, as soon as she saw him.

"I feel like crap," he responded.

As they were walking to the car, he proceeded to tell her about the events leading to the hearing, including the raid on the office, his meeting with the FBI, the arrest and subsequent arrests of Draper and Ford. The conversation continued over breakfast and well into the morning.

"What a story!" she was flabbergasted.

"Judy, it's far from complete. How about working with me to see if we can unfold what's going on? We have all the pieces in regards to Draper and Ford, but we need to find out how Stanier, Styles, and this guy Ernie Mueller are involved. They even asked me if I've visited India. What's that all about?"

"We don't know that they are involved."

"Then, why would a federal grand jury ask me questions about them?"

"I have no clue. Okay, where do we go from here?" asked Smythe.

"I have to think this out. One thing is for sure, Judy: we shouldn't discuss this with anybody and, of course, when there's a conclusion of any sort, I will collaborate with you on a story."

"I know. I just don't know where begin," she admitted.

On the way back to Palm Beach Airport, Downes got messages that Sol Perlin, Tony Sprano, Art Lavelle, and George McLoud had called. He returned McLoud's call in Toronto.

"Hello," answered McLoud, obviously with a cigarette drooping from his mouth and gasping for breath.

"George, Terry Downes returning your call."

"Terry! What in the fuck is goin' on?" he screamed.

"I don't know, George. You probably know more about what's going on than me."

"Buuullshit! All I know is that, if the government doesn't get anybody to step in for Draper, they're going to take over the bank."

"I figured that, George, but I'm staying as far away from that bank as I can right now," said Downes.

"Please Terry, come down to St. Kitts. I'll be here next week. We can talk about everything. There are so many things going on down here."

"Yeah, I know, George," said Downes, sounding disinterested.

"Please!" McLoud pleaded.

"I'll think about it," said Downes and hung up. "He wants me to meet him in St. Kitts" he told Smythe.

"You should go. Maybe McLoud can answer some questions, as long as he's not arrested."

"I'm sure they wouldn't let him into St. Kitts, if he were a problem."

"I guess not," she said.

"Say, why don't we both go? I can do some snooping around while you meet with McLoud," she suggested.

"Can you get the time off?" he asked.

"I'll have to tell the editor that I'm working on a story that could be huge. He generally lets me do what I have to do. Besides, it's not like we'll be gone for more than a few days."

"Okay, let's think about it," he said.

CHAPTER 13

Don Draper and Tim Ford had been convicted of multiple charges in a Canadian court and were serving ten- to fifteen-year sentences in a federal prison in Toronto. Upon completion of those sentences, they faced fifteen to twenty years in the U.S.

Since his initial involvement with Draper and Ford, Downes had returned to St. Kitts on a few occasions and by now had established good relationships with local businesspeople.

First Investors Trust was still in operation and McLoud was still its "managing director," although Henry Blackstone appeared to have more control over the day-to-day activities. Draper and Ford's equity interest in the bank had been forfeited and it was unclear who the de-facto owners of the bank were.

On a hot and humid Monday morning in late October 1989, Downes, while sitting in his office working on bids for the county, received a call from a guy in Delhi, India.

"May I speak to Mr. Downes, please?" a caller said, with an Indian accent.

"Yes," replied Downes .

"Yes, my name is Anwar Rhami. I am a reporter for the Delhi Times in Delhi, India. How are you today, sir?"

"Fine, thank you."

"Sir, Mr. Downes, I am calling from Delhi, India, and I was wondering if you could help me, please. I have in my possession a copy of a numbered account that was sent to me anonymously, which was opened in your bank, First Investors Trust CompanyLimited, in St. Kitts, West Indies."

"You have a what?" asked Downes.

He heard what the caller had said, broken English and all, but he was so befuddled that the guy had mentioned his name associated with First Investors Trust.

"Yes, sir, Mr. Downes. I have in front of me a copy of a numbered-account agreement on the letterhead of the First Investors Trust Company Limited. Also, I have a letter on First Investors letterhead, signed by Terry Downes, that references the account number to a Mr. Syed Singh for the benefit of a Mr. Jai Kumar. The account shows deposits of over fifty million American dollars and withdrawal activity until the account was closed. Can you confirm this account to be legitimate?"

"I really don't know what you're talking about," said Downes, struggling for his words.

"Yes, sir, Mr. Downes. Could you let me have a fax number? I will fax this document to you, then you can confirm the account, if you will," asked Rhami.

"No, I don't think so," he said, wondering if he should give it to him or not. Maybe it would have been good to see what this was all about. "I need to speak to my lawyer and see what he says," he said.

"Why not tell me if this is a transaction that you handled, Mr. Downes?"

"I don't need to talk anymore about this. St. Kitts has strict privacy laws," he said, and hung up.

"'Numbered account,' 'fifty million dollars,' 'my bank,' 'newspaper reporter,' 'India'.... What the hell is going on, and who the hell is Syed Singh or Jai Kumar?" Downes wondered out loud. " And how the hell did he obtain the name of the depositor?"

"Kumar is the socialist candidate for Prime Minister in the elections next month against Gandhi. Holy Shit." said Downes to himself out loud.

Having thought that this part of his life was behind him—after all it had been over two years since his grand-jury testimony—he started to recall specific questions that had been asked of him which, at the time, seemed unrelated to the case.

Downes's mind was racing as he played the call, in his mind, over and over thinking about the grand-jury testimony and the questions that had been asked.

Two hours later, he received another call. This time, the call was from London: "Mr. Downes, this is Alistair Brown. I'm an investigative reporter with The London Observer. I need to know if you recall a recent numbered-account agreement that you opened in your bank in St. Kitts, First Investors Trust Company Limited, in the name of Syed Singh. I have a copy of the account agreement and a letter, signed by you, which references the account to Jai Kumar."

Downes was stunned and realized that something big was going on, and that he could be in the middle of it. "What's this about?" he asked.

"We were mysteriously sent a copy of a numbered account after we were told that it references Mr Kumar. The account is for the benefit of Mr. Kumar, and your signature appears on the letter as the managing director of First Investors Trust Company," said Brown. "Mr Kumar is campaigning for prime minister of India in their general election next month."

"Holy crap," Downes said to himself. "You realize, Mr. Brown, that the laws in St. Kitts concerning numbered accounts prevent the disclosure of such confidential information," he explained.

"I understand but upon inquiry, we were told that the account belonged to Mr Kumar and all I'm looking for is your confirmation or denial that such a transaction actually occurred."

"I'm sorry, Mr. Brown. I can't help you. Sorry!" he said and hung up, not thinking to refer him to Art Lavelle.

Immediately after hanging up with the newspaper reporter, he placed a call to George McLoud at his apartment in Toronto, to see what he had to say about these calls.

"George, Terry Downes."

"Terry, how are you?" he asked, coughing and spluttering.

"I'm not very good, George. I need to know what's going on."

"We were expecting your call," he said with a nervous chuckle.

"You were what?" screamed Downes.

"Terry, I can't talk about this over the phone. I need you to come up here."

"Oh, really? I need an explanation now, George. Somebody has been forging my fuckin' signature."

"Sorry, I can't talk about it over the phone, Terry. There's a 7:30 flight to Toronto leaving Miami tomorrow morning—Air Canada. There will be a round-trip ticket waiting for you at the ticket counter. The flight gets in around 10:45, and I'll arrange for somebody to pick you up."

"George, please tell me what's going on," Downes demanded again.

"Just be on that flight," he said abruptly and hung up.

Having no sleep that night and wondering what this was all about and whether this was connected to the events involving Draper and Ford, Downes nervously left his home at five a.m. and drove the seventy miles to Miami Airport.

The first-class ticket was for 7:45 a.m., arriving in Toronto at eleven a.m., and had a return flight at eight p.m., arriving in Miami at eleven p.m.

During the flight to Toronto, he ran a number of different scenarios through his mind and wondered if this was the iceberg that had been referred to by Pete Sankowitz when he was taking his testimony two years earlier.

Wednesday, October 18, 1989

Terry Downes arrived on time at Toronto International Airport and breezed through immigration and customs. He was expecting a driver to be waiting with some sort of sign, but didn't see anything as he made his way through the reception area to a restroom, where he needed to freshen up and look for McLoud's telephone number.

Standing at a sink while he splashed water on his face, a voice said, "Are you Terry Downes?"

Downes looked in the mirror and saw a guy dressed in a black topcoat with dark glasses and a black flat-top chauffeur's hat. "Who are you?" he asked.

"Please follow me."

"Follow you where, and who are you?" said Downes, with his legs starting to tremble.

"To my car," said the driver.

"Who are you, and where are we going?" asked Downes, turning around to face the man.

"You are Terry Downes, right?" asked the driver.

"Yes, now who are you?"

"I'm a driver for Mr. McLoud and I'm here to take you to a meeting. I saw you in the reception area and you fit the description of the Terry Downes I'm supposed to pick up. I didn't have time to make up a name sign," said the driver.

Downes reached for a towel to dry his hands and face, picked up his briefcase, and nervously followed the driver out of the men's room.

They headed for a black Lincoln town car parked directly outside the revolving doors of the main terminal, in a spot next to a sign that read, "Positively No Waiting."

"Where is this place?" asked Downes, with a nervous tone.

"On the outskirts of Toronto."

Downes checked the inside of the car before getting in the back seat. "Who's at the meeting?" he asked, trying to get a heads-up and sounding a little concerned.

"I don't know," said the driver, displaying a real economy for words.

After a forty-five-minute drive, they took an exit off a main highway onto a less-traveled road and then to a side road where they drove a couple of miles through a heavily wooded area. The driver slowed down as they pulled up to a huge wrought-iron, remote-controlled gate, which opened after the driver dialed a number from his mobile phone. They proceeded down a long driveway lined with oak and maple trees to a huge Victorian-styled residence.

On a very cold morning, they made their way past the immaculately manicured grounds of the house, where a group of yard maintenance people were cleaning leaves and taking care of the exotic plants and shrubbery.

The driver stopped and parked near the entrance to the house, next to a number of late-model limousines, and quickly exited the car to open the passenger door.

A crowd of Indian people, dressed in their traditional saris, gathered at the entrance to the house, in the middle of which stood George McLoud and another gentleman waiting for Downes to get out of the car. With a cigarette in his mouth and wearing the same clothes he had on when Downes had last seen him in St.Kitts, he hollered, "Terry, welcome. Glad you could make it."

"Did I have a choice, George? Somebody has a lot of explaining to do," Downes was angry.

"Yeah, no problem, Terry. Everything's good, I'd like you to meet a very good friend of mine: Terry Downes, meet Ernie Mueller," said McLoud, knowing that he would be surprised to meet him there.

"Pleased to meet you," said Mueller, extending his hand..

"Sure," said Downes curtly.

"How was your flight?"

"The flight was fine."

"Well, let's see if we can explain everything to you, so that you can enjoy your flight back," said Mueller.

Still standing in the entranceway to the house, Mueller turned and said, "I'd like you to meet my spiritual leader and partner in some of my ventures, Chandrasastari Murkarji. We call him Sastari, a name that he prefers."

At that, a portly man in his late forties approached, wearing traditional white cotton robes, with a red dot on his forehead.

Downes made the mistake of extending his hand as Sastari backed off, clasped his hands as if in prayer, bowed, and said, "Namaste."

"Let's go inside and relax," said Mueller.

Downes assumed that this was Mueller's home. What a place, he thought.

He was led to a library just inside the house on the left. Mueller led the way and following him were Sastari and McLoud.

The house, or mansion, had been built in 1947 and once owned by a prominent Canadian politician. It had twelve bedrooms, ten bathrooms, two kitchens—each as big as Downes's home—library, two huge dining rooms, theater, billiard room, two pools—one indoors—a six-car garage, etc., etc. It sat on fifteen acres of the most luxurious property he'd ever seen. The driveway was lined with exotic plants and old oak trees, which had been placed in perfect locations, accentuating the entire landscape.

"George, why don't we let Terry and Sastari talk for a few minutes? I have someone on hold on the phone," suggested Mueller, not telling him that it was the newspaper reporter, Anwar Rhami, from Delhi.

Mueller opened the door to a huge library with fifteen-foot ceilings and bookshelves from floor to ceiling. A wooden ladder on a roller track was leaning against the shelves for easy access to books out of reach. An old English roll-top desk was positioned facing a ceiling-high window with leaded twelve-inch square panes overlooking a Japanese flower garden.

Worn, antique Persian rugs partially covered a random-width, oak-wood floor boards and a large desk with leather and brass-top inlays was centered toward the rear of the room. Two black leather couches, long enough to seat six people, were neatly placed along the sides of the room, both with matching leather-and-bronze-topped coffee tables. Each had antique cigar boxes and crystal ashtrays placed on both ends.

On the right side of the room was a TV monitor showing the Headline News Channel, where the ticker tape for instant updates of the stock market and another similar monitor showed options trading from the Chicago Board of Trade.

In ornate picture frames, numerous photographs of Mueller and his family, as well as Mueller and his friends and business associates, were placed on the desk. Some hung as a collage on the right side of the dark mahogany paneled walls. One of four Queen Anne chairs was facing one of the couches.

Downes entered the room, Sastari followed, and Mueller closed the door behind them.

"Mr. Downes, my name is Chandrasastari. My friends call me Sastari. Thank you for visiting with us today," he said in perfect English.

Downes remained quiet, looked him square in the eyes, and concentrated on every word he said.

Sastari was around forty-five years old, although it was difficult to tell. He had a long patched beard and a red dot in the middle of his forehead. He sported a large gold chain with a medallion of sorts around his neck and wore a Rolex President watch studded with diamonds. Gold bracelets were hanging on both wrists and a huge diamond ring on the pinkie finger of his left hand.

Downes had always had the feeling that Indians and Pakistanis were dirty and seldom bathed. No matter how much jewelry they wore or scent or perfume they used, they still appeared dirty. Growing up in England, he recalled the reputation they had as being thieves and cheats and whose standard of living was generally that of paupers.

"As you may know, I'm a spiritual man. I am the leader of the Hindu people around the world," said Sastari. He paused and waited for a response or a reaction.

Was this guy for real or what? thought Downes.

"I am also a businessman and a friend of many Western world leaders—an international broker, you might say. I handle financial affairs for countries that require confidentiality, and it could involve, at times, billions of dollars."

Downes's eyes didn't leave his. He paused again, still waiting for a reaction. Sastari hadn't asked him a question, so Downes didn't say anything.

"Here, let me show you my album with photographs of me and my friends and business associates," he said, as he got up from his chair and walked over to the roll-top desk.

Sastari provided him with a large, gold-leafed album, which he placed on the coffee table and motioned him to open. The first page showed a picture of Sastari with the Sultan of Brunei. Downes flipped the page and there he was with Margaret Thatcher; then with François Mitterrand, Helmut Kohl, Jimmy Carter, Elizabeth Taylor, and so on and on. It was a pretty impressive collection of photographs of Sastari with world leaders and celebrities. But what did this have to do with him?

"These people are my friends, and I have access to them at any time. I work with them personally and professionally. I am also a spiritual advisor to many other Hollywood celebrities and well-known businessmen."

"Are you Mr. Mueller's spiritual advisor, or is your relationship with him strictly business?" Downes asked, sarcastically.

"Both," said Sastari, with a glare.

The door opened and Mueller and McLoud entered, followed by a maid in uniform carrying a silver tray with coffee, tea, and cookies.

"I'm sure you're ready for a little snack, Terry. Help yourself, please," said Mueller.

Mueller and McLoud both grabbed a chair and took a seat alongside Sastari. Downes felt like he was being prepped for a shocking revelation.

He was.

Jacques "Ernie" Mueller was extraordinarily wealthy. His main business was batteries and he owned the largest manufacturing company in the world, located in Mumbai, India. He held major interests in Canadian and Indian financial institutions and his political connections, especially with Indian dignitaries, gave him access to a number of lucrative ventures.

Mueller had made his big money brokering deals with his best friend Omar Khallehki, the world's renowned arms broker, and his spiritual man Sastari. He was also the "validator" and the missing link in the Draper-Ford drug conspiracy, although he had escaped prosecution, even investigation. His involvement was well concealed, and he had been able to pick up and not miss a beat when Draper and Ford were convicted and sent to prison.

Mueller had always stood in the background. He would seldom have his name involved with any of his deals, and would hide behind different corporate veils which he constantly changed.

It had been Draper who showed him how to structure his enterprises, to hide cash, and shelter income from the IRS.

Mueller was a corporate chameleon. He did billions of dollars of business with the Indian government and had numerous politicians, Indian and Canadian, in his pocket. Mueller had come a long way since his days of owning and operating a string of strip clubs in Toronto.

George McLoud was one of his bagmen, and Mueller took care of him, as a result of favors rendered by McLoud when he was employed by the City of Toronto and worked in the mayor's office in a public-relations capacity.

Although his name didn't appear on any document or was ever mentioned in any conversation, Mueller was behind the forming of First Investors Trust Corporation Limited. He had also been initially involved in the hotel project in St. Kitts, but pulled out of the deal when he found out that McLoud had mentioned the deal and his name to several people.

Mueller had been the final say in what Draper and Ford were involved in. He made sure that the flow of cash was restricted and that projects suffered before money would be wired so as to not make the source of funds look too obvious. He was known, and referred to, as "the Professor."

So when Ford started flaunting his newly found wealth, Mueller was furious. This was something that couldn't be tolerated. It had escalated to the point where Mueller had to terminate his involvement with both Draper and Ford, even if he had to sacrifice his equity position in a number of ventures that the two guys operated.

"Terry, the reason we asked you to join us today is because we have a business matter that needs to be resolved right away, and we need your help in resolving it," said Mueller very matter-of-factly.

Downes started to feel very anxious and seriously concerned that he had somehow been involved in an international scheme that was way over his head.

Sastari sat with a scary stare focused directly at Downes. George McLoud, cigarette protruding out of the corner of his mouth, sat with his fat ass hanging over the seat and a sneaky grin on his face.

"As you probably have gathered, we are involved in large financial transactions around the world, especially in India, where trade with the United States and Canada is at an all-time high. My friend Omar Khallehki, who you will meet, together with Sastari have established this wonderful relationship with the political leaders of India, the results of which have contributed to their strong economy. This has been made possible by working with a duly elected democratic government in the largest democracy in the world," said Mueller with his hands clasped and looking toward the ceiling.

Why in the hell does he want me to meet Khallehki? Downes wondered. He had heard of him, of course—he was known as the world's biggest arms broker. Khallehki supposedly took ten percent of the gross on all weapons sold to different countries and he didn't care whom or what they were fighting for.

"When general elections take place and governments change, it makes us very nervous, especially in a country like India, where it is very easy to completely change the political landscape from a democratic form of government to socialism and possibly communism. The general election takes place in India in three weeks. Running for office is a gentleman by the name of Jai Kumar, former minister of finance in Mr. Devi's government," said Mueller.

Downes was already anticipating what he was about to hear.

"Kumar is a socialist, and if he wins the election, trade as we know it today will disappear and the country will be set back fifty years. He has also been accused of taking kickbacks from defense contracts while he was defense minister, after being fired as minister of finance in Devi's government. Mr. Devi has been trying to remove him from his government ever since he took office, but was unable to do so because of the politics in their parliament. Kumar has a huge following, mostly millions of peasants in India. Many world leaders have discussed with Sastari the negative impact of him being prime minister of India."

"So, how does this affect me?" asked Downes.

"When situations like this come up, we have to do whatever it takes to stop them from coming to fruition. The action taken at times looks and sounds deceptive, but believe me, it is always within the best interests of democracy and we are the good guys, the guys who wear the white hats," explained Mueller, with a smile on his face.

"So now, how does this affect you?" he continued. "Well, first let me say this: We know that Kumar has been taking kickbacks and misappropriating funds from the treasury for a long time. There have been a number of internal investigations conducted, but nothing conclusive revealed, mainly because of corruption within the political offices that Mr. Devi has been trying to correct."

Please get to the point, thought Downes.

"We needed to be sure that Kumar does not get elected. It was widely known that he was involved in a number of fraudulent activities which were being covered up by his cronies in government. So, what we did was bring them to light by showing the Indian people proof that he had hidden absconded money and, therefore, was bad for the country. We fabricated a numbered account in First Investors Trust Corporation in the name of Mr. Kumar's brother, Syed Singh, with Kumar being the beneficiary, and we superimposed your signature on the account as managing director of the bank, authenticating the transactions. And, by the way, officially notarized. The account shows numerous deposits totaling fifty million dollars. We also recorded withdrawal activity in the account covering a period of several months, until we showed the account as being closed," said Mueller.

"Why couldn't he authenticate the account?" asked Downes, pointing to McLoud and getting madder than hell.

"That would have raised too many suspicions. You add credibility to what we're trying to do, Terry. Besides, we needed George to arrange for the immigration records to show Singh's people entering St. Kitts at the time that the activity in the account was recorded," replied Mueller.

Downes couldn't believe what was going on and how they could arbitrarily forge his name and make him responsible for affecting the outcome of a country's general election. This was way beyond his imagination. The only thing he could imagine was the worldwide implications this could have and the consequences of the truth being told.

Sastari just sat there staring at him, expressionless, while McLoud sat with a contemptible grin on his face, to the extent that the cigarette sticking out of the corner of his mouth would allow. Downes wanted to smack him. What a fucking moron! he thought.

Mueller took a sip of coffee and said, "We then faxed a copy of the account to six major newspapers around the world, hoping that they would contact you for confirmation that the account and the transactions had been legitimate. So, yes, George was expecting your call."

"Why didn't you contact me before you sent the faxes?" Downes asked, angrily.

"Because you would have denied any knowledge," replied Mueller.

"Unbelievable," said Downes.

"And what we would like from you, Terry, is your cooperation…to the extent that you will confirm the transaction as being legitimate," said McLoud.

"Fuck you, George," he said, spontaneously.

"Look, Terry, whether you like this situation or not, you are involved. But let me just say this: you will be handsomely rewarded—in a way that will change your life," said Mueller.

"And if I don't cooperate…" he let the conjecture linger.

"Let's not dwell on that. I'm confident that you'll see the benefit to the world in what we're asking you to do. With absolutely no risk or downside to you," he replied.

"This is bullshit!" said Downes, holding his head in his hands.

"Let's get something to eat. We have lunch waiting for us," said Mueller, before Downes had a chance to continue venting out his wrath.

After what he had just heard, he really wasn't hungry. The knot in his stomach simply wouldn't allow him to eat.

The dining room was spectacular. Seated for lunch were a host of Indian people, most of whom were "disciples" of Sastari—the ladies wearing saris and the men loose-flowing Kurtas with pajama pants, all with red dots on their foreheads.

Downes was introduced to an older-looking Indian gentleman named Babbi, who appeared to be Sastari's right-hand man in his business dealings. As Babbi clasped his hands, he whispered, "Mr. Downes, thank you so much for being here. The prime minister sends his most appreciation for assisting him in these difficult times."

Jesus Christ! he thought. Devi knows about my involvement!

It appeared as though it was a foregone conclusion that he would go along with their plan. Ahmed Devi had contacted Sastari and Babbi and prayed that they could help him.

Devi needed to be sure that Kumar would not get elected, for it would be catastrophic for the country, so he claimed, and worse for him and his close friends. For sure, the deals with Sastari and Mueller would come to an end and investigations into the prior weapons transactions could ruin Devi's political career.

Sastari contacted Mueller about the dilemma and Mueller talked with McLoud, who came up with a "splendid" way of discrediting Singh shortly before the elections.

Babbi was ecstatic about the plan and what this huge favor meant to Devi. At the same time, it would help the Holy Man's business partners. He didn't even consider the fact that Downes may not go along with them.

The table was laid out with huge crystal vases containing fresh-cut flowers and large silver bowls of fruits and nuts, with a place-setting for twenty-two people. Bowls of saffron-laced rice were scattered with curried vegetables and other vegetarian sauces popular in Southern India. There were small bowls of cucumber in yogurt and Nan bread, poppadoms, and flavored ghee placed at each end.

The fragrances of the food permeated the extra-warm house. Together with the scents and perfumes of the guests, it felt like actually being in New Delhi.

Downes helped himself to a very small portion and, after a couple of bites, politely excused himself from the table. He felt nauseous, hot, and miserable—and it wasn't because of the food.

He found his way to the foyer and thought he would take a little walk around the grounds to get his head straight, but the security guards and Mueller's driver were watching every move as he walked between the Mercedes and the Rolls parked in the driveway.

Still feeling uncomfortable, he returned to the library and gazed through the window at the Japanese garden, trying to gather his thoughts. What should he do next? he asked himself. Play hardball with these guys and see what happens, or reach some compromise that would allow him to walk away without the risk of retribution.

Mueller, Sastari, and McLoud went into the library and took their seats—Mueller still eating out of a fruit bowl; McLoud lighting a cigarette, openly burping in the process; and Sastari resuming his stares at Downes.

"You didn't eat much, Terry," said Mueller.

"How in the hell can I eat, having just been told that I was set up in a major international scam?"

"It's not as bad as it sounds," said Mueller.

"Oh yeah, tell me what I'm missing here."

"I don't think you understand what we're asking of you. All we need is for you to verbally confirm the transaction with the guys that called you."

"Oh, is that all?"

"That's all. I still have one of them on the phone—on hold—right now," Mueller said.

"And what if I decline?" he asked.

"We are not asking you to write or sign anything, and if by chance questions are raised at a later date, you can deny having ever said anything, and we will claim that you were never here," said Mueller, with McLoud looking so smug.

"Terry, we're not in the business of threatening anybody or forcing people to do things. It would destroy us if we did that. You have been caught in the middle of a potentially ugly situation and we want to help get you out of it," he continued.

"I don't think I was caught in the middle of anything. I didn't sign that document. This piece of shit forged my name," barked Downes, pointing his finger at McLoud. "Furthermore, I am not and never was the managing director of that so-called bank. So, I guess he forged my name on that document also…right, George?"

"I was told that you were. Isn't that one of the reasons why Draper hired you?" asked Mueller.

"No, I was asked if I would be a director and I didn't give him an answer until we left the lawyer's office two days later. I didn't sign anything," argued Downes.

"Well, it's my understanding that you signed the documents while you were there, in anticipation of your acceptance," said Mueller.

"No, I didn't," snapped Downes.

"Well, Draper and Ford forfeited their roles when they were convicted, and we thought you would take over the bank," said McLoud.

"That does not give you the right to forge my signature, George! Jesus Christ!"

"Well, we did, and now we have to deal with it," said Mueller, trying to stave off a battle of words between McLoud and Downes.

"You mean I have to deal with it, right, Ernie?"

"Right," said Mueller. "So you're involved, Terry, whether you like it or not. We all know what Draper and Ford were doing at the bank. It would be unfortunate to have your name disclosed in a smear campaign with the Indian government after you compiled a fake numbered account," Mueller went on, bearing a strange look on his face. "We have the resources and contacts to make anything look the way we want, so please, it is in your best interest to work with us, not against us," he concluded, very sternly.

McLoud removed the cigarette from his mouth and smiled broadly.

"Look, take this as an initial small gesture on our part for your willingness to work with us on this matter. We want you on our team," said Mueller.

Downes wouldn't touch the large brown envelope that Mueller had just placed on the table in front of him, but he imagined that it was a sizable amount of cash.

"I need to call my lawyer," said Downes, afraid that they may say no.

"By all means, but remember what I said, Terry: you are involved, whether you like it or not," said Mueller, waving his hand toward the phone.

They stood up and left the room, allowing Downes some privacy to make a call, although he was sure they were listening to the conversation.

Thank God Judy answered her phone! he thought. She was quite surprised to hear from him. He tried to explain the predicament that he was in and that he was in a meeting with McLoud, Mueller, and Sastari. He asked that she meet him the next morning in West Palm for breakfast.

They reconvened their meeting after taking a phone-call break, and Mueller started talking before he sat down. "What did your lawyer say?" he asked.

Downes just stared at him and said, "He said, 'Be careful.'"

"Terry, we would like you to meet Mr. Khallehki at his home in New York. He would like to discuss a business proposition with you. Sastari will be there to make the introduction. We've made arrangements for you to be there the day after tomorrow," said Mueller.

"Is this another attempt to get me to confirm this phony transaction?" asked Downes.

"What we want you to say is, 'Yes, that is my signature and the account is legitimate.' However, if you're not willing to do this, we would ask that you say, 'Due to the rigid privacy laws in St. Kitts, I'm afraid I cannot comment at this time.' Would you, at least, say that and then we would take this one step at a time?"

Downes thought for a minute and said, "Ok!"

Mueller made the calls to the reporters and Downes gave them his formal response.

Ernie Mueller was hoping that he would create enough controversy to propel the newspapers to run a story, anyway, without the confirmation that they needed. Indian and British newspapers were notorious for publishing stories with little or no collaboration, and it was widely known that Indian politicians could coerce the Indian newspapers to publish pretty much anything they wanted.

Downes felt terrible about doing this, but at least he hadn't lied. And he may very well have precluded harm to him, his family, and his business. As soon as the session was over, McLoud told him that a reservation had been made for him on a flight from West Palm Beach to New York, on the following day, for his visit with Omar Khallehki.

CHAPTER 14

Jai Kumar was born in the Rathore Royal Family of Manda in Allahabad, United Provinces, British India, in 1932. He studied at the Colonel Brown Cambridge School, Dehradun, for five years and entered local politics in Allahabad during the Nehru era.

He was appointed Chief Minister of Uttar Pradesh in 1980 by Indira Gandhi, when the Congress came back to power after the Janata Party interregnum. As chief minister, Kumar cracked down hard on the banditry problem, which was particularly severe in the rural districts of the southwest of India.

During his term as finance minister, he oversaw the reduction of gold smuggling by reducing gold taxes and the excellent tactic of giving the police a portion of the smuggled gold that they found. He also gave extraordinary powers to the Enforcement Directorate of the Finance Ministry, the wing of the ministry charged with tracking down tax evaders.

Devi was forced to fire him as finance minister, possibly because of many of the raids that were being conducted on industrialists who had financially supported the Congress in the past. However, Kumar's popularity was so high that only a lateral move was possible: to the Defense Ministry.

As minister of defense, Kumar began to investigate the notoriously murky world of defense procurement. After a while, word began to spread that he possessed information about a major defense contract that could damage the prime minister's reputation. Before he could act on it, he was dismissed from the cabinet and, in response, resigned his membership in the Congress Party and the Lok Sabha, the Indian Parliament's Lower House.

Ernie Mueller and his associates knew that, if Kumar were elected prime minister, it would have a big impact on future business and possibly result in their being implicated in previous illegal arms deals. Kumar's popularity was on the rise and the chances of his winning the election were high, since he had gained the support of India's masses.

An assassination plan of Kumar was prohibitive. First, it would create such a furor in the country and lead to civil unrest; second, there was not enough time to plan an assassination and be sure it would be properly covered up.

Prime Minister Devi was very much afraid that Kumar would win the election, for he was ahead in the polls and telling the Indian people what they wanted to hear. Mueller had to act fast and the only way to affect the voting, Sastari confirmed, was to orchestrate a major scandal.

If the international and Indian newspapers could publish a story of significant importance portraying Kumar as a rogue and have evidence to support the story, voters could be swayed.

Chandrasastari was a controversial Indian tantric, one who could allegedly perform miracles.

He was born in 1950 and left home at an early age to become a disciple of Upadhyay Amar Muni and Tantra Pandit Gopinath Kaviraj. He lived in the jungles of Bihar, meditating, and claimed to have obtained siddhi(miraculous powers).

He was the favorite "godman" for the rich and famous and self-professed leader of the Hindu religion. He was a fabulously rich power broker, an international jet-setter, and a Rasputin-like figure, but also a spiritual man who gave advice and counsel to numerous international celebrities and world leaders.

Omar Khallehki, an international arms dealer who at one time was the world's richest man, was Sastari's personal friend and business partner.

Sastari had palatial homes in Beverly Hills, California, and New Delhi, India, and an army of security personnel and attendants who minded the queue of visitors to his homes. He also took residence in a condo on New York City's Fifth Avenue, one floor below Khallehki's residence on the forty-fifth floor. Khallehki owned the condo but it was there just for Sastari.

Sastari, or Holy Man as he was known, was Omar Khallehki's personal guru and best friend. He was also Ernie Mueller's spiritual advisor and business partner. The three of them were tight—very tight.

Sastari was a short, fat man with long black hair, always bearing an un-groomed, long black beard and the red dot on the forehead. He usually wore white cotton, long dhoti skirts with white cotton shawls and Indian sandals. He was always accompanied by a team of advisors (disciples) that included chefs, personal secretaries, spiritual advisors, and gophers.

When entertainers or other public figures needed him, they were made to wait for appointments, sometimes for weeks. Whenever they visited him at the sumptuous Balmoral Towers condo on Fifth Avenue, New York City, they were treated just like everybody else. They very seldom arranged for Sastari to visit them, since he traveled with his entire entourage and the logistics of housing his troupe was prohibitive, plus, of course, his fees did not include travel expenses for which he expected full reimbursement.

He was the go-to person for arms deals that needed to be kept under the radar, and in doing so, he hid behind his religious and spiritual position in life. When he was contacted by representatives of countries or factions that needed arms or required money be "parked" for other reasons, they were given priority treatment.

A typical transaction would be: when a foreign government official, mercenary, dictator, or terrorist organization needed certain weapons, they would get in touch with Sastari either directly or through a contact in India. The deal would be referred to Khallehki as the broker and he would order the arms through his small chain of contacts, of which Mueller was one. The commissions could range in the millions of dollars, most of which were deposited in accounts at Carib Bank in St. Kitts, care of First Investors Trust Company Ltd., before being wired out to other banks and back to financial outlet of Sastari's choice.

George McLoud managed the accounts.

CHAPTER 15

Downes met with Judy Smythe after he got back from Toronto and described his meeting in as much detail as he could. Her reaction was one of amazement. She couldn't wait to hear what the New York meeting would be all about.

Again, a first-class ticket was awaiting him at the airport-round-trip, same-day, West Palm Beach to La Guardia, N.Y. Specific instructions were given to Downes to go to Balmoral Towers on Fifth Avenue and tell the doorman that he had an appointment with Sastari in apartment 43F. Sastari would meet with him and then take him to Khallehki's place one floor above.

The entrance to Balmoral Towers was somewhat unpretentious, under a big black awning with a single set of revolving doors. The building housed a number of celebrities, but the top-two-floors, sixteen-thousand-square-feet, belonged to Omar Khallehki.

Downes was greeted by a doorman in a posh-looking green uniform with gold embroidery, who accompanied him inside to verify his appointment with Sastari. A call was made and he was escorted to a private elevator, where a uniformed operator wearing white gloves took him to Forty Three F and waited with him until someone answered the door.

Several minutes later, the door opened and he was greeted by a short Indian fellow dressed in traditional Indian clothes. He welcomed

Downes and asked that he take a seat on a large sofa where five or six other people were waiting to see Sastari. He saw a pile of shoes at the door, so he removed his shoes before taking a seat.

The condo was relatively small and very warm, with a stench of cheap perfume and Indian cooking, resembling that of Ernie Mueller's house.

As he entered and took a seat, people waiting to see Sastari stood up, clasped their hands, slightly bowed, and whispered 'Namaste'.

There were a number of Indian people there, Sastari's followers and disciples, some of whom Downes recalled seeing at Ernie Mueller's house.

Sastari used his bedroom as an office of sorts, for it was in this room where he would hold his private meetings. People from all walks of life would make appointments to see him, but were required to wait in the living room until called upon by his secretary. These people could be foreign dignitaries, prominent businessmen, or guys like Downes from whom Sastari needed favors to facilitate a big deal. No matter who it was, they were required to wait in uncomfortable conditions until Sastari was ready to see them.

The furniture and fixtures in the condo, although seemingly expensive, were not well-maintained. There were stains on the furniture and chipped or broken ornaments. The floors were dirty, and the doors and the walls had never seen a coat of paint.

The visitors sat quietly, either reading or in meditation, waiting for the little Indian guy to tell them, "His Holiness will see you now."

After waiting almost three hours, seeing a couple of people come and go and wondering what the hell he was doing there, the little Indian guy approached Downes and whispered, "His Holiness will see you now."

He was escorted down a hallway, where the little Indian guy knocked and opened the door and showed him into Sastari's bedroom. Very strange, Downes thought.

"Namaste, and thank you for coming. You are a very wise man," said Sastari.

Standing by his side and smiling was Babbi, whom Downes had met at Mueller's house.

"You have met Babbi, my business assistant. He is quite familiar with the situation," said Sastari.

"Namaste," said Babbi.

"Thank you," replied Downes.

Sastari's bedroom was huge, with a king-sized bed and a sitting area where he conducted his meetings. The walls were bare, dirty blinds covered the windows, the lighting was dim, and the room, very warm and uncomfortable. There was a statue of 'Shiva' on a nightstand, together with pictures of Sastari with some dignitaries. Otherwise the room was bare, with just three or four chairs and the bed.

Sastari pointed to a chair and stared at him, his eyes glazed and his hands clasped, "Please have a seat," he said.

Sastari talked briefly about his personal mission and how all Hindus looked upon him as their savior and, philosophically, about "some things in life that we must do, which may not be popular with everyone."

He told Downes about his longtime friend Ahmed Devi and how he and his mother had helped India become an emerging economy and how important it was for Devi to get re-elected. Downes just listened. It was the most eerie conversation, one with which he felt completely out of sync.

"We are blessed with having Ahmed Devi as our leader in India. Ties between India and America are very strong, and this will continue if he remains in office. He is a wonderful person who comes from a reputable family. He is a humanitarian and is solving the poverty crisis in India, and we need him to remain in office, Mr. Downes. If Mr. Kumar is elected, all this will go away and India will resort to standards of living that were prevalent fifty years ago. Furthermore, it will leave India vulnerable to attack from Pakistan. You can help prevent this, Mr. Downes. We would be forever indebted to you," pleaded Sastari.

He spoke about his friends, the entertainers and the world leaders, how he helped them, and the billion-dollar deals that he brokered, which took a lot of his time.

It was soon apparent to Downes that Sastari's main purpose was to make money. His religious beliefs and spiritual following were a means to an end.

Sastari thanked him for taking the time to visit with him and Ernie Mueller who, he said, was his main business partner and a very good friend of India.

Babbi just sat and stared at Downes. After just ten minutes of conversation, Sastari suggested that they go to see "Omar."

Babbi rose immediately and opened the door, with Sastari leading the way down the hall. Upon entering the living room, everybody nervously stood up and bowed, except one guy who kneeled down on the floor kissed Sastari's feet.

Downes slipped on his shoes and followed Sastari and Babbi outside into the hallway and to the stairwell, where they climbed the stairs to the next floor.

It was unusual to see a controlled-access door in a stairwell, until he realized that Omar Khallehki occupied the entire floor and the one above.

Sastari punched in an access code, which led them into a small holding area, and then another access-controlled door where he entered another code. Security cameras were positioned to cover every square foot of space.

Omar Khallehki was a billionaire Turkish–Saudi Arabian arms dealer. He was noted for his engagements with high society in both the English- and Arab-speaking worlds, and for his involvement in the arms-for-hostages deals and numerous other controversial deals.

Khallehki owned a U.S. corporation called Trinity Holding Company which, among other things, built the Trinity Center in Denver, Colorado. It was this property that had purportedly been used as collateral to get financing from Ernie Mueller to fund the Iran-Contra deal.

Khallehki was implicated in the Iran-Contra Affair as a key middleman in the arms-for-hostages exchange, along with Iranian arms dealer Manucher Ghorbanifar, and in a complex series of events, was found to have borrowed money for the arms purchases from Ernie Mueller.

Among Khallehki's clients were defense contractors such as Lockheed Corporation, Raytheon, Grumman, and Northrop. A shrewd businessman, he covered his financial tracks by establishing front companies in Switzerland and Liechtenstein and bank accounts in other tax-haven countries that offered strict privacy laws, such as St. Kitts, to handle his commissions and develop contacts.

Most of the deals were in excess of one hundred million dollars and involved arms purchases through the Indian friends of Sastari's or, for that matter, anyone who had the money. These customers could be from the Western world or underdeveloped countries, dictatorships, mercenaries sponsored by governments, friend or foe of the U.S. or Canada...it didn't matter.

Arms purchases could involve a number of different manufacturers and complexities, and could take months or years to fulfill. Weapons components, such as missile-guidance systems, were popular, and Khallehki and Mueller knew exactly whom to go to when it came to defense contractors and/or political officials such as Senator Douglas Styles.

Huge amounts of money would be "parked" with Sastari until the deal could be fulfilled, and the negotiated commissions could range from three point five percent to fifteen percent. After people were paid off—politicians, company executives, and lobbyists of defense contractors—and logistical expenses paid, the group could still net as much as five to seven percent. Most deals were kept out of the public eye, usually a condition for the transaction, due to the fact that many of them were illegal.

Khallehki was a Judas when it came to business. He didn't care who was fighting whom, as long as there was fighting. He sold arms to anyone who had the money, and they always did. He thrived on international conflicts. Sastari added spiritual trust. Mueller was the end game and had a book of names to call on for any type of weapon, including nuclear components. Mueller generally arranged the delivery through different merchant-marine outlets. Omar Khallehki was, at the time, the richest man in the world.

Downes was completely flabbergasted when he entered Khallehki's home. It occupied the top two floors of the Balmoral Towers with a three-hundred-sixty-degree, floor-to-ceiling panoramic view of Manhattan. The ornate furnishings and the paintings, the sculptures, floor and wall coverings, and the grand piano in one of the lounges were magnificent.

He was greeted by a young, armed Arab gentleman in a smart business suit who offered to show Downes one of the offices where, on display, were photographs of Khallehki with many world leaders, celebrities, family members and front pages of magazines that featured his picture.

Downes was told that the residence had over one hundred rooms and that it had originally made up the sixteen condominiums once owned by a renowned Greek tycoon.

Sastari had disappeared while Downes was being shown the office, but he and Babbi reappeared just in time to see Khallehki enter the room.

"Mr. Downes, welcome, welcome! So glad that you could make it," Khallehki said, with a huge smile.

"Thank you," said Downes.

Khallehki whispered something to Sastari, and he and Babbi left without saying anything.

Khallehki was a short, stout man with a big midriff wearing an open-neck white dress shirt with black pants and brown sandals. In Arab countries, being overweight is usually associated with wealth.

Khallehki had just been extradited to the U.S. and released on bail, after having been arrested and held in Switzerland, accused of concealing funds. He wore a security bracelet around his ankle, which was a part of his release, and confined to his residence. He never mentioned anything about it, but it must have been quite embarrassing for him, for the press portrayed him as an international villain as a result of a relatively minor offense. He was ultimately acquitted of all charges against him.

They walked across the room, passing the grand piano, to a plush overstuffed sofa and a gold coffee table with Arabic markings, the likes of which Downes had never seen before. He tried to suppress his excitement at seeing such a magnificent place but was truly overwhelmed.

As he took a seat, a butler presented a silver tray of fruits and nuts and another with coffee and tea. Khallehki sat in a chair facing him.

"So, I understand you met with Ernie and Sastari in Toronto."

"I did."

"They thought it good for us to chat about ways in which I can help get the situation resolved with the account in St. Kitts," said Khallehki.

He talked about his friend Ahmed Devi and explained to Downes the significance of his help and the rewards that he would receive for his assistance.

The conversation with Omar Khallehki was more of a plea for help on his part than anything else, but Khallehki appeared surprised and disappointed when Downes told his side of the story—how he had been set up and became an innocent party to this mess.

Khallehki had not been told the whole story. He did say that all governments and their officials were deceitful and that there were times when we were all subjected to unconventional tactics to achieve fair and equitable solutions.

He respected the fact that Downes couldn't lie about the numbered account, but stressed, yet again, how important it was that he knew of the impact on the world if Kumar were elected. Khallehki was a very gracious and dignified man; he would never appear to be one of the world's renowned and infamous arms dealers.

After a short but interesting meeting, Downes left the "palace," caught a cab to the airport, and the plane home. He had a chance to reflect on the day. What a day.

Downes returned to West Palm Beach and, on the following morning, met with Judy Smythe. She was most interested in hearing about his meeting in New York, the international implications, and whether there was any connection between Mueller, his Indian friends, First Investors Trust Company, and drug trafficking.

Downes had first met Smythe soon after he had left First Community Bank. She was writing a piece for the 'Palm Beach Banker' on Bruce Stanier, the "dynamic banker," and interviewed Downes trying to get his opinion of the guy after having worked for him for eighteen months.

At the time of their interview, Downes wasn't very complimentary but was also careful not to burn his bridges with Stanier or First

Community Bank. Smythe was careful in her article not to quote things that he had told her off the record.

He had also bumped into her at a couple of local fund-raisers and afterwards she always made a point of contacting him whenever she needed his opinion on banking matters. From time to time, she would quote him in her articles. She was a highly respected reporter for the Journal and a person with whom Downes had gained a lot of trust and respect.

Smythe had also started some background work in preparation for another article on Stanier and First Community, since there were a number of rumors floating around, especially in the gay community, concerning Stanier and his friends in Tallahassee and Washington. Also, the bank had received lower ratings from the "bank monitor" and from Wall Street as a result of lackluster earnings, even though South Florida continued to be in a very bullish real-estate market.

Smythe had also heard about the political violence in St. Kitts and the deals with South American drug cartels, which she suspected were related to politics. The problem was a lot bigger than she had originally thought.

In essence, the Labour Party members wanted to increase their wealth through illicit business, more so than the PDM Party, and the end result was violence. St. Kitts had become the most violent country, per capita, in the Caribbean and there were constant threats to the lives of politicians and their families as drug deals continued to rise.

Smythe didn't realize that drug peddling wasn't the only problem in St. Kitts. It appeared as though a number of crisis situations in India were being resolved or brokered in St. Kitts, primarily because Mueller was involved in most of them and he knew that they would be kept out of the public eye if negotiated and closed on this remote island.

It had been generally known that, in order to do business in St. Kitts, one must have a government official as a partner, usually a majority interest partner. It was either that or pay exorbitant fees to the government officials each time their approval was needed.

This type of payola was encouraged by the government, considering that their employees, including the prime minister, were very poorly paid even by their own standards.

Evidence of payoffs or some other form of subsidy could be seen in the standard of living and the lifestyles of top government officials. A number of them supported more than one family and could not possibly afford the support payments—not to mention the big homes and the late-model cars—on their meager salaries.

Government officials in St. Kitts were encouraged to take equity interests in projects that were financed by foreign investors. It was also an unwritten policy to inflate license fees and take kickbacks, the amount of which depended on what the investors were prepared to pay or what the deal could afford. These fees or kickbacks were often distributed amongst a number of government officials.

CHAPTER 16

Sunday, December 3, 1989

In spite of it all, on December 2, 1989, three weeks after attempts to smear him and his campaign, Jai Kumar was elected the tenth prime minister of India.

The attempt to discredit Kumar and influence the outcome of the general election failed. An article appeared in the Delhi Times but it was after the election, and what was published was a true account of what had happened, except that Downes was implicated in a fabricated attempt to discredit the new prime minister.

The headlines in the Delhi Times read, "American Businessman Allegedly Involved in PM Scam":

"American businessman Terry Downes, a resident of South Florida, USA, and apparent Managing Director of First Investors Trust Company Ltd., an offshore bank in St. Kitts, West Indies, has been implicated in an attempt to discredit the newly elected Prime Minister of India, Jai Kumar. Three weeks prior to the election, the Times received, from an anonymous source, a faxed copy of a numbered account in First Investors and a letter referencing the account to Aleyja Singh, for the benefit of Prime Minister Jai Kumar. The account showed cash deposits and withdrawals totaling over fifty million dollars, over a period of eighteen months, before the account was closed in October of this year.

Mr. Downes, who would not confirm or deny the legitimacy of the account, claimed that he could not comment on it when interviewed by the Times, since St. Kitts had very strict privacy laws that prohibited disclosure of any information pertaining to its customers or directors.

When asked about the matter, it was revealed by Syed Singh that he had never visited the island of St. Kitts and offered to share his passport as evidence.

The prime minister has not commented publicly, but according to unnamed sources, is said to be livid about the accusations and pledges retribution against the perpetrators of these unbelievable accusations.

The incident is currently under investigation by the Central Bureau of Investigation."

The impact that the election results had on Mueller, Khallehki, and Sastari was devastating; the impact of the article in the Delhi Times on Downes was worse. Fortunately, the story had not been picked up by the API and, of course, neither Mueller nor McLoud nor anyone else would be implicated in the dastardly event.

The real reason why there was so much adversity toward Jai Kumar, to the point of putting together the smear campaign, was his pledge to open an investigation into corruption charges in government. These charges included illegal arms deals and kickbacks received by government officials.

It was apparent that Sastari, Khallehki, and Mueller had been able to get a lot of business done through the Gandhi government.

Shortly after taking office, Jai Kumar's government formally opened a criminal investigation into allegations of official corruption in a 1986 weapons purchase by the Indian Army.

Gandhi, who headed the government when it decided to purchase four hundred and ten howitzers from a Swedish arms manufacturer, maintained that no illegal payments were made when the deal had been made with the government.

But reports in the Indian and Swedish press had named Gandhi administration officials, who appeared to have taken part in a cover-up of multimillion-dollar commissions paid on the $1.4-billion arms sale. Of course, Sastari was in the middle of this controversy as having parked the money for the purchase. He had been responsible for the payout of commissions to government officials, all known to Gandhi.

The director of India's Criminal Bureau of Investigation, Rajendra Shekhar, said that former Prime Minister Rajiv Gandhi could be called in for questioning. Upon this announcement, Ernie Mueller went into damage control and arranged a meeting with Sastari and Khallehki to make sure that they had their bases covered.

Tuesday, December 5, 1989

Upon the news that Kumar had won the election, Downes figured that there would be plenty of repercussions. He hadn't heard, of course, from Mueller or McLoud and he wasn't particularly interested in contacting either one of them. Judy Smythe had accumulated a lot of information and she was determined to write a story on the St. Kitts connection.

Smythe visited Downes's office in West Palm Beach to talk about the next step in her attempt to connect all the dots on this mission of intrigue. After a couple of hours of reviewing her notes and confirming the details of Downes's visit with Mueller, she concluded that the next step would be to visit St. Kitts and attempt to gather collaborating witnesses to many parts of the story.

"Terry, is there anyone in St. Kitts who would talk to me about the operations of the bank?" she asked.

"The problem down there is that everybody has their own agenda, and the amount of truthful information that they are willing to give you strictly depends on what you have to give them. Under the circumstances, I don't think McLoud will talk to us. Henry Blackstone will only tell us as much as he thinks we should know. And if we talk to Dennis Fisk, he will not say anything unless there is money in it for him."

"How about the girls in the office?"

"I remember meeting Sophie Albrightson, who worked in the office but I doubt that she would know anything, and furthermore she would probably be too scared to talk to anybody."

"Well, let's try. It seems they are the only option we have," suggested Smythe, looking for the banks' number in a Rolodex file and picking up the phone.

After fifteen to twenty attempts to get through, the phone finally answered: "Hello, First Investors, can I help you?" said a very faint voice with an off-island accent.

"Hello, this is Judy Smythe from the Palm Beach Journal calling from Florida. Who is this?"

"This is Sophie Albrightson."

"Hi Sophie, how are you?"

"Fine." Albrightson was not a very talkative person. Polite, yes; pleasant, yes; but not a conversationalist.

"Sophie, I'm planning a trip to St. Kitts this week and was wondering if I could spend some time with you. I would like to talk about the bank.."

"Why do you want to talk to me?" asked Albrightson.

"I'm a newspaper reporter and am writing an article on St. Kitts and offshore banking."

"Then I think you need to talk to Mr. McLoud, and he's not here."

"No, Sophie, I would prefer talking to you. I think you can be more helpful than Mr. McLoud."

"I don't think it's right for me to talk to a newspaper reporter without Mr. McLoud knowing."

"When will Mr. McLoud be back?"

"I'm not sure. He's in Toronto."

"Sophie, our conversation will be in the strictest confidence, and if there are things that you would prefer off the record, I will give you my word that it won't be repeated."

"No, I think you should talk to Mr. McLoud," she insisted.

"Okay, Sophie, but if you should change your mind, you can call me at any time," said Smythe, leaving her number. Disappointed, she hung up the phone. "I'm going, anyway," she turned to Downes. "You want to come with me?"

Meanwhile, Downes had received a copy of his grand-jury testimony and shared with Smythe some files that he had kept when Meadowbrook was shut down. They met with Janice Radico, who had agreed to assist them after they told her that the Draper and Ford saga had had other implications.

"They asked me about the cash received for sales of homes and property, how it was accounted for, whether anybody was skimming cash from the sales, and whether or not I received money to keep quiet," said Radico.

"Were they?" asked Smythe.

"Yes. I tried to keep track of the receipts and made sure they were deposited to the bank account, but there were a few occasions when property was sold and the customer paid in cash and would bring in suitcases full of money at closing. It was always Dutch Cramer who had these customers, and the closing statements were always changed to reflect different amounts," replied Radico.

"What happened to the cash?" asked Downes.

"I have no clue. I know that it wasn't deposited into our bank accounts. But I do know that building materials were showing up on job sites and I didn't get invoices for payment. The same with subcontractors: they were often paid in cash."

"Did any money ever go to St. Kitts?" asked Smythe.

"Not that I'm aware, but we did wire money to an account in Jersey, which I was told was for 'the Professor,' whenever we sold something."

When she was first hired, Radico had been told that both Draper and Ford were very private people and she was not to talk to employees or anyone else about their business. At the grand-jury hearing, apparently the jurors didn't quiz her as much as they did Downes, but the assistant U.S. attorney did spend considerable time asking her questions about the flow of funds and to whom she wrote checks, most of which were covered in her conversation with the FBI and DEA.

They tried to track down Draper's girlfriend, Arma Lozo, who had received a subpoena and pleaded the fifth at the grand-jury hearing; she had returned home to Colombia.

Thursday, December 7, 1989

Downes and Smythe arrived in St. Kitts after a grueling second leg of the flight from San Juan, Puerto Rico. The American Eagle flight was miserable with frightening turbulence all the way through. By the time they arrived, four p.m. local time, they felt completely drained, and it was too late to call people in hopes of setting up meetings.

They decided to eat dinner at the hotel, the Ocean Terrace restaurant, a quaint, small eatery five minutes from Basseterre. They dined outdoors amid tall, lit lanterns placed around the terrace, covered in flowery vines. There were concrete squares in the form of stepping stones placed over grass with moss growing loosely over the surface, creating a natural ambiance. It was a typical, relatively upscale Caribbean restaurant, with fresh-cut flowers neatly placed on each table on top of pure white-linen tablecloths.

Smythe and Downes had known each other for over two years and had shared, ever since, a great professional relationship. She had divorced her husband of five years and had no children. They had never really talked about their private lives, although he had made her aware of his marital problems several months earlier. He said words to the effect that "It's great to be away from her. We got divorced last month..." when she asked if his wife minded that he went out of town with another woman.

They ordered a bottle of wine and studied the menu for a couple of minutes. Neither of them had decided yet on anything to eat when a young lady asked them if they cared to order.

Smythe looked great: an attractive woman—a lot more so when dressed in casual clothes—and with a great personality, which made her that much more attractive. Downes thought she knew that he was physically attracted to her but, up to this point, had never made it look obvious. He wasn't sure what she thought of him, outside of their professional relationship.

Friday, December 8, 1989

With very little sleep and reliving the events of the last several hours, they both showered, together, and Downes went to his room and got ready for a day of uncertainties.

They decided that Smythe would contact Sophie Albrightson and try to get some time with her, while Downes would contact Dennis Fisk or anyone else in the inner circle, such as Walter Jones, founder of the PDM Party, or Sir Brian Ashe, former Governor General. Both of those guys would know what was going on, but the question was whether they would talk to him.

Smythe called the bank and Albrightson answered on the first ring.

"Hi Sophie, this is Judy Smythe from the Palm Beach Journal."

"Hi Judy"

"I'm here in St. Kitts and was wondering if we could meet for a few minutes."

Smythe sensed a little caution in Albrightson's voice and feared that she would decline, but welcomed her "Okay, I'm here all day if you want to stop by."

"How about in thirty minutes?"

"That's fine. Nobody else is expected today. Mr. McLoud is in Toronto, and I don't know when he'll be back."

"Okay, I'll be there in thirty minutes," said Smythe.

"Yes, yes, yes!" she shouted, jumping with joy. She grabbed her notebook, shoved it in her valise, and made sure that her tape recorder had good battery power. She gave Downes a kiss on the cheek and told him to wish her luck.

"I'll catch up with you later in the day. If I can't reach you at the hotel, just leave a message at the desk," she said as she was running out the door.

Smythe was dressed in a pair of white slacks, a pink top, and flat shoes so as to look relaxed and casual and fit in with the tourists.

By this time, Downes had visited St. Kitts four times since being introduced to the island by Draper and Ford. Each time he had developed a bit of a friendship with a cab driver named Rufus Caple.

Caple was a real character. He was a cut above all other cabbies and regarded himself as a businessman who aspired to having other cabbies work for him. He was around his early to mid-thirties, had a full beard, but was almost bald.

Caple was a hustler and knew everybody and everything that was going on in St. Kitts. He had never been off the island. While other cabbies were hanging out at the Circus, the center of Basseterre, waiting for fares, Caple would be working his contacts for future business. He was seldom seen waiting in line for fares at the airport or at the port for cruise-ship passengers, since his schedule was filled with reservations and commitments already made. He had been able to buy a new Toyota mini bus and was the only cabbie in town that both accepted advance reservations and was reliable enough to keep them. His customers included many government officials, businesspeople, and even tourists returning to the island. A tremendous source.

The Circus was the heart of the city, a crowded place where dozens of cabbies hung out and tourists mulled around shopping at the tiny stores, and where the local ladies were set up with tables and chairs outside, selling fresh fruit, trinkets, cotton clothes, handmade flip-flops, and braiding hair.

The problem Downes had with Caple was the difficulty in understanding him. He had a strong Kittitean accent that incorporated local phrases and pronunciations, but Caple was patient with him and generally repeated himself two or three times.

Smythe arrived at the bank and was immediately greeted by Albrightson, the only one in the office.

Sophie Albrightson had come to St. Kitts from Oslo, Norway, on vacation four years earlier, fallen in love with the island and its people, and decided to stay. She applied for a work permit and found a job as a clerk working for George McLoud. She lived in a tiny room above a small convenience store in Basseterre with hardly the living amenities that she had been used to in her home country, but she was very happy and would never go back.

She was tall, blonde, and naturally attractive. She didn't wear makeup and her hair was simply combed straight. There was a certain shyness to her that, at first meeting, was usually construed as being uncooperative but became very personable and quite witty after talking to her for a while. Over her four years of living on the island, she had become very wise regarding the culture and mannerisms of the local people.

The events of the last few months, however, had left her very concerned and had forced her to look elsewhere for employment. She had been casually asked about working for other companies, but had decided to wait and see what was going to happen to McLoud's "hotel project," in which she had been promised a top administrative position.

Albrightson was dressed in a yellow cotton dress with flat shoes, clearly prepared to deal with another uncertain day.

The office looked empty and void of any business activity. The front door was left open and there was a comfortable breeze flowing into the office, the only problem being the periodic interruption by local people selling their wares.

"Sophie, you know that I'm a reporter and you also know that I'm a colleague of Terry Downes, who you knew when Draper and Ford were involved with the First Investors."

"Yes, I know. I've met Mr. Downes. He is a director of the bank."

"Well, he was asked to be, but I don't think he officially accepted the position."

"Judy, I don't know if I should talk to you or not. As I said when you called, I think it best that you talk to Mr. McLoud first."

"Fair enough, but let me ask you this: when did McLoud leave for Canada?"

"Two days ago."

"Have you heard from him since leaving?"

"No, I haven't."

"Isn't that odd that he wouldn't call you?"

"Yes, he usually calls every day when he's in Toronto."

"Sophie, I don't think Mr. McLoud will be coming back," Smythe's tone was sober.

This was quite a ballsy comment to make, since Smythe didn't have any reason to believe he wouldn't be back...except that there was a lot of damage control going on as a result of the general election result in India.

"That may explain why Mr. Blackstone asked me to go to George's apartment and gather his belongings," Albrightson was pensive.

"Did you ask him why he wanted you to do that?"

"No, I never ask questions; I just do what they tell me. I think Mr. McLoud could be in a lot of trouble if he returns."

"Why do you say that, Sophie?"

"There were some Indian people here last week, and I could hear them talking in the room. They were demanding that George tell them about the phony account and asked about Mr. Downes. They first offered him money then they threatened him. I know they met with the prime minister and Mr. Blackstone, but I don't know what the outcome was."

"Okay, I'll talk to you as long as you don't mention my name."

"That's fine. You have my word."

"And I don't want to talk here. It would be best if we met somewhere else so people won't see me talking to you."

"I agree. How about if you come to my hotel room tonight? I'm staying at the Ocean Terrace."

"What time?" Albrightson wiped her eyes.

"How about eight?"

Smythe was elated. She left the bank after assuring Albrightson of complete confidentiality and letting her know that this would help her. She also couldn't wait to tell Downes of her meeting. In the meantime, she decided that she would take a walk around the town. Simultaneously, she would think about the questions to ask and the information she needed.

When she called Downes back at the hotel, Smythe sounded ecstatic: "I met with Sophie Albrightson and she's ready to talk—eight p.m. in my room."

"Do you think I should be there?" asked Downes.

"Let's see how it goes first. I don't want to scare her away."

"Thanks a lot."

"You know I didn't mean it that way," Smythe reassured.

"Okay. Where are you now?"

"Just doing some window shopping at the Dockside Mall, why?"

"I'm trying to get to see Henry Blackstone and maybe you would like to join me. Call me in an hour or so. He should have returned my call by then."

CHAPTER 17

Downes met Rufus in the lounge area of the hotel, where he gave him a hug and a welcome. They took a seat and Downes gave him a leather briefcase that he had promised him so that he could look the part, for which Caple was most appreciative. He also gave him a hundred-dollar bill so he wouldn't feel bad about keeping him from business. Caple told Downes he had about one hour to spare.

"So, how are you Rufus?"

"Great, mon, great. Life's treating me good, mon."

"So, what's goin' on on this beautiful island?"

"What d'ya need to know, mon?"

"Tell me about the bank and George McLoud."

"Fat George!" he said, bursting with laughter and flashing his pearly white teeth. "I tink he's in trouble, mon. I picked up lots 'a Indian fellas from de airport an took 'em to de bank an' to 'is flat."

"What were they doing here?"

"Dey wanted ta know 'bout da count dat Fat George made up, mon, an wanted ta know 'bout you. Dey bad people, mon. Ya need to watch yer back."

"Rufus, how do you know all this?"

"I know evrythin', mon," Caple laughed.

"Where's George now, Rufus?" asked Downes, knowing the answer.

"I's back in Toronto. If 'e comes back, somethin' bad will appen."

"Rufus, what do you know about that phony account set up at the bank for some Indian politician?"

He looked around the room, laughed, and said, "Fat George set up an account at 'is bank so dat dis guy in India would lose de election. It was for fifty million dollars, 'sept dere was no money, mon. Dis was a big problem, we ad Indian people all over de place."

"Who else is involved in this deal?"

"Tis 'ard to say. I tink Dennis Fisk, maybe Henry Blackstone, an' maybe uders, mon."

The information that Caple gave Downes was good, and he was generally reliable, so he asked if they could meet again, before he left to go over a few other things.

"Yeah, mon. Just call me," Caple said, holding his finger to his lips.

Downes went back to his room to make some calls and to review the notes of his conversation with Caple. He called Henry Blackstone and left a message, as he did with Dennis Fisk. He also placed a call to the prime minister, Dr. Kendall Rudolph, but didn't expect that he would call him back.

Albrightson showed up at Smythe's room at 8:30 p.m. Downes was anxiously standing by in his own room, watching television.

"Hi Sophie, come in and make yourself comfortable," said Smythe, opening the door.

The room was okay. It had a small coffee table with a couple of chairs and was relatively clean and tidy. Smythe had the windows open and the gentle noise of the surf could be heard as the breeze from the Atlantic Ocean was ruffling the curtains.

"Is this okay for you, or would you like me to close the window and turn on the air-conditioning?" asked Smythe.

"No, this is fine."

"Okay. First of all, I want to thank you for doing this. I know how tough it must be for you."

"No problem," said Albrightson.

"Before we get started, I don't know whether you know this or not, but Terry Downes is here with me and since he has been involved in the scheme of things, I was wondering if you minded if he joined us."

"Good. I've only met him once or twice, but I don't mind if he joins us."

Smythe knocked on the connecting door to their adjoining rooms. Downes carried his own chair and greeted Albrightson: "Hi Sophie, you remember me?"

"Of course."

"Thanks for doing this, Sophie," he said.

"No problem."

"Judy, would you like me to give Sophie the background on why we're here?" asked Downes.

"Sure."

"While it is true that Judy is writing an article on St. Kitts and offshore banking, the reason why we're here is much more involved," Downes explained.

He proceeded to tell Albrightson how he had gotten involved with Draper and Ford, the raid, his testimony in front of a federal grand jury, and his thinking that it had been all over when they were convicted of drug trafficking and so on and so forth.

Albrightson sat in amazement as he told her about the phony account and showed her the article in the Delhi Times.

"Sophie, could you talk to us about George McLoud?" he asked.

"What do you want to know?"

"What was he up to, what kind of deals was he involved in, and with whom?"

"First of all, I don't think anybody likes Fat George. He is crude, dirty, and obnoxious; has some very bad personal habits; has no respect for women; and the only time he sounds civil is when he's talking to his boss," Albrightson said, with a look of disdain.

"Who's his boss?" asked Smythe.

"Well, it was Don Draper but now I don't know. I know he answers to Ernie Mueller, 'the Professor', but he also takes orders from Dennis Fisk, the Deputy Prime Minister."

"How long have you worked with McLoud?" asked Downes.

"About four years."

"How did you meet him?" asked Smythe.

"I had only been here a few days and I was walking past the building when I noticed furniture being moved into the office, so I went inside and met George. I told him that I had office experience and he offered to get me a work permit through Henry Blackstone, and then he hired me."

"Who organized the bank? Who were the founders?" Smythe kept probing.

"I don't know who all the original founders were, but when I came, there were Don Draper, Tim Ford, and George. The corporate records show that Dennis Fisk is a stakeholder on behalf of himself and three other people in government. I don't know who they are. I don't know who owns the bank now. Mr. Blackstone has all the corporate records."

"Do you know if Ernie Mueller is involved in the bank?" asked Downes.

"I don't know what his involvement is. All I know is that he is George's boss and when he calls, George gets very nervous and polite. George told me once that Ernie is in charge of everything and if he called when he was out of the office, I was to get in touch with him right away. He also told me never to mention his name but just refer to him as 'The Professor,'" she said.

"What about transactions at the bank? Could you tell us about them?" asked Smythe.

"I must have your word that this is not repeated, because I could end up in serious trouble with the government," said Albrightson, nervously.

"You have our word," Smythe promised.

"As far as the funds coming in and going out, you need to talk to Doreen. I know nothing about who sent the money. The numbered account journal is kept by her .

"Who else has access to the journal?" prodded Downes.

Well, all the records are kept by Doreen, under Fisk's supervision. He has a staff of ladies in his chambers that take care of records."

"Wait, you mean that McLoud doesn't handle all transactions?" asked Downes

"The bank was taking in millions of dollars, mostly in wires from other banks from different countries. We sent most of the money out to other banks the same day or the day after we received them. There was also a lot of cash that would be brought in by tourists that were friends of George's and, at times, Dennis Fisk would bring people here with cash to deposit."

"What did you do with the cash?" asked Downes.

"George would sit in the room, count it, and then have somebody from Carib Bank pick it up and deposit it in our account there. He would tell Doreen which account it should go into, or it was for a CD."

"Would you be able to guess how much money the bank received over the past four years?" asked Downes.

"I can only guess from what I processed. Doreen handled many of the transactions, but when I look at the deposits in the bank statements, I would say many millions. But Mr. Blackstone handles other accounts from India, so it could be a lot more than what I know. You know this money doesn't belong to the bank; it's for our customers, and some of them are governments of countries," explained Albrightson.

"Yes, we know," said Smythe, smiling.

"Most of the money was wired back out and some went into numbered accounts or certificates of deposit," Albrightson elaborated.

"Can you tell us who some of them are?" asked Downes.

"No, sorry, I really can't do that."

"If I mentioned some names, could you say 'yes' or 'no'?" he asked.

"Okay, but I would recognize company names better," she said.

"Omar Khallehki."

"I've heard his name."

"Chandrasastari Murkarji, or maybe just Sastari."

"I've heard the 'Sastari' name."

"Ernie Mueller, you know."

"Yes, 'the Professor.'"

"Ed Devine," asked Smythe.

"Yes, he's building condos in Frigate Bay. He's asked me a lot of questions about what we do at the bank, he's very friendly."

"James, or Jim, North."

"Yes, he's Devine's partner."

"Bruce Stanier," asked Downes.

"Yes, he is a beneficiary on an account. I don't recall which one."

"Syed Singh."

Albrightson sat back and tears began to flow down her cheeks, while Smythe handed her a Kleenex. "I'm very sorry," she said, with her head in her hands.

"Sorry for what, Sophie?" asked Smythe.

"George told me to make out a numbered account and type in some transactions totaling fifty million dollars and to forge Terry's signature as managing director on a letter that referenced the number to the account. It was for a person named Syed Singh and Jai Kumar as the beneficiary. He gave me five hundred dollars to do it. He also told me that I would get a good job in the new hotel. At first I said no, but then he told me that you knew about it and it was no big deal," sobbed Albrightson looking at Downes..

"He also arranged for immigration records from Mr. Blackstone to show that Syed Singh had entered the country at the time the deposits and withdrawals were shown on the numbered account," she continued. "I don't think there was such a person."

This was great news for Downes and Smythe. Now they knew that if Mueller ever denied knowing about the account, they would have a witness who had actually forged the account. They both believed that Albrightson would now tell them everything she knew about the bank and the people involved. Downes had heard about the hotel that McLoud was involved in from his previous visits and had expressed some interest in developing the property himself.

"I knew it was wrong, but I was assured that nothing would come of it. But then I overheard him talking to Doreen, saying that he needed something faxed to some newspapers and it had to be anonymous, so he asked her to go to the post office to fax it," said Albrightson.

"Did you know why he wanted you to do this?" asked Downes.

"No, not until you just told me, but I suspected that there was something going on when all these Indian people were coming here and wanting to talk to Mr. McLoud, asking about you, Terry, and where they could find you. They were really nasty people."

"What about other wires: where do they come from?"

"Wires come in from all over the world, but the money is only in our accounts for a day or so. Then we send wires to different banks to the attention of different companies."

"Which banks do you generally send the money to?" asked Downes.

"Doreen handles all the wires, but I have seen the transfer forms for BCCI Bank on the Cayman Islands, a Swiss bank, a bank on Jersey Island, one in Florida, and a bank in Liechtenstein," replied Albrightson.

In addition to laundering drug money, Downes and Smythe had suspected that First Investors was being used for other illicit activities. They needed to know the connection between Khallehki, Sastari, and Mueller as it related to the Indian politicians and First Investors since they couldn't accept that they would go to these extremes "for God and Country" alone, without personal benefit.

The activity in the bank, per Albrightson's description, indicated a huge money-laundering scheme that involved a number of influential people.

"What about Stanier, Devine, and North?" asked Downes.

"I don't know much about either one, except that Mr. Stanier is the beneficiary of an account in the name of a company in Florida and funds are wired to Barnett Bank. I don't think Devine is involved in any account, but I know that North is a friend of Stanier's and he and Devine are involved in a building project in Frigate Bay."

"What about Dennis Fisk? How is he involved?" asked Smythe.

"Mr. Fisk used to send people to the bank with money to deposit. George would take care of them. He cannot have an account with the bank but, as I said, he does own a stake in the bank. He handles all the government matters for George and Mr. Blackstone—all the legal matters," explained Albrightson.

"What about loans, Sophie? Who borrows money from the bank?" Downes pumped her.

"There are lots of loans. There are loans to companies in Canada, Florida, Europe, and to foreign companies that have a business here. Almost all customers that have deposit accounts have loans. I don't believe they are all loans though, since I seldom hear about the money being paid back," she added.

"Does George or Doreen keep a record of the loans?" asked Smythe.

"If they do, I've never seen or heard of it."

"Has the bank paid any money to the owners?" asked Downes.

"Well, Mr. Fisk and his friends in government receive bonuses; so has Mr. Blackstone and, of course, George. I know this because I have withdrawn cash from our bank account in Carib and given it to George."

"How much?" asked Smythe.

"The last check was for one hundred thousand dollars. We had to make special arrangements to get the cash."

"But there is nothing that shows Mueller's involvement?" asked Downes.

"The only time I've heard his name mentioned was from George. He told me once that he was responsible for the building of the new road from Frigate Bay to the Southern Point. He also said that Mueller gets all of the assembly work done in St. Kitts for a company that he owns in Canada. Oh, and he does a lot of business with both Mr. Khallehki and Mr. Sastari."

"What kind of business?" asked Smythe.

"I don't know, but the money is sent to the bank and then wired out on their behalf."

"Where are the bank records kept, Sophie?" Smythe went on.

"In Mr. Blackstone's or Mr. Fisk's office."

"What records are in the files?" Smythe pressed on.

"I don't think there's much. George was not one to keep records. The files are identified by company or code, and we keep copies of incoming and outgoing wires—notes made by George, names of people, and telephone numbers. He had to have money available when customers requested termination of their agreements. Doreen kept track of expiration and redemption dates and George had to make sure money was available. The only files that contain agreements or any formal papers are in the numbered-accounts file and the certificates."

"That must have been nerve wrecking," said Downes.

"Is there any chance you can get copies of the records?" Smythe inquired.

"I don't think so. Ever since those Indian men were here, Mr. Blackstone's office has taken over everything. Doreen and Jazzi have moved over there and he has asked me to move also."

"What did the Indian guys want?" asked Downes.

"Well, I only overheard the conversations that George and Mr. Blackstone had with them, and they were demanding to know about the account for Syed Singh. I heard them asking for copies of the law that affected offshore banks. They wanted to know who was authorized to open accounts and needed to know how to reach you, Terry."

"Did you give them my telephone number?"

"No, but I gave it to the newspaper reporters who called asking for your address. George said it was okay to give it to them."

"How long were they here?" asked Smythe.

"I think two or three days. I know they went to see George's flat because Rufus took them, and when George came into the office the next day, he was really upset. They tried to break in, but some people told them they would call the police. George and Mr. Blackstone called 'the Professor' in the office after they met with the prime minister."

"Are you still doing business?" asked Downes.

"We haven't conducted any business here the last few weeks, but maybe Doreen is getting wires and everything at her new office. We've been asked if the bank is for sale by some stranger, though. I think he was a part of the Indian group. Also, Mr. Blackstone asked me if I would go to George's apartment over the weekend and pack all his belongings. Maybe he's not coming back."

"Do you mind if we come with you?" asked Smythe.

"No, I don't mind."

Downes and Smythe chatted with Albrightson for quite some time and when they wrapped it up, they both felt as though she had been very candid and would supply them with other information as it became known to her.

CHAPTER 18

Henry Blackstone returned Downes's call late in the evening. They had met with Sophie Albrightson and left a message saying that he would meet them at the hotel at eight a.m. the following morning, unless they heard otherwise.

Henry Blackstone was the prime minister's solicitor and had been the country's ambassador to South Korea and Taiwan. Born in St. Kitts and educated at Oxford University, Blackstone followed the footsteps of his father, George Blackstone, a prominent lawyer and good citizen of St. Kitts.

Blackstone soon gained the respect of the legal community throughout the Leeward Islands and built a fairly decent-sized clientele, representing offshore clients looking to do business in St. Kitts. He played a major role in assisting Dr. Kendall Rudolph, the prime minister, in gaining independence from Britain. Blackstone had also helped write the law governing offshore banks, so he was the guy that George McLoud first searched out in 1982, when he was looking at chartering an offshore bank for Ernie Mueller.

Blackstone was thrilled at the possibility of St. Kitts having its first offshore bank. He was further thrilled at the notion of earning over one hundred thousand dollars in legal fees, which McLoud, on behalf of Mueller, was only too pleased to pay. He was invited to serve on the board of First Investors Trust and McLoud soon found out that, as long as Blackstone was taken care of, there wasn't too much that he wouldn't agree to.

Blackstone was shrewd and hid behind the privacy laws that he wrote. So whenever any questions were raised regarding the legitimacy of the transactions within the bank, he knew he didn't have to reveal a thing.

Ernie Mueller was ecstatic that McLoud had found somebody like Blackstone—somebody who had the ear of the prime minister; the legal knowledge to bail them out of tricky situations, if any arose; and a willingness to take chances, as long as the rewards were there.

Blackstone's only problem in the community was that he couldn't stay away from the women. In addition to his two kids by his current wife, he had two by a previous wife and had impregnated two other women with whom he had one child each. He had to make a lot of money, by St. Kitts' standards, to support a wife, an ex-wife, two girlfriends, and six kids.

Henry Blackstone's chambers were located about a hundred yards from First Investors, just off the Circle in Basseterre, on the second floor of an all-wood building that, over the years, had seen several coats of different-colored paint. Access to the offices were from stairs from a grocery store on the ground floor—something the owners of the store didn't like—or an outdoor staircase that was a challenge to climb, since many steps were either broken or missing. There were no window panes in the building, just wooden shutters, and a couple of them had come unfastened and were swinging freely in the breeze. Inside, the wood floor was painted pale blue and had been worn down to the bare wood in areas most trafficked.

As is usually the case in office buildings, there were more people employed than were needed, and it wasn't unusual to see ladies hanging around with nothing to do. Work efficiency didn't seem important in the workplace.

Monday, December 11, 1989

Eight a.m.:

Downes and Smythe sat in the restaurant in the hotel sipping coffee, smiling at each other, after another glorious night together without much sleep, waiting for Henry Blackstone to arrive.

"What a trip," said Smythe, breaking the ice.

"It's been great so far. Now all we need is to have just as much success getting information as we've had making love."

Smythe blushed, smiled, and said, "I hope we come close."

Henry Blackstone arrived around 9:30, apologizing for his tardiness. He was dressed in a typical island business suit, loosely fitting short sleeve open-neck shirt with matching pants.

"How are you, Henry?" asked Downes, shaking his hand.

"Fine, Terry, and you?"

"Very good."

"Henry, I would like you to meet Judy Smythe. Judy is a reporter for the Palm Beach Journal, in South Florida, and a good friend. Henry is the prime minister's attorney, represents offshore companies, and is a director at First Investors Trust."

"Pleased to meet you."

"Well, what brings you to St. Kitts this time, Terry? And what brings a newspaper reporter here with you?" asked Blackstone, knowing perfectly well why they were there.

"Judy is an investigative reporter and she's writing an article on St. Kitts and offshore banking. Of course, when I found out that my signature had been forged, disclosing a name on a numbered account at the bank, something that has received international attention, she became a lot more interested, and so did I."

"Let's order some breakfast," suggested Smythe.

Blackstone looked around the restaurant and said, "We are in some troubling times in St. Kitts. We have our internal political issues, we have economic issues, and we have issues brought upon us from outside sources."

The waitress came with a beautiful display of fresh fruits and a tray of bread and pastries. Pots of coffee, tea, and fruit juices were left on the table. It was a beautiful morning, with clear blue skies and a nice Atlantic breeze.

"Henry, I know the country is in a bit of turmoil right now, but you may have people in government who have an interest in the issues brought upon you by outside sources," said Downes, trying to be as diplomatic as he could.

"I was told that my name had been forged in disclosing a name on a numbered account by the people behind it," Downes carried on, "and I was asked to confirm that the account was legitimate, whereupon I became part of a conspiracy to affect the outcome of the general elections in India. As you know, despite it all, the person they had wanted discredited won the election, anyway. However, an article appeared in the Delhi Times implicating me in the conspiracy. George McLoud orchestrated this deal for some pretty important people and he needed the help from somebody in government who could falsify immigration records," said Downes, showing him the article.

Blackstone read the article, had no reaction, and said, "How can I help you?"

"What interest does Jacques 'Ernie' Mueller, or this guy Sastari, have in First Investors?" asked Downes.

"As far as I know, they have no interest," replied Blackstone.

"Henry, c'mon! They are the ones, along with George McLoud, who put this smear campaign together," Downes sounded quite angry.

"I heard that there could be a problem when we were visited by the Indians," said Blackstone, nonchalantly.

"I got calls from newspaper reporters from India and London asking me to confirm that I had opened a numbered account in the name of Syed Singh for the benefit of Jai Kumar, the recently elected prime minister of India. The account showed activity of fifty million dollars. I went to Toronto to get some explanation from McLoud. I was introduced to this guy, Ernie Mueller, and some guru named Sastari, and they admitted forging my name on this bogus account. And you, Henry, not only handle the legal work for the bank, you are also the custodian for all the records. You must have known about it," said Downes, getting right to the point.

"Well, I was shown a copy of the account by the CBI guys from India, and I told them and I'll tell you: I knew nothing about it and will not comment any further. This is a matter that has to be resolved by McLoud and whoever else was supposed to be involved. If a formal complaint is filed, I will address the matter at that time," said Blackstone.

"There are many suspicions about the transactions in the bank," Blackstone continued, "but it is none of our business where the funds come from or what they represent. You know about the strict privacy laws that we have governing the bank."

"I do, but when the bank is being used in such a sinister way, don't you think that something should be done about it?" asked Downes.

"What would you suggest?"

"How about talking to McLoud and finding out how he got the immigration records to reflect that Syed Singh was making continual visits to St. Kitts?"

"I did, before he left for Toronto. He denied knowing anything."

"Well, obviously he's lying."

The conversation was getting to be confrontational, and although Blackstone was keeping his cool, Downes's voice was getting louder and Smythe was tapping him on the shoulder to keep it down.

Blackstone spoke in a very deliberate, calculated way, emphasizing the syllables in each word, typical of West Indies' diction.

"Terry, I think you're making too much out of this. If McLoud, as you say, fabricated an account, it didn't work. I don't think the CBI will be back and I'm sure that they have closed the case," said Blackstone, offering Downes some solace.

"Henry, I don't buy the reason they gave me for trying to set this guy up. They said it was because Rajiv Gandhi, the former prime minister, had asked them to make sure he didn't win the election because Kumar was a socialist and a crook. I believe there's more to it than that. Further, and most important, my name has been tarnished and I need to get it cleared up. I can't afford to have my name involved with these guys and I would like to get a statement from the government of St.

Kitts exonerating me of any involvement in a conspiracy to discredit an international political figure," Downes demanded.

"You know that is not going to happen, Terry. This has nothing to do with St.Kitts" said Blackstone.

They were not getting anywhere with Henry Blackstone. He was not about to reveal anything that could come back and bite him, especially since he knew he could be quoted in a U.S. newspaper. He did say, however, that he didn't think George McLoud would be coming back to St. Kitts. When Downes asked him why, he thought for a second about it and replied, just intuition.

They thanked Blackstone for his time and asked that he get in touch with them if there was anything with which he thought he could help them.

CHAPTER 19

Dennis Fisk literally had his hands in everything that was going on in St. Kitts. His constituents idolized him, although his colleagues in government generally loathed him.

As minister of tourism, he was responsible for the development and promotion of all tourism activities, including the coordination of hotel and casino projects, cruise-ship activity, and coordinating flights from major airports around the world. As such, he had opportunities to take payoffs, kickbacks, or to partner with investors if government approvals were needed on their projects. They always did.

Dennis Fisk made no bones about his ability to get things done for the right price. He was involved with the harbor-extension project, which would facilitate large cruise ships, not to mention the permits required for the ships to moor at the new dock. He had his hands in airline schedules and carriers, customs, and bonded warehouses and could move goods rapidly through the normal process—for a price. Any foreign investor planning on building a hotel/casino or any other building project went through Dennis Fisk for permits and cabinet approval.

The fact that Fisk was minister of tourism gave him a hammer; his also being the deputy prime minister gave him a wrecking ball. He had a secretary, six assistants and twelve clerks and had an office suite one floor below the prime minister's.

Fisk lived with his wife and three teenage kids in a very comfortable home just outside of Basseterre. He also supported two or three girlfriends and their three kids whom Fisk had fathered. Being a womanizer in St.Kitts could be very expensive, since the law required mandatory family support for children born out of wedlock and for their mothers.

Fisk was the consummate politician and had been a founding member of the Political Democratic Movement Party (PDM), along with Prime Minister Rudolph and a well-known lawyer named Walter Jones.

The prime minister tolerated Fisk, although he was continually challenged by members of his own party about the inherent conflicts of interest that he, Fisk, was involved in by wearing a number of different hats. Jealousy was their problem.

Fisk's office, of which he saw very little, was always cluttered with promotional pieces, books, magazines, legal documents, and files, which made it difficult for him to manage his different ventures efficiently.

He was responsible for getting foreign investors to develop the Dockside Mall, a quaint little upscale shopping mall which housed some of the finest stores from New York and London. He had spearheaded the dock-extension project and convinced major airlines to schedule flights into St. Kitts. In addition, he single-handedly took on the hotel/casino project and got an agreement with the owners to sell the property—through him.

Terry Downes and Judy Smythe asked Fisk to meet them for lunch at their hotel—out of the public view, they hoped.

Monday, December 11

One-thirty p.m.:
Fisk was one hour late, but nobody stuck to a rigid time schedule on the islands, anyway. Hell, not many people kept track of time, period.

Dennis Fisk walked through the lobby of the hotel, shaking hands and stopping to chat with someone who needed to know what the government was doing about power outages.

"We're working very hard to resolve this problem. Don't forget: it affects me as well, and I don't like being without electricity any more than you do," was his response, as he continued to walk past the inquirer.

"Hi Dennis, thanks for stopping over," Downes said, bearing a welcoming smile.

"Hello, Terry. And who's this lovely lady?"

"Hello, Mr. Fisk. I'm Judy Smythe."

"Pleased to meet you, and welcome to St. St. Kitts"

"Thank you."

"What brings you to our beautiful country? I hope it's to invest money here," said the deputy prime minister, in his usual charming way.

"No," said Smythe, smiling. "I wish it were. I'm a newspaper reporter."

"Oh, really? And what are you reporting?"

Downes explained to Fisk the background and why they were there, and his response was much the same as Blackstone's. In fact, for all they knew, Blackstone could have contacted him, after he had left them, to tip him off on what they were trying to accomplish.

So Downes tried another tactic: "Dennis, you are aware of my interest in pursuing the hotel project in Frigate Bay. I have a proposal to present to you and the PM for financing the project. But there are issues here that concern me. I'm sure you've heard about the numbered account with my forged signature and the attempt to affect the outcome of the general elections in India."

"Yes, I did hear something about that."

"As I'm sure you understand, I can't afford to have my name associated with this scandal and I need to get it cleared up," Downes said. "For one thing, it will affect my chances of getting permanent financing for the hotel, not to mention the effect it will have back home."

"I understand, but Kumar was elected, anyway, so it didn't do much good," said Fisk, with a broad grin.

Downes showed Fisk the article in the Delhi Times and said, "Are you aware of this?"

"What do you want me to do?" asked Fisk, after reading the article.

"We need to know what Ernie Mueller is doing in St. Kitts," asked Downes.

"I've never met Ernie Mueller."

"I didn't ask you if you've met him, Dennis. I need to know what he's up to. He's the guy who orchestrated this phony account. Wasn't he involved in the hotel project before Draper and Ford were arrested?"

"Yes, he was. George McLoud was waiting for him to authorize the payment of the initial costs of securing the property, but then he backed off," replied Fisk. "That's all I can help you with. His involvement with the bank, if any, is confidential. Maybe Henry can help you," he added, hoping that Downes would change the subject.

"There is nothing that goes on in St. Kitts without your knowing, Dennis. Are you saying that Mueller doesn't have his hand in any business venture here?" asked Downes.

"I'm saying that if he does, I don't know about it."

"Okay, what's the story with McLoud? Why did he leave unexpectedly and why have all the bank records been moved to Henry Blackstone's office?" asked Downes.

"When we were visited by the Indian people, George left. Nobody knew that he was leaving and nobody knows if he's coming back," replied Fisk.

They ordered a light lunch, although there was an uncomfortable feeling between them and neither of them was really hungry. Downes knew Fisk was holding back on a lot of information and there was no reason for him to divulge anything to them, except that he wanted Downes to close on the hotel deal.

The subject was changed after they had placed their order and introduced a little brevity in the conversation. Downes thought, underneath it all, that Fisk was just an opportunist and would take advantage of all the loopholes that allowed him to line his pockets at the expense of foreigners. The problem that Fisk had was that he talked openly about it and this created animosity between him and his colleagues in government.

"Mr. Fisk, who do you think is behind all the political violence in St. Kitts?" asked Smythe.

"It wouldn't be fair for me to name one individual who I think is behind the violence. It is political and therefore involves the actions of a group of people," he replied.

"You have never had this kind of violence in your entire history, and now you have the reputation of being the murder capital of the Caribbean," she said.

"People in St. Kitts have become very passionate about their political beliefs," said Fisk.

"What about drug trafficking? Who's involved in this?" asked Downes.

Fisk smiled, wiped the perspiration off his forehead, and said, "If we knew this, the culprits would be in prison."

"You must realize that these problems could have a dramatic effect on tourism," Smythe reminded him.

"I do, and we currently have a detective from Scotland Yard assisting us in combating this problem."

"Oh, really?" said Downes, looking and sounding quite surprised. "Could we get in touch with him?"

"Of course. His name is Inspector Clive Townsend, and he is staying here at the Ocean Terrace."

It was pretty obvious that Fisk was not going to tell them anything. His answers were much the same as Blackstone's—empty. He was uncomfortable talking about First Investors and their questions about drugs and violence. He couldn't wait to excuse himself from the table. Besides, he had an important real-estate closing that he needed to attend.

Both Smythe and Downes believed that Henry Blackstone and Dennis Fisk were either directly involved in illicit activities or at least aware of them, and were being paid to turn a blind eye. They knew that Fisk was delivering cash to the bank; that Blackstone must have been aware of the immigration favors to support Syed Singh's fabricated entrance into St. Kitts; and based on what Sophie Albrightson had told them, they suspected that Mueller, Sastari, and Khallehki were using the bank for illegal transactions.

Then there was McLoud, possibly coordinating whatever was going on. They were also of the opinion that the political violence and the growing drug trade on the island were somehow tied together.

St. Kitts was the perfect place to broker business, legal or otherwise. It was off the beaten tracks, a tax haven, had strict privacy laws, and a few powerful politicians who could make a lot of things happen. And one knew that things were happening because politicians were living way beyond their meager pay scales as civil servants.

"I think the reason for the increase in crime rate on the island is because of power struggles involving some big drug dealers. This country has slept along for many years, and now they see an opportunity for big money. In order for guys like Mueller and Sastari to do whatever they're doing, you'd better believe they have the help of top government officials. I haven't figured out who those names are, but you have to figure that Blackstone and Fisk are involved to some degree," said Smythe.

Downes tried several times to reach George McLoud in Toronto, to no avail. He also placed calls to Ernie Mueller, Sastari, and Omar Khallehki's offices and left messages. All of a sudden, no one was interested in talking to him, which was not surprising. Their mission had failed, so why talk to him?

In the meantime, Downes tried to reach Scotland Yard's Detective Clive Townsend in room 322. No answer. He placed another call to the prime minister's office, hoping to get a meeting to discuss his financing plan for the hotel, and left another message.

By this time, both of their rooms were cluttered with paper and notes of their conversations. Smythe had a habit of sticking sheets of paper on the walls showing timelines, questions, answers, etc.

They had asked the front desk not to clean their rooms until they requested, so as to make sure that all the papers were removed from the walls and hidden away before the maids entered.

Downes was scratching his head, trying to figure out their next move, when he received a call from Albrightson saying that she had just received a call from George McLoud's sister in Toronto, wondering how she could reach him. It had been over a week since George had left unannounced for Toronto. Albrightson, very wisely, took the lady's number and told her that she didn't know where George was, but she would try to contact him and have him call her.

Downes wrote down the number and thanked her for her good judgment. By now, he began thinking maybe McLoud had never gone back to Toronto. Before calling the sister back, he decided to get confirmation that McLoud had actually left the island by calling the airlines, to see if his name had been listed on the manifest on the day he was supposed to have left.

"Sorry, Mr. Downes, we can't divulge that information without the written authority of the government," was the answer he got from all three airlines that had flights connecting cities to Toronto that day. He tried contacting immigration and got the same answer.

The only person who he knew could assist him was Henry Blackstone: "Henry, I need a favor: George's sister in Toronto is trying to locate him and, according to her, not only is he not answering his phone, it looks like he's never returned to his apartment. Before I call her back, I would like to see if he actually left St. Kitts. I called the airlines to see if they could confirm his having been on a flight the day he was supposed to have left, and they said that I need government approval. Could you help me?"

"Of course, Terry. I'll call you back."

Detective Clive Townsend called back while he was on the phone, and the prime minister's office called to apologize but the PM would not be available to meet with him since he had appointments for the next several days and then he would be off island for a week or so. Downes was told to call back in two weeks to make an appointment.

Albrightson called, saying that McLoud's sister had called again, very worried, since he had missed two doctors' appointments.

Within thirty minutes, Henry Blackstone called back saying, "Terry, we have confirmation that George McLoud was on American Eagle flight 102 to San Juan, Puerto Rico, leaving at 8:30 a.m. with a connecting flight to Toronto. Would you like a copy of the manifest?"

"Yes please, Henry, and thank you."

"No problem. Call me if you need anything else."

He called McLoud's sister wondering if, God forbid, she looked anything like him. "Hi, this is Terry Downes calling from St. Kitts. I'm a business associate of George's."

"Oh, Mr. Downes, could you tell me where George is?"

"He should be in Toronto. I have confirmation that he left on December 4 on American Eagle flight 102 to San Juan, with a connecting Air Canada flight to Toronto arriving at 4:20 p.m."

"Well, there must be a problem because he would never come back without me knowing. I always pick him up at the airport because he doesn't drive in Toronto. He didn't tell me he was coming back, and I found out that he missed two doctors' appointments, so he should have returned for those."

"Maybe he caught a cab," Downes said, knowing in his mind that McLoud hadn't made it back to Toronto.

"I have keys to his apartment and I know he hasn't been there in several weeks," the sister sounded aggrieved.

"Please don't worry. I'm sure there's some explanation. Let me do some more checking and I will call you back."

"Oh, please, thank you," she said, in a voice of desperation, "You know he takes a lot of medication and requires doctors' visits quite often."

"I'll get back to you," said Downes.

Smythe and Downes were conjecturing over the "what ifs" and trying to figure out where McLoud could be. "We know that if something happened to him, it would have been in Toronto," said Downes.

"Do we know that he actually caught the connecting flight in San Juan?" asked Smythe.

"We didn't check the manifest, and it should be easy to check immigration in Toronto," he replied. "Let's do that. In the meantime, I want to make sure he left the country."

"What do you mean? Blackstone told us he was on that flight," Smythe was surprised.

"I haven't seen the manifest yet, and even if I see his name, somebody could have traveled in his place. George knew a lot, and if somebody wanted him out of the way, they would make sure it would be done without a trace. Just a hunch," he said.

Downes called Rufus Caple and asked him to check with his buddies to see if anybody recalled seeing McLoud going to the airport, in the airport, or boarding the plane he had been supposed to be on. Caple also knew people who worked in immigration, so he asked him to check with them.

CHAPTER 20

Monday, December 11

Four p.m.:
Downes had finally made contact with Inspector Townsend and arranged to meet him in the hotel bar. He decided to meet him alone and leave Judy Smythe available for any important calls. She would have him paged if anything came up.

Townsend was in his late fifties and nearing retirement. He had spent his entire career with the Yard and more recently investigating unsolved crimes in British Commonwealth countries. He had been in St. Kitts for eight days after Scotland Yard had been asked by Henry Blackstone, on behalf of the prime minister, to assist in the investigation of the brutal slaying of Charles Bison, a member of the Labour Party and a suspected contact person with a Colombian drug cartel, something that Blackstone hadn't disclosed in their conversation.

At first, Townsend was very cautious in revealing any information regarding his investigation, which Downes understood and respected. He wouldn't even admit that he had been investigating a crime, but said he had been teaching local police the fundamentals of detective work.

He warmed up a little after Downes explained why he was on the island. He had heard of the mystery numbered account, but said that it was outside of the boundaries of what he was there for. Downes asked him if he could help him find the whereabouts of McLoud, and Townsend said that he could check immigration in Toronto to see the last time McLoud had entered the country.

Townsend really wasn't interested in the bank, Mueller, McLoud, or the infamous numbered account—unless, of course, there was evidence to suggest that they were related to Charles Bison's murder. If this were the case, Downes was told in no uncertain terms and with typical British arrogance, that he was to turn over all evidence to him, making sure that nothing would stand in the way of his investigation.

Okay, whatever, Downes thought, but he did appreciate Townsend's help with Canadian immigration.

Rufus Caple had gotten back to Downes with information that he kind of expected. After having asked his cabbie buddies, the airport porters, and his friends in the terminal, nobody had recalled seeing Fat George leave to go to the airport, in the airport waiting room, or boarding the airplane. Everybody knew, or knew of, Fat George. He just couldn't have ventured outside the bank or his condo without someone's knowledge of it.

Terry Downes was now confident that McLoud had not left St. Kitts and thought that he could be dead. The question was twofold: who was behind changing the flight manifest and who had traveled in his place?

Downes was at a bit of a loss on where to go from here. A lot rested on what Townsend could find out from Canadian immigration. As he walked over to the hotel's front desk to see if there were any messages, he stopped to call Smythe in her room and asked her to meet him for a drink in the lounge.

"Ah, Mr. Downes, there is a message for you on your room phone. You can pick it up at this phone by dialing your room number and pressing 001," said the clerk, handing him a house phone.

"Mr. Downes, it is imperative that you and your colleague leave St. Kitts immediately. Failure to do so could have dire consequences," was the message left by an unrecognizable voice with a well-defined West Indies accent.

Smythe was standing behind him and noticed the look on his face as he turned around. "What's up?" she asked.

"Listen to this," he said, handing her the phone and redialing the number.

"Holy shit, what do we do now?"

"Let's go back to the room."

They taped the message and played it back time and again, searching for any clues.

"I guess we've been asking the wrong questions," said Smythe.

"Or the right ones."

"The problem here is, we don't know who to trust," she added.

"So far, the only two people who I think we can confide in are Sophie and Rufus. One is a bank clerk and the other a cab driver. But I think, at least for now, we should stay right here and make sure that we are both together at all times. We shouldn't answer the door, unless we know who it is, and we should stay away from the patio door, although nobody could get in, since there's nothing between us and the beach," said Downes.

"Okay, and then what?" she asked.

"We play it by ear, since neither one of us wants to leave, right?"

"Right."

Smythe suggested that they call the head of police—which Downes didn't think was such a good idea—then have Albrightson or Caple come over to the room and see if there was a safe house or a place other than the one-hundred-fifty-dollar-per-night room they were presently in, where they could stay and feel safe. He thought that was a better plan, so he called Rufus and asked him to stop over.

Clive Townsend called to tell Downes that the last time George McLoud had re-entered Canada had been three months before and had not re-entered on the date Downes had given him. Townsend suggested that they call the police department. This guy was so full of ideas.

"Why don't you call Henry Blackstone? He told me that he had a copy of the flight manifest showing McLoud being on the flight to Puerto Rico," Downes suggested.

Downes called McLoud's sister, as he said he would, and she was hysterical. He told her that he could have gone somewhere else from San Juan, a notion that she immediately rejected. He then told her that he would get the local authorities involved in his apparent disappearance. He suggested that she talk to the Toronto Police Department to see if they could start an investigation.

A knock on the door resulted in both Smythe and Downes jumping up, wondering who it could be, forgetting for the moment that they had asked Caple to stop over. They let Rufus listen to the message. They also informed him of George McLoud's apparent disappearance and the attempted cover-up. Rufus smiled, scratched his big bushy beard, and said, "I don't know da voice, but dese are bad people, mon. 'Tis de island Mafia."

"What island Mafia?" Downes's eyebrows were raised.

"Deres a group of people from de islands dat traffic in drugs and dat are controlled by big people, mon—from Antigua. Dey 'av people on St. Barts and Anguilla. Dey bad people, mon."

"How does this affect us, Rufus?" asked Smythe.

"And how did this affect George McLoud?" asked Downes, rhetorically.

"I tink Fat George was da banka for do's Canadian big guys, but he knew a lot, mon, 'bout who was 'andlin' drugs an' I tink dey go rid of 'im."

"How would they get rid of him, Rufus? He weighed four hundred pounds plus?" Smythe's tone was at once amused and perplexed.

"I'll aks around. Dey could 'ave got 'im on a boat. I'll find out. But you must be careful, mon. Dese people, dey kill for nutt'n, mon."

Rufus thought that the best place for them was right where they were. They agreed. He also said that he shouldn't come to their room, and if they had to meet he would borrow a friend's cab and pick them up outside the hotel. Downes decided to give up his room and he would move in with Smythe, which was no problem with him.

The one strange thing was, to their knowledge, nobody from Canada had called concerning the whereabouts of McLoud—just his sister.

Tuesday, December 12, 1989

The next morning, Albrightson stopped by to take them to McLoud's condo to see if there was any evidence of foul play. At first they were leery of going anywhere off the hotel's premises, considering the last twenty-four hours' circumstances. However, there was no investigation being conducted and McLoud's place was not a crime scene. Their true main concern was the threatening telephone message, but the condo was only a few miles from their hotel and there were three of them, so they figured they would be okay.

The condo was in a small complex on the ground floor of a two-story building—a fairly new construction on the beach and in a great location. It was a small, one-bedroom, one-bathroom condo with modern appliances and white-tiled floor. There was barely any furniture: a bed and a nightstand in the bedroom, a table and chair in the dining area, and a reclining chair and a small television in the living room. It had just the bare necessities for one person.

As they entered, it appeared obvious that McLoud had not intended to leave, certainly not for good. There were clothes in the closet, albeit not many, together with a suitcase. There was little food in the refrigerator, mostly junk food, and a few personal items and toiletries which he would have taken with him had he been leaving the country for an extended period. There was also medicine in the bathroom that he took on a daily basis. They looked for any files or papers that he may have brought back from the office, but found nothing.

"George always carried a briefcase with him. We always made fun of him because he would carry it everywhere, even to the bathroom. We all wondered what was so important that he never left it out of his sight," said Albrightson.

Interesting, thought Downes, thinking where it could be.

There was no sign of a struggle, either, and the place looked surprisingly neat and clean.

Albrightson told Downes and Smythe that all expenses associated with the condo—rent, utilities, maid service, and condo dues—were paid for by a company in Canada and, she thought, had already been prepaid until the year's end.

Downes suggested that Albrightson should not pack up all of McLoud's belongings, as had been requested by Henry Blackstone, and that they don't disturb anything in the condo. He and Smythe explained their reasons: McLoud's apparent disappearance. Albrightson agreed and would tell Blackstone that she didn't have time to do it. They asked her to stop by their room again just so the three of them could go over a few more things.

CHAPTER 21

It was another gorgeous day, with lots of people on the beach, especially the Caribbean side of the island, where the sand was volcanic black. There were parasailing enthusiasts, boat rentals, and diving events, and the hordes of vendors gathered on the beach with the usual hawking of T-shirts, trinkets, beach clothes, and cold drinks. Reggae music was blaring and people were having a great time.

Back at the room, Albrightson announced that she and Rufus were now living together. Downes looked at Smythe and she at him, both wondering if they should say, "Great!" or "Is that where Rufus gets his information?" or "Why didn't you tell us before?"

In any event, Downes broke the brief silence by saying, "That's okay, but be careful. You have a lot of information and you may be vulnerable, just like we are. Now, listen to this":

He played the tape for her and she got a little scared. "I will tell Rufus the same thing," Downes added.

"Also, you must be careful what you tell Rufus about the bank, not because you don't trust him, but because you would be breaking the law," Smythe reminded her.

"I really haven't told him anything, because he's never asked. Rufus knows most of the people in St. Kitts and he has his own sources of information. It's amazing how much information cab drivers pick up on this small island. He probably knows more than I do about the affairs of the bank," Albrightson chuckled slightly.

"How long have you known him?" asked Smythe.

"Well, I've known Rufus since I first arrived here from Norway, but we've been dating for only three months. I just moved in with him last week. I still have my little flat in Basseterre."

"Sophie, is there anything else that you could tell us about the bank and the transactions that you processed, or do you have any notes or documents that you could share with us?" Smythe continued.

"I'm sure that there are still notes and stuff at the office."

"Is there any way we could see them?" asked Downes.

"I suppose I could collect them and bring them to you."

"Why don't we go over your daily work, that is, what you did when George was there?" suggested Smythe.

"Okay, but my work was usually given to me by Doreen, and it was different each day."

"That's okay. Just tell us everything that you did, who you spoke to, and what McLoud would talk about," Smythe proposed.

"My job was to do all the stuff that was not important. I ran errands, anything that George needed I would get—like soft drinks, ice cream, personal items. I made sure that the office was always neat and tidy, that files were put away, etc. I answered the phone. He would never talk to me, or any of us for that matter. He spent most of the time on the phone in the little office."

"Who would call you guys?" interrupted Downes.

"For a while, we were getting calls from neighboring islands about jobs for the new hotel. George had told everybody that he had investors who were going to build a hotel in Frigate Bay and he would be looking for all kinds of help. But most calls were either for George or Doreen. Nobody called for me," she laughed.

"Give us some names of people that would call," asked Smythe.

"Henry Blackstone and Dennis Fisk called for George and Doreen quite frequently. Ed Devine would call for George. When Draper and Ford were involved, they would call for George all the time. Whenever Ernie Mueller called, he would have his secretary place the call and she called from a number in Jersey. Walter Jones called once in a while, and we would get calls from the power and the telephone company about paying our bills."

"Could we get the telephone bills?" Smythe interrupted this time.

"Yes, but all the bills are now in Henry Blackstone's office. Whenever George would want to talk to somebody privately, he would dial an international number. Henry and Dennis have the same number, and I'm sure a lot of other people do, too. They all had code names whenever they called. The reason I know this is because when people called for George and he was either on the phone or out of the office, they would often ask that he call a code name at a certain time. He kept the names on a sheet of paper in his desk. Even Henry's office would call and ask me to tell him to call a code name at a certain time. I think the number is untraceable because they wanted to make sure they complied with the privacy laws and didn't want anybody tracing their calls. The calls never showed up on our telephone bill."

Downes looked at Smythe and thought that they were finally having a bit of a breakthrough.

"So, you think they had conference calls on this number? Can you get it for us?" asked Smythe.

"Yes. Whenever he made the call, he would go into the private room with a notepad," replied Albrightson.

"Do you think Doreen would talk to us?" asked Downes.

"Only if Henry hasn't paid child support. You know: she's one of his girlfriends and she has two kids with him."

"So, what else did you do?" Smythe probed.

"Sometimes, after a telephone meeting in the private room, George would ask me to prepare wiring instructions to transfer money."

"Can you tell us where these funds were wired to?" asked Downes.

"There were about ten or twelve wires a month. Most of the time, they would go to different accounts either at BCCI in Grand Cayman or First Jersey Bank in Jersey."

"What was the amount of average wire?" asked Smythe.

"I don't know. Some were in the millions and some in the tens of thousands."

"Okay. What else did you do?" asked Downes.

"I kept a file on the bills to be paid and entered them into the computer."

"What programs did you have on the computer?" was Smythe's following question.

"We had Lotus 123 and Word Perfect. I would type letters or reports for George."

"What type of letters and reports?" Downes was curious.

"Could you download your files onto a floppy disk?" Smythe cut in.

"Sure, but you have to show me how to do it," Albrightson replied.

"They were mainly letters to different builders and contractors about the new hotel."

"And the reports?"

"I've also typed reports mainly for the hotel project for the government."

"Sophie, is there a list of numbered accounts?" asked Downes.

"Yes, but I haven't seen it."

"What about loans?" Smythe added.

"Same, but I don't think there are many loans that are paid back."

"Why not?" Smythe's eyebrows were slightly frowned.

"I don't know, but I can tell you that there are quite a number of loans made to Florida companies, and the money is wired to a company called Greenbriar NV in Jersey," said Albrightson.

"Do you recall the names of the Florida companies?" asked Downes.

"I remember seeing the name Rainbow Farms and a company called New Southfield, but the money was always sent to Greenbriar NV in Jersey."

"And those loans are usually not paid back?" Downes's curiosity also went up a notch.

"Not to my knowledge. I overheard Doreen asking George if they were to be paid back, and he saying that she should not worry about it."

"So, that's where they got the money to fund the operations in Wellington!" Smythe's eyes were wide open now.

"Have you ever seen or heard of any transactions at the bank that involved arms deals?" asked Downes.

"I don't understand what you mean."

"That is, if they were selling or brokering weapons to different countries."

"Well, I know that there were funds wired to our account from banks in India, which were immediately wired to other banks, especially to accounts at BCCI on the Cayman Islands. These were usually for large sums of money, and we were told which banks, accounts, and amounts to be wired. Once, I overheard George talking to "the Professor" about us not making any money on funds that an Indian man was responsible for," Albrightson explained.

"Was the Indian man's name Sastari?"

"I think so, but the funds were sent from another name and wired to a company at BCCI."

Unbelievable...simply incredible! they thought. Smythe was excited, for the pieces were slowly coming together. Now they needed to get some evidence and get to know the connection with the Indian government.

Before Albrightson left, they spent a few minutes going over some safety precautions. They also thanked her profusely for the information and promised her that they would keep everything confidential.

They decided to file a missing-persons report with the police department on behalf of McLoud's sister. It was quite amazing that, in fact, nobody else seemed to care.

Downes received the manifest from Blackstone and it was clear that McLoud's name had been added—after the fact. "Does Henry think I'm stupid or what?" Downes laughed.

"Oh, Fat George will show up! He's too big to go missing. He's probably taking a rest in San Juan," said MacCallister Crutchen, the police chief taking the report.

"Well, would it make any difference if I told you that all of his clothes and suitcase are still in his condo?" Downes snapped.

Crutchen chuckled and said, "I didn't think Fat George had any extra clothes. He's been wearing the same stuff since he first came here, ha, ha, ha!"

"Do you think you can start an investigation?" asked Downes.

"We don't investigate somebody who went missing in Puerto Rico, especially a non-citizen."

Downes started to argue with the old bastard, but then he thought better and decided that he would do his own thing. He didn't even tell him about the change in the flight manifest.

CHAPTER 22

Dr. Walter Jones lived with his wife and three kids in a large home on a quiet road just outside of Frigate Bay. There were two sides to Dr. Jones: one was the lawyer from Anguilla who had helped form the People's Democratic Movement (PDM) Party, practiced law in St. Kitts, had assisted in writing law for the country, former ambassador to the United Nations, an avid fisherman, and devoted family man. The other was the drug trafficker.

In the mid-seventies, Jones had met a Colombian businessman, Carlos Lotero, at the United Nations in New York, where he was attending a trade seminar. At the time, Lotero was searching for opportunities to expand his business and considered the Caribbean a perfect new market for his product: cocaine.

Lotero was a lieutenant in the Calli drug cartel and was becoming concerned with the United States' attempt to control the trafficking at its major ports. He was interested in establishing business with people closer to Colombia, where the waters were much safer to transport their product. The Bahamas was becoming too risky and many shipments had already been seized by joint U.S. and Bahamian law enforcement.

The attraction of big money was very appealing to Jones, since his law practice was not providing the income that he needed to support his lifestyle. His professional position in the community and ambassadorships were more form than substance. The timing was perfect. He was aware of both the Draper and Ford's and First Investors fiascos and knew that Ernie Mueller would be interested in working with him. Jones was also aware of the favors owed him by Prime Minister Kendall Rudolph, since it had been Jones, who had largely been responsible for Rudolph's election.

Jones did a lot of research before contacting his sources. He concluded that this new venture would be highly rewarded and, if everybody cooperated, with very low risk. Jones contacted Ernie Mueller, said that he had a huge opportunity, and needed a partner with North American contacts to join him in a very lucrative business venture. Mueller, not one for talking on the phone, asked Jones to travel to Toronto and meet him at his home.

Jones got a taste of what money could buy when they met and was anxious to have Mueller as a partner: "Ernie," he expounded enthusiastically, "our shores are virtually unprotected. Shipments could be dropped by plane or sea without any problem. My friends in government would not interrupt, provided that I take care of them, and the chief of police is my brother-in-law, who likewise would not interrupt. In fact, he could be a big help in transporting the shipments to a location for further delivery."

Mueller was expressionless and listened intently to what Herbert was saying.

"The infrastructure is in place, Ernie," Jones proceeded. "I have access to people who will deliver the shipments to St. Kitts and move the product within. I have protection in place and I am working with some people in the U.S. who will buy the product and offload it from a ship's container using fast boats for entry into the U.S. We could do the same around the Canadian border.

"We pay fifteen hundred American dollars per kilo for processed cocaine and twenty-five hundred dollars for heroin," Herbert went on. "The wholesale price is fifteen thousand and twenty-five thousand dollars, respectively. The street value for a kilo of coke in the U.S. is around sixty-five thousand dollars and heroin is one hundred and thirty thousand."

"What about payment?" asked Mueller.

"Payment is cash. However, if we can pay in Colombian pesos, we will get all kinds of favors thrown at us. The reason being is that the U.S. dollar is not used in Colombia and those guys need pesos to operate their businesses. Ordinarily, they would sell dollars on the black market and pay a hefty price. We can pay in pesos through our contacts at Carib Bank. Also, once we've established business, they will allow us to wire the payment," said Jones.

"The minimum purchase with these guys is one thousand kilos. We should figure a sale price of fifteen million dollars, leaving a gross profit of around thirteen million. The investor will want five million, so figure two million for expenses and that leaves a net of six million, of which I want seventy percent," said Mueller, with a very stern look.

Jones laughed, "Ernie, I would be shocked if you had asked for anything less. But that doesn't work for me. After all, I have all the risk."

"And I have to answer to my investors, expose the bank, and arrange for distributors," Mueller countered, with a straight face. "Not to mention the favors we need at Carib Bank."

"Okay, okay! Fifty percent of the net," said Jones.

"Sixty-five percent," Mueller insisted.

They shook hands on sixty-forty. Once they began using their own money, it would be fifty-fifty.

Jones lived very well in his nice home, a Range Rover and Mercedes in the garage, jet-skis, a thirty-foot Grady White fishing boat, the Max II, and all the gear he needed to support his favorite pastime. The other home was in St. Johns, Antigua, where he conducted most of his business. He and his family often traveled to exotic places around the world and life was very good. People obviously associated his wealth with both his legal practice and political stature on the island.

Downes tried to locate Ed Devine but found out that he had not been on the island for the past few days. He and Smythe decided to risk leaving the hotel and hopped into their little Citroën rental car to look at the condos that Devine and Jim North—the infamous former vice chairman of First Community Bank—had been building in St.

Kitts. It looked as though one-third of the condos had been occupied and the remainder was still under construction.

The project was made up of luxury townhouses, about one hundred of them, at the top of a peak overlooking the ocean, where the Caribbean met the Atlantic. It was probably the best property on the island, providing a fantastic view. They took down the number on a sign which read, "Landmark Properties: Luxury Townhouses—Purchase or Lease."

Ed Devine and Tim Ford had met Jim North at a polo game in Wellington, Florida. After discussing the land-development opportunities over a few glasses of Champagne, they agreed to meet and discuss specific deals in which the bank could make a lot of money. At their follow-up luncheon, Ford was accompanied by Bruce Stanier and Doug Styles and the four of them chatted about opportunities that, in Stanier's words, better suited them personally rather than through the bank. Of course, First Community funded the deals at very low interest rates, no fees and no equity interests.

When the feds raided Meadowbrook, Ed Devine was arrested and held in custody but released due to lack of evidence—the conclusion by the DEA had been: Devine's role in the conspiracy, if any, was minor.

Since Stanier, Styles, and North had made a lot of money with Tim Ford before the house of cards collapsed, they had no problem doing business with Devine. After all, he had made the original introduction to the opportunities.

Ed Devine not only knew of the opportunities in St. Kitts, he also knew of George McLoud and First Investors. He had knowledge, from Tim Ford, that investment properties on the island were a perfect way to launder drug money. And having access to an offshore bank obviously made it even more attractive.

Devine contacted McLoud who referred him to Walter Jones.

In order to legitimize his law practice, from time to time Jones represented clients buying or selling real estate in St. Kitts. He happened to have a client who had twenty acres of land for sale on Timothy Beach. Bruce Stanier was aware of the property and intrigued by the way he could launder money through a building project.

Ed Devine and Jim North traveled to St. Kitts to get acquainted with the island and meet with Walter Jones, who in turn had been referred to them by George McLoud.

When Herbert met with Devine and North, he told them that the property would cost $1.75 million and for one hundred thousand dollars, he could get the zoning and permits pushed through the government in order to develop the property and build townhouses. Of course, this fee was not to be construed as the fee for the actual permits, as required by the government, but a fee to be split between Jones and Fisk for pushing the building officials to provide the permits without delay.

After reviewing the property and discussing the costs and logistics of the project with Devine, they agreed to pay the property's asking price and the one-hundred-thousand-dollar payola. They would stay in St. Kitts until a closing could be scheduled, and the funds wired from Funding Inc. at Barnett Bank, in North Palm Beach, to Walter Jones trust account at Barclays Bank.

The following day, the $1.75 million was wired to Jones trust account, one hundred thousand to his personal account and an initial four hundred fifty thousand to a new account inside Barclays Bank's "Landmark Construction Account." The total $2.4 million was the proceeds of a loan from First Community Bank to Scott Bartholomay, Executive Vice President of Funding Inc. On the books of First Community, the loan had been made to Boynton Properties for the acquisition of land for a strip shopping center in Boynton Beach.

Architects and engineers from South Florida, friends of Bruce Stanier's, had been retained, and working drawings for mechanical and electrical had been put to paper.

After a few post-closing glasses of Scotch, Jones posed the question as to whether there would be an appetite to partner in on some deals where the return on investment was huge and the risk minimal.

Jones explained the process, but not before he had checked out Jim North and Ed Devine.

Devine was to get a salary plus all living expenses paid while he was construction manager, as well as five percent of the net cash flow of each townhouse sold. North got the same salary, seven percent of the net cash flow and a big bonus at the completion of the project. The average price of the condos was seven hundred thousand dollars and the net cash flow was around two hundred thousand.

Within a couple of days, an additional $1.5 million was wired to the construction account at Carib Bank to begin excavation and utilities. Devine had hired local laborers, a couple of guys from Antigua, and several people on call from other islands.

Devine and North were the talk of the town and had no problem getting help for the project. The only problem was, North was in over his head and before long, had completely lost track of costs.

CHAPTER 23

Since taking office as India's Prime Minister, Jai Kumar was being faced with crisis after crisis. His main campaign pledge had been to aggressively pursue the prosecution of those involved in taking kickbacks and other illegal activities, which were taking place in India's defense-procurement program. This was something he had attempted to pursue while minister of finance and defense, but his actions had been thwarted by political leaders, including then–Prime Minister Rajiv Gandhi.

Kumar was also aware of the illegal arms trading between India and rogue nations and knew that the people behind the smear campaign against him were those either directly or indirectly involved in brokering large, illegal weapons deals. He suspected that some weapons deals were even involving Pakistan, India's staunch enemy, from which hailed the main threat of a full-scale nuclear war being waged.

When Kumar heard of the bogus numbered account, he was furious and determined to "get to the bottom of this incredible attack on [his] character." He waited until the election was over to wage a full-scale investigation into the "lies and fabrication" by those who were afraid of him, including a visit to St. Kitts by India's head of the Central Bureau of Investigation and a meeting with Prime Minister Rudolph.

Kumar knew that Sastari had been involved, along with others in the Gandhi camp, and vowed to destroy everybody who had been a part and parcel to this conspiracy.

There were other issues that he and his political party, Janata Dal, faced, all of which was music to the ears of people like Sastari and Ernie Mueller, who longed for a confidence vote in parliament.

In the meantime, their enterprise—including Khallehki and others—was suffering. Commitments were left unfilled and demands for the return of money were being made. Worse still, the carrying-out of skirmishes around the world was being affected due to the lack of weapons that heretofore had been virtually guaranteed.

Mueller realized that they were running the risk of being investigated by the Indian government and decided to put a hold on all pending transactions until he had a better sense of where everything was going.

Sastari and Khallehki agreed.

To see all the families dressed for church was quite a sight. The guys wore suits and ties and the ladies wore flowered dresses with matching purses and the most flamboyant headwear. The kids wore their best clothes, the boys in long pants and generally coat and tie and the girls with their best Sunday dresses and matching shoes. The churches were full. It appeared that everybody attended church on Sunday.

Sophie Albrightson delivered a large, brown cardboard filing box filled with loose papers, broken pencils, paper clips, and other miscellaneous crap that she'd gathered from the drawers of McLoud's desk and empty cabinets.

It was what remained after Doreen had cleaned out his desk and filing cabinet amidst the bits of stale food and candy wrappers. Some of the papers had been lodged in the back of the drawers and would have gone unnoticed had Albrightson not searched every inch of the desk and the remaining files.

She arranged, as Downes and Smythe had suggested, to have a cabbie other than Rufus Caple bring her over to the room.

Downes, Smythe, and Albrightson sat on the floor of the room rummaging through the stuff in the box and placing the items of interest on the bed. Downes and Smythe were like a couple of kids in a candy store.

Included in the box were blank deposit slips for the different accounts they had in Carib Bank, unused checks, blank wire-transfer forms, and incomplete Lotus spreadsheets. There were numerous sheets of paper torn from a spiral notebook that had notes and looked like they were for some kind of reference. One in particular had the names Apex (1), Apex (2), and Apex (3) with bank account numbers alongside.

"Who or what is Apex?" Downes asked Albrightson.

"It's a company set up specifically to have money wired into. The wires are from different banks all over the world, but mostly from the Bank of India."

"How many bank accounts does First Trust have in Carib Bank?" asked Smythe.

"I don't know. They were opening and closing accounts all the time. George has a contact person there who he deals with all the time, and I know that George takes care of him because he has asked me to deliver cash to that person in a DHL envelope. Anyway, I know that the companies, or people, that were wiring money didn't change, and Apex is a big account. When the wires come in, they are referenced to an account number, and then 'for credit to,' which would be First Investors Trust Company Limited. Never would the name appear—that's for internal purposes only," Albrightson explained.

"Interesting. So, McLoud had to keep track of the names and corresponding account numbers?" asked Downes.

"Doreen did that, and sometimes the other lady. Her name is Jasmine—Jazzi. She's one of Dennis Fisk's girlfriends. They have two kids...and she's only nineteen."

"Then they wired out the money?" asked Smythe.

"Yes, sometimes on the same day. I don't understand why they sent the wire to us. Why couldn't they wire the money directly, right?"

Downes and Smythe understood why alright.

"Did they wire the same amount out as they received?" asked Smythe.

"Yes, I think so, but I think sometimes George would take out a fee and that would go into another account."

"So, you think that the money you would receive was always zeroed out?" Smythe probed.

"Yes, but I think there was always a small balance in the accounts to keep them open."

"What other names can you remember?" asked Downes.

"There was Excelsior (1), (2), and (3), etc.; Greenbriar NV; and then I remember a company in Canada for which I just had a number."

"Bingo!" shouted Smythe. "Look at this!" She had come across three sheets of paper clipped together with company names, contact names, account numbers, some kind of code and amounts, and it was dated April 12, 1989.

Unbelievable! This is what I'm talking about," Downes shouted. He leaned over and gave Smythe a big kiss on the cheek and then the same on Albrightsons'.

The names Mueller, Sastari, Khallehki, and others whom he didn't recall were cross-referenced to different shipments. Further, the sheets showed dates, amounts, arms supplier, destination, and even the logistics of how the shipments were to be handled.

Khallehki's name was alongside Sastari's on all Apex and Excelsior accounts. "The Professor's" name was alongside Quantum Holdings, Pitroyal Limited, and Paradox Investments Limited. Downes recalled seeing these names on the organization chart that Bob Krieder had distributed at their meeting in Miami. The amounts of money noted were in the hundreds of thousands and represented commissions collected on deals.

"Sophie, do you know anything about this list?" asked Downes.

"No. George was forever scribbling notes on pieces of paper. He would give them to Doreen and she would file them under the code number."

"And Henry Blackstone has those files, right, Sophie?"

"Yes, in locked file cabinets in his chambers."

"What do you think was going on here, Sophie?" asked Smythe.

"I really don't know, but whatever it was, or still is, it involves a lot of countries and a lot of money. I know that the money for Excelsior is wired to a bank in Liechtenstein, some to Saudi Arabia, and some to Jersey, but never to Canada and never to people; always to company accounts.

"It has never occurred to me that anything was wrong," a pensive Sophie Albrightson added, in a solemn voice.

CHAPTER 24

There had developed, over the years, a group of thugs operating out of Antigua which had been involved with and controlled the local drug-trafficking business and other illegal activities on neighboring islands. The "island Mafia," as the group was known, consisted of small, unorganized street gangs that terrorized local businesses and controlled local prostitution and drug dealing.

From time to time, they were recruited by the bigger dealers as runners, in moving shipments from drop-off points to intermediary locations before being transported to final destinations. The gangs were compensated with a very small piece of the shipments, which they peddled between the islands.

The setup was simple and effective: word would be passed to the local leader on the island whenever a shipment was to be delivered. He and four or five helpers would drive their vans to the drop-off point at Fort Charles, an abandoned old British fort on the northwest side of the island. They waited for the sight and noise of small, twin-engine planes and signaled the planes with two intermittent flashes from a powerful flashlight. The planes would, then, make several passes at the drop-off point before completing their missions.

The packages were retrieved, counted, loaded into vans, and transported to a number of different locations used for storage, until the word was given to take them to a makeshift pier on the southernmost point of the island. The financial arrangements would have already been made.

These storage locations frequently changed and the helpers wouldn't know until en route to their final destination. The locations could be an abandoned warehouse, the garage of someone's home, a hole-in-the-ground at a remote location, even a church rectory. All locations were known to the chief of police, and he was always advised beforehand about the shipments.

When the packages arrived at the makeshift pier, they would be counted again and loaded onto waiting boats, minus the local 'rake', and then transported to a waiting merchant ship positioned about twenty miles off shore.

The routine occurred, on average, once every couple of months and it could involve as much as three thousand kilos of cocaine.

Sri Lanka was in the middle of a civil war in 1989 and had been so since July 1983. This magnificent country located in the Indian Ocean at the southern tip of India, with its phenomenal beaches and wonderful culture, had gained independence from Britain in 1948 but remained as Ceylon until 1972, when a new constitution was adopted. By 1986, the country was on the verge of devastation by the on-again-off-again civil war fought between a separatist faction and the Sinhalese government.

The Liberation Tigers of Tamil Eelam (LTTE), also known as the Tamil Tigers, were a separatist group in Sri Lanka and since the early eighties had been fighting for a homeland for ethnic Tamils, who had felt persecuted by Sri Lanka's ethnic majority.

The Tamils were an ethnic group living in southern India (mainly in the state of Tamil Nadu) and on Sri Lanka, an island of twenty million people. Most Tamils lived in northern and eastern Sri Lanka and in the early nineties comprised approximately ten percent of the island population.

The LTTE was notorious for having pioneered the suicide-bomb jacket as well as the use of women in suicide attacks. They were blamed for many high-level assassinations, over two hundred suicide attacks, and its war against the government had cost over fifty thousand lives.

Both their religion—mostly Hindu—and their Tamil language set them apart from the eighty percent of Sri Lankans, who were Sinhalese members of a largely Buddhist, Sinhala-speaking ethnic group. When Sri Lanka was ruled as Ceylon by the British, most Sri Lankans regarded the Tamil minority as collaborators with imperial rule and resented the Tamils' perceived preferential treatment. Ever since Sri Lanka had become independent in 1948, the Sinhalese majority had been dominating the country. The remainder of Sri Lanka's population included ethnic Muslims as well as Tamil and Sinhalese Christians.

The LTTE had broadened its objectives and targeted a number of buildings to be bombed, not to mention politicians to be assassinated. They needed weapons, munitions, and financial support, especially for maintaining the Sea Tigers, the sea-operating wing of the LTTE.

The Sea Tigers had a number of small-but-powerful, light fiberglass boats equipped with four two-hundred-and-fifty-horsepower outboard engines which carried machine guns and grenade launchers. When not involved in training or operations, the boats would be loaded on large trailers and hidden in the dense jungle southwest of Mullaitivu District in Northeast Sri Lanka.

They also manned large merchant vessels, sailing under different flags, used for smuggling equipment and drugs from neighboring countries. Since there were no large ports under LTTE control, they offloaded their shipments onto the smaller vessels that could land on the beaches or the small, shallow river inlets near the northern town of Mannar.

The LTTE had established a solid relationship with some of the poppy growers in Afghanistan and would arrange for shipments of opium to be delivered to various points in Pakistan and India, before making their way to the makeshift heroin labs dotted around the desolate areas of Tamil Nadu. These shipments were protected by a number of LTTE sympathizers throughout Afghanistan, India, and Pakistan and there were very few incidents of interception by authorities.

Since its inception in 1984, the LTTE had built a well-organized international network of drug smuggling, and its large band of supporters provided the peddlers, traffickers, and bulk distributors with the necessary protection.

Sastari was very sympathetic toward the Tamils who were, for the most part, impoverished and in desperate need of a better life. As devout Hindus, they were Sastari's most fervent supporters and prayed to him as the official godman of the Hindu religion.

Judy Smythe had become obsessed with the entire situation in St. Kitts and was determined to unravel the connection between Ernie Mueller, Sastari, and Khallehki in Canada; the possible involvement of Bruce Stanier and friends in the U.S.; possibly Blackstone and Fisk, and who knows whoever else in St. Kitts; and the politicians in India.

There was no doubt in Smythe's mind that there were ongoing multimillion-dollar illegal arms transactions that were known to, and possibly involved in, a number of foreign governments and/or terrorist groups. Furthermore, she believed that there was a major drug ring involving a cartel in South America which connected in St. Kitts for distribution of drugs to several points in the U.S., Canada, and Europe. Smythe suspected that this operation had originated from the fallout of the Draper/Ford conspiracy failure and involved some of the same players who also took part in the arms deals.

Smythe and Downes had been in St. Kitts for eight days and while they had gathered a few evidentiary documents and hours of taped incriminating conversation, they still hadn't obtained absolute proof that would convince Smythe's boss to run a story. The notes in "the box" had been a good start, but they still needed evidence that would support their findings and suspicions. Then there was the problem of whom they could trust, especially in law enforcement and all the way up to, possibly including, the prime minister.

Smythe and Downes had confirmed that the numbered account sent to at least two foreign newspapers was bogus and that the immigration record of George McLoud's leaving the island had been falsified. Further, they had testimony and evidence concerning coded bank accounts in First Investors, which helped create a complicated web of financial transactions very difficult to trace. They knew that, through a non-traceable number, conference calls were being used for strategy and deal-making meetings. They suspected that a number of people in St Kitts were involved up to their 'necks', as evidenced by McLoud's disappearance and the threat against the two of them.

Smythe had made up her mind that she would stay on the island until she could get some resolution to the issues and complete her investigative report, notwithstanding the risk of bodily harm or her losing her job at the Palm Beach Journal.

As far as Downes was concerned, his schedule allowed him to stay but his wallet rendered the stay prohibitive. His credit cards were being maxed out and the cash supply drained. Nevertheless, he was just as determined as ever to reveal what appeared to be a massive and complex international conspiracy in illegal weapons dealing and drug trafficking.

Wednesday, December 13, 1989

Smythe made several attempts to reach Henry Blackstone, but to no avail. She sat in the waiting area of his office for two hours, trying at least to make an appointment to see him. His assistants claimed that his schedule was full for the foreseeable future. She met Doreen and Jasmine, both of whom gave her a frightening stare as if to warn her that she was not welcome.

The same occurred when Downes called Dennis Fisk's office: "I'm sorry, Mr. Downes. Mr. Fisk is not available at the present time. I would be happy to take a message and have him contact you," was the answer he got whenever he tried to speak to Fisk. Several times he asked if he could make an appointment to see Fisk, but he was told that his agenda was fully booked with government matters within the upcoming weeks.

Downes tried again to reach Ed Devine and Jim North and left messages for both, knowing that they were on the island. Under normal circumstances, he thought they would return his calls right away. But these were a far cry from normal circumstances.

Walter Jones knew that they wanted to talk to him, and for a while they thought about parking their butts in front of his house so that he could see that they were not going to go away.

Downes had placed another call to the prime minister's office and asked his assistant to tell him he needed fifteen minutes to go over a financing proposal for the new hotel project. Alas, no return calls. The frustration was becoming unbearable.

Downes knew that Ed Devine was a big drinker. While working at Meadowbrook, he remembered that it was a ritual for him to be at the local tavern after work, so he decided to take a chance and go out for a drink at the closest drinking hole to his building project.

The Monkey Bar was a tourist-y place, offering rum drinks in coconuts, pineapples, and decorative glasses. It was 4:30 p.m. and the bar was packed. Reggae music was blasting as Downes walked over to the bar area looking for Ed Devine without any clue as to his true identity…and there he was, bigger than life.

"Ed, how are you, buddy?" he shouted, slapping him on the back.

Looking stunned, Devine forced a smile and shouted, "Terry, I was going to call you tonight."

Yeah, right! Downes thought.

"What's up? You wanna a drink?" Devine asked, hoping he would decline.

"No thanks, Ed. I need to talk to you."

"Can it wait till later, Terry? I'm in the middle of something."

"No, Ed. I just need a couple of minutes. I would appreciate it. It's really important."

Devine finished his scotch, slammed his glass on the bar and excused himself from a group of middle-aged women he was trying to hit on. "Let's go outside, then. It's too noisy in here."

They walked out of the bar to the end of the gravel parking lot and out of the noise of the music.

"Ed, you know why I'm here and you know I have a newspaper reporter with me who's writing an article about St. Kitts and offshore banking on the island. We would like to meet with you and ask a few questions."

"I ain't involved in nothin' illegal, and I ain't talking to you or your fuckin' newspaper reporter friend."

"Look, asshole, I know about you, North, and Stanier. I know about the financing of drug purchases and I know how you get the money to finance projects like these," Downes said, pointing up the hill to the townhouse project.

"Fuck you. You have nothing," said Devine, walking back toward the bar.

Downes kind of figured that he would get that reaction and was prepared for the consequences. He also thought it was best to hang it out there and see what happens.

In the meantime, Smythe had established quite a bond with Albrightson, who was prepared to do anything to assist them unravel the issues. When Downes arrived back at the room, the two women were chatting about the activity in the bank and repeating a lot of what the three of them had already discussed.

The one thing that Downes found interesting, and possibly very helpful, was the fact that Blackstone had asked Albrightson to prepare to move her desk into his chambers, for he planned to close the bank office.

Downes told them about his very brief conversation with Ed Devine while Smythe made notes and nodded, as if to say, "We have another notch."

CHAPTER 25

Thursday, December 14, 1989

Downes received a call from the prime minister's office asking if he could meet with him at seven p.m. at his office in Basseterre, since there had been a break in his busy schedule. He was taken completely by surprise and concluded that he should go alone, but not before he confirmed the appointment, as suggested by Smythe, just in case he was being set up. At the risk of sounding paranoid, he called the prime minister's office and confirmed the seven-p.m. appointment.

The government office building was located on Front Street, somewhat off the beaten track, in a refurbished section of town. The building was shaped like a big, dirty box with pale blue panels and ugly, odd-sized air-condition units protruding out of the windows. Inside the building was an open atrium with a stagnant water fountain in the middle, which looked and smelled like it had never operated. One of the three small elevators had an OUT OF ORDER sign attached to the door with multiple layers of scotch tape.

Downes was less than impressed. In fact, he felt very uneasy even if this was the government headquarters. The building was dark and quiet with one policeman at the entrance, who casually asked for his ID upon entering.

When he arrived, there was a power outage, an accepted problem that left fifty percent of the country out of power every other day as a result of the old, main generator system's inability to meet the electricity demands. This was under government review and feasibility studies were being conducted to acquire a new system—a campaign promise from PM Kendall Rudolph.

Downes climbed the six flights of stairs in the hot, dirty, and smelly stairwell to the top floor where the offices of the government officials were housed. An auxiliary generator was working, which provided electricity to the floor and the welcomed air-conditioning.

It was seven p.m. and the building was empty except the top floor, where two middle-aged ladies were busy at their typewriters. They knew who Downes was and politely greeted him and offered him a cold drink. "Please have a seat. The prime minister will be with you shortly," said one of the assistants.

Kendall Alfonse Rudolph, M.D., was born and raised in Antigua. He received his education in the best schools in St. Kitts and in 1956 received a scholarship to the University of the West Indies. After graduation, he did his internship at the Kingston Public Hospital in Kingston, Jamaica, and returned to St. Kitts in 1964 as a qualified physician.

In 1965, along with Dennis Fisk and Walter Jones, he became a founding member of the People's Discretion Movement Party, formed in opposition to the ruling Labour Party. In 1966, he campaigned for a political seat in the general elections and lost. He left St. Kitts shortly thereafter and went to the Bahamas, and then to Pittsburgh, Pennsylvania, to pursue post-graduate work. He subsequently returned to St. Kitts to resume his medical practice and political career.

In 1971 and 1975 he campaigned again for a seat in the general election, and he lost both times. He finally won in 1979, when a seat became vacant as a result of the incumbent's death. It was Sir Brian Ashe, the former Governor General, who campaigned heavily for Rudolph and was later credited for his election.

Three years later, as prime minister, Dr Rudolph led the nation into full independence from Great Britain.

Dr. Kendall Rudolph was a quiet, unassuming man and a shrewd politician, but much overwhelmed by internal strife and by perennially being at loggerheads with a strong opposition party.

The reception area was small, with four workstations for the prime minister's assistants and another room with two workstations and a lounge area. There were two other offices with the doors closed and a space for visitors, consisting of two well-used couches and a glass-top coffee table with magazines and promotional flyers on St. Kitts.

"The prime minister will see you now," said the lady who had greeted him. She walked him into his office, announced Downes's presence, and politely closed the door behind her.

The prime minister's office was small but very comfortable, with an attached conference room that seated twenty. A huge map of St. Kitts was draped to a wall of his office and showed the islands' different parishes. Pictures of the independence celebration covered another wall. On his antique desk was a much coveted picture of him and Queen Elizabeth II taken at the time of St. Kitts and Nevis' independence.

"Hello, Mr. Downes. So sorry it took so long to arrange to see you. I hope I didn't cause any inconvenience," said the prime minister.

Downes really didn't know how to address the him, so he just went with Dr. Rudo;ph. "Thank you for seeing me, Dr. Rudo;ph."

"Please, have a seat," he said, extending his hand to a couch then taking a seat facing him. "I understand that you would like to discuss financing for the hotel project in Frigate Bay."

"I do, sir, yes," he answered, nervously.

"I understand that you have discussed your plan with Dennis Fisk and he advised that you run it by me, since it will require cabinet approval."

"Correct. In essence, sir, the plan calls for the government of St. Kitts to allow me to sell one hundred passports to qualified expatriates and foreign nationals for one hundred fifty thousand dollars each.

"They would receive a one-bedroom efficiency condominium in the hotel complex for one hundred thousand dollars," Downes went on, "and the government would receive a fee of fifty thousand. This would provide ten million dollars for the project and five million to the government.

"The benefits are threefold," he kept on. "The first is, we get the project off the ground; the second, the government makes money; and the third, it will stimulate the economy by bringing wealthy individuals into the country. The benefit to them is that they will have a permanent residence in a beautiful condo and will have a passport that will allow them to obtain a visa to visit the U.S. As soon as we raise enough money, I will apply for permanent mortgage financing with a local bank."

"This sounds very intriguing, Mr. Downes. Would the funds be escrowed until all the money has been raised?" asked Dr. Rudolph.

"Yes, sir. There will be an escrow agreement which will outline the terms to be approved by the government."

"Do you believe that you can raise the money?"

"Absolutely."

"Excellent. When could I get a formal proposal from you?"

"In a few days."

"Good, then. I'll look forward to getting it." The prime minister paused for just a second. "Now, I understand that you have other business that brings you to St. Kitts," he said, with a slight smile.

Great! Downes thought. Rudo;ph himself had brought it up, so he didn't have to run the risk of masking the real reason for his appointment. "Well, yes, I do," he said.

"Would you mind telling me about it?"

With Rudo;ph listening intently, Downes proceeded to give him a blow-by-blow account of events leading to his current visit and the fact that he had a newspaper reporter with him who wanted to write an article about St. Kitts and offshore banking.

After he finished, he told the prime minister that he was on the island because he had a personal interest in getting to the bottom of why his name had been involved in an international scandal, lest it affect his credibility in St. Kitts if his name weren't cleared. Downes showed him a copy of the article in the Delhi Times.

Rudolph was noticeably shaken. However, he never acknowledged knowing about the bogus account or the fact that he had a meeting with the Indian guys from the Central Bureau of Investigation. "I am horrified that these activities are going on in St. Kitts. I am further horrified that local people are involved, and to think that some of them may be government officials leaves me speechless. I have to tell you, though, that I am aware of drug trafficking happening here, which I thought was under control," said Rudolph.

"We have had two murders here over the past few weeks, and I requested Scotland Yard's assistance in bringing those responsible to justice. There are so many rumors, but my chief of police can never seem to get the evidence that he needs," Dr. Rudolph's countenance darkened.

"Dr. Rudolph, I want you to know that I have no interest in causing any additional problems for you or your country. On the contrary, I will assist and cooperate with Scotland Yard and the local authorities to whatever extent they wish," said Downes.

"When you have completed your work, could I review it with you and your colleague, before it's published? As to your colleague's writing an article on offshore banking, she needs to chat with Henry Blackstone."

"Of course," said Downes, smiling.

He left the government building at 9:40 and felt that he had the support and conviction of the prime minister.

Thursday, December 14, 1989

Ten p.m.:

Upon returning to their room, Downes was surprised to see Rufus Caple waiting with Sophie Albrightson and Judy Smythe for his return.

"They killed him," said Smythe.

"Killed who?"

"George McLoud," she said.

"Dey fount 'im down by the Salt Pond. He bin ded for ten days."

"How did you find this out, Rufus?" asked Downes.

"I no dis guy. He works at de morgue, mon. Some tourists walking down an unpathed road toward the Great Salt Pond had discovered the body after detecting dis smell."

On the morning of December 4, the day after the conference call with Mueller and the day before Downes and Smythe arrived in St. Kitts, McLoud had ordered a cab to pick him up and take him to the office. He had made arrangements to have someone pick up his car, have new tires installed, and wanted it taken care of before he returned from Toronto. He was to leave for Toronto the following morning.

"Mista George!" the cabbie had shouted, banging on the door.

McLoud opened the door, cigarette in mouth, and walked toward an old, beat-up Subaru cab. He carried with him his briefcase and got in the cab without saying a word.

There was only one way to Basseterre from Frigate Bay, across a couple of hills and then a couple of miles on a flat road through the sugarcane fields. At the top of the first hill, to the left, there was the fitness club owned in part by Dennis Fisk. A minivan was parked in the parking lot with two guys standing alongside it.

McLoud's cab approached the gym, the driver made a quick left turn into the parking lot and pulled up alongside the waiting minivan.

"What the fuck is going on?" screamed McLoud.

"Shut up, George, and just do as we say," screamed one of the thugs opening the passenger door and thrusting a small caliber semiautomatic in his face. The other wrapped him with masking tape and covered his head with a burlap sack.

"Where we goin'?" asked McLoud, in a state of panic.

Nobody answered as they pushed him in the minivan's back seat with his hands crudely taped behind him leaving his briefcase on the front seat of the cab.

They headed back toward Frigate Bay and then on to Conaree Beach to the local Episcopal Church, with McLoud pleading for them to let him go. "Please, please, whatever you want. Is it money? I can get you money. Drugs? Please, what's it all about?" he cried.

There was no response from either of the goons flanking his huge body in the second row of seats. They pulled up to the church rectory on Conaree Beach, north of Frigates Bay, where one of the guys jumped out to see if everything was in order.

Given the all-clear, with the sack covering his head and his arms tied to his body with the heavy-duty masking tape, McLoud was pushed and pulled out of the minivan. They quickly led him into the rectory and into a dark room, where he was guided into a chair.

McLoud was breathing very heavily and his heart ready to explode, as a man in khaki shorts, New York Yankee's T-shirt, and baseball cap emerged from the corner of the dark room. "Mr. McLoud, I have some questions for you and, from the answers I get, I will determine whether you get to live or die," said the man in the shadows, with a rich Russian accent.

McLoud could hardly talk. He was utterly exhausted but knew that he had to tell them everything. And so he did, without any of the persuasive methods that the Russian had available to him.

He told the Russian of the deals that had been made through First Investors Trust, the names of the players, and how they had been coordinated. McLoud even told him of the money involved and how it had been laundered, as well as the names of the St. Kitts government officials involved—all with a minimum of questions.

Once satisfied that he had gotten all the information out of McLoud that he could, the Russian motioned to his comrades that he was done and to please take him back to his office. "Thank you, Mr. McLoud, you have been most helpful," said the Russian as the bag was placed back over his head.

McLoud was led out of the church rectory and back into the white minivan, where the cabbie was waiting. Still shaking and sweating, he asked if he could have a cigarette and be taken back to his flat in Frigate Bay rather than the office. There was no answer.

As they drove past his condo complex, the minivan bouncing over the unpaved road, McLoud screamed out, "Where are you taking me? Where are we going?"

The cabbie had been instructed to take a dirt road toward the Great Salt Pond. "Where are we going, please?" McLoud cried out, with his head still covered and hands tied behind him.

"Keep going," instructed one of the thugs.

They pulled up along a desolate stretch of dirty beach where locals likely dumped their trash and where the sandy, dirt road ended. One of the thugs got out of the van and pulled McLoud toward him, while the other pushed until he fell out of the van.

With McLoud screaming and crying not to hurt him, one of them brandished the small-caliber semiautomatic and shot him in the back of the head. McLoud rolled over, dead from the gunshot. The shooter, then, shot once more into the head of his lifeless body.

They had planned on dumping the body in the pond, but never realized how heavy McLoud would be. They simply couldn't drag him to the water. Concerned that some tourists may have heard the shots, they left him where they had shot him and drove back to the fitness club, where the cabbie was given one thousand dollars and told never to mention his fare or he would suffer the same fate. Shaking, the cabbie grabbed the money and jumped out of the minivan and into his Subaru.

The coroner's office had concluded that McLoud had been dead for approximately ten days. It also confirmed that he had been killed at the spot where his body had been found.

Despite what people thought of McLoud, he hadn't deserved that, Downes thought, but he wasn't surprised. McLoud had been missing for several days and they knew he hadn't left the island. The four of them sat around and discussed who would want him dead. The other question was: where was the briefcase?

Friday, December 15, 1989

Nine a.m.:

News of McLoud's murder made headlines on the local radio station and in the St. Kitts newspaper, and it didn't take long for Chief of Police MacCallister Crutchen to pay Downes a visit at the hotel.

"Mr. Downes, do you have a few minutes?"

"Sure, come in," he waved the chief in. "This is Judy Smythe. Judy, this is MacCallister Crutchen, Chief of Police."

"Pleased to meet you," she said.

"I wanted to talk alone, if I could," requested Crutchen.

"Judy knows everything that I know, but if you want to talk alone, you'll have to come back another time," Downes said, rather curtly.

"Very well," said Crutchen. "I don't mind if she stays."

Crutchen wanted to know everything they knew about George McLoud. He had no idea who had been responsible for the man's death or what the motive could have been. No wonder Dr. Rudolph had requested the help from Scotland Yard. Investigating a murder was way beyond Crutchen's level of competency.

Downes only answered the questions that were pretty obvious and, after forty-five minutes of boring, unimportant dribble, Crutchen excused himself and left.

Rufus Caple had been told of a cab driver who had been carrying a lot of cash around and with no reasonable explanation about how he had gotten it.

The cab-driving profession in Basseterre was like a fraternity. Everybody knew what everybody else was involved in, be it women, gambling, drugs, or simply maintaining an honest, clean family lifestyle. When somebody's lifestyle changed this dramatically and in so short a time, everybody invariably would know about it.

Caple called Downes to tell him that there was talk amongst the cabbies that Freddie Little had done an "extra" job for some off-island guys and thought it might be a good idea to talk to him. Downes told Caple to ask Little where he had gotten his newfound wealth and immediately tell him if he thought something smells fishy.

CHAPTER 26

Douglas "Dougie" Styles had come a long way since Downes had met him at First Community Bank. Within eight years, he had risen from Florida State Representative to U.S. Congressman and member of the Senate Arms Committee. He was highly respected as a junior Congressman, and his colleagues thought that he had a great future in the Republican Party. He had maintained his relationship with Bruce Stanier, for he had provided much of the campaign funds that had helped him win elections.

Styles had never admitted to being gay and, over the years, managed to sidestep all the questions raised by the media in this regard. His friends and acquaintances knew but he had succeeded at staying out of discussion on whether he was or wasn't.

Styles was a millionaire and, although the income he declared on his tax return was far from accurate he had been, and still was, indirectly involved in some very shady deals, which had provided him equities in foreign companies proven to have been recipients of laundered money. The dividends he received from those companies had never been reported nor had the cash gotten from Stanier.

Styles got involved in illegal deals when he and Stanier had decided to purchase a tract of land in Wellington from Tim Ford in 1985. The deal had been financed by First Community Bank, but the borrower had been a company owned by Stanier and Styles. The company had no history, no credit substance, and the $1.2-million loan had never been approved by the loan committee or by the board of the bank. The property had subsequently been flipped for $1.4 million and the loan paid off.

After the deal had been closed, Ford asked them if they would be interested in a partnership interest developing a tract of land and building high-end homes in the new Wellington Aero Club. Ford had also offered to pay back their cash contribution within ninety days, and triple their investment. He explained that he was involved in some lucrative, offshore, risk-free financial deals where the returns on his investment were being placed in offshore banks and managed by foreign corporations that he had control of.

They jumped at the opportunity, but Stanier hastened to add that First Community could not be involved for obvious reasons and that the initial cash would come from one of his own companies.

The deal was done. Stanier invested two hundred thousand dollars cash and promised Styles fifty percent of the profit. Within ninety days, he received notification from Ford that his six hundred thousand dollars was available and awaited instruction on the amount's disbursement. They maintained their equity interest in the project.

Ford accomplished what he had set out to do. Now he had a banker and a politician in his pocket.

In the late eighties and early nineties, the illegal arms business could be divided into two categories: those imported into embargoed countries where internal strife existed, in which case the arsenal was comprised of small to medium-sized weapons; and those imported into embargoed countries desirous of boosting their defense strategies in anticipation of external conflicts, in which case the arsenal was made up of medium- to large-sized weapons.

It has always been—and will always remain—extremely difficult to trace or control illegal trading of arms, especially when it involves a Third World country such as Ethiopia, Angola, Somalia, or Sudan, which wants to obtain weapons from any of the hundreds of manufacturers around the world. It becomes even more difficult when payment for the arms is made in drugs.

There were many manufacturers of weapons that sold their products to embargoed countries and were unbeknownst to them, including some in the U.S. There were occasions during which weapons would be relocated from their pre approved intended destination and there were times when shipments were meant to be diverted as a result of payoffs or other favors.

When looking through each piece of paper found in "the box," Judy Smythe and Sophie Albrightson came across a scribbled note that simply read "Colombia–Tupolev 10 mill." The note had been placed in a "Need Disposition" file.

With all of his followers around the world, Sastari had little trouble getting business and had seldom turned business away, even when there had been drugs involved. He knew about the distribution network in place in St. Kitts and that the drugs could quickly be disposed of and the money laundered without a trace.

He also knew that he could make additional money from the sale of drugs.

Friday, December 15, 1989

Ten-thirty a.m.:

Shortly after Chief of Police Crutchen left, Downes and Smythe were paid a visit by Inspector Clive Townsend from Scotland Yard. "Could I have a few minutes?" he asked.

"Sure, come in," said Downes, rather ignoring the fact that Sophie Albrightson was also there and might not want Mr. Townsend to know that she had been cooperating with them. He quickly realized it and wasn't so sure that he wanted Townsend to know it, either. In any event, Albrightson was in the bathroom and decided to stay there until the inspector had left.

"As you may know, we had an incident recently that may be associated with the two murders that I have been investigating," said Townsend.

"Really?" Downes said, feigning surprise. "I heard about McLoud getting murdered, but I thought that he was robbed or something."

"Yeah, right," said Townsend, in his typical British way. "Do you know who would want him killed?" he asked.

"I have no idea," replied Downes.

"You know that his immigration status was changed on the day he was supposed to have left for Canada. Any idea of who would have done that?" he asked.

"No, I thought you were investigating that. You confirmed that he had not arrived in Canada, remember?" replied Downes.

"Yes, but at the time it had no bearing on what I was investigating."

"Well, we know this: McLoud didn't leave the island, and the airline manifest said he did, according to Henry Blackstone."

"And you think the motive was robbery?" Townsend's tone was sarcastic.

"Inspector, I don't know what the motive was. I'm not the cop here. Talk to the chief of police."

"I have, and I need you to be more forthcoming with information. I'm investigating two murders, both committed without a trace of evidence. Now we have another one. I have to believe there's some connection," Townsend's tone was quickly becoming one of frustration. "When was the last time you saw McLoud?" he asked.

"When I was here a few months ago."

"What type of banking business does First Investors Trust engage in?"

"Ask Henry Blackstone," Downes replied.

"Okay, Mr. Downes, it's clear that you'll only tell me what you think I need to know."

Downes shrugged his shoulders thinking to himself, *I gave you the opportunity to work with me. Now I'll contact you if I think you can help us.*

After Townsend left, Albrightson came out of the bathroom and said, "I bet Rufus can find out who killed him. He knows everybody on the island, and they know he can be trusted."

Rufus called later in the afternoon saying that he had talked to Freddie Little and was sure that Little knew something about McLoud's murder. When Downes asked him why he thought that, he said, "He 'ad Fat George's case in 'is cab, mon."

Smythe got a phone message from her editor saying that he'd been trying to reach her for two days and insisting that she return to her office with a complete report.

This had not been anticipated; now they would need to decide what to do. Should she ignore the message and avoid her boss—which could lead to her dismissal or at least the editor's establishing an antagonizing attitude toward her that could have an impact on publishing her story—or should she go back and try to get him to assist her in completing the story?

There was plenty of work to do in Florida, such as getting interviews with Douglas Styles and Bruce Stanier or any of their current or former staff, maybe a conference with the FDIC or the State Banking Department regarding the probable irregularities at First Community Bank. Maybe even a trip to Toronto to track down Ernie Mueller and any of his lieutenants. Smythe also wanted to go to New York and attempt to locate Sastari and Omar Khallehki.

They opted for her to return to West Palm Beach. Downes would stay and continue gathering information.

CHAPTER 27

Downes's relationship with Jim North during his employment with First Community Bank had not been good. He found him to be a sneaky, conniving, flamboyant little dickhead who had no redeeming features whatsoever.

If one were to guess the line of business North was in, after seeing and engaging him in a short conversation, one would have never guessed banking but more like a bookie. So it was no surprise to hear that he had been handling sales of condos in a project in which he had part ownership and whose construction costs came from suspected dope money.

It was also no surprise that he was still in cahoots with Bruce Stanier. His main reason for still being in St. Kitts was not just to sell the townhouses but to keep Devine "honest" and protect Stanier's interests. North was also there to avail himself of any other lucrative deals in which he could get involved.

North had made subtle inferences to Henry Blackstone that he had banking knowledge, if Blackstone ever needed somebody else to manage the bank, even though North knew full well that this in fact was Ernie Mueller's bank.

Henry Blackstone had discussed with Mueller the possibility of North helping out at the bank, but Mueller would have no part of it. Giving somebody knowledge of what they were doing could be disastrous, plus he didn't know this guy. Things were working fine, and even if McLoud was no longer around they would work around it. Mueller wasn't about to dilute the secrecy that he had built over the past few years and place himself in a vulnerable position, not to mention what Sastari and Khallehki would have thought of it.

North often frequented Antigua, just for a day at a time. That island had better casinos—St. Kitts had only one—and plenty of good-looking hookers—St. Kitts had none. He usually stayed at the Wharf Hotel Casino and became quite friendly with the owner, Victor Poslov.

Poslov knew a lot about North, his days as a banker, his involvement with Stanier, and the townhouse project in St. Kitts, which he also knew was being built with drug money.

It wasn't long before North was being supplied with free hookers from Poslov and comps in food and beverage at the hotel, as well as transportation, similar to the comps that were given to Dennis Fisk. Poslov had confided in Fisk to the point where he had asked him if he would like to make some money on the side.

Poslov had asked Fisk to make sure that a flight manifest would show George McLoud leaving the country on a specific day. That assignment alone made Fisk five thousand dollars.

Rufus Caple picked up Downes and drove to the Circle, where they waited for Freddie Little's cab to show up. The Subaru was not hard to find, since Little was always either waiting for a fare at the airport or at the docks. Other than that, he hung out like all the other cabbies at the Circle. Caple reached him on his radio and found him waiting in line at the cruise ship, where he had just dropped off a couple of passengers.

"Freddie, need to talk, mon," shouted Caple.

Little got out of his cab and walked over toward them.

"Git in da cah, mon!" demanded Caple.

Little was a young—maybe twenty years old—native of St. Kitts. The cab he drove belonged to a friend of his, and he was paid fifty cents per fare plus one-third of the tips. He lived with his parents, had dropped out of school when he was fifteen, had no skills, and was always heading for trouble.

"Freddie, dis is my fren, Mista Downes. He workin' wid da police," said Caple, as Little climbed into the back seat.

"Freddie, I understand you just made a lot of money. Where did you get it?" asked Downes, leaning over his seat.

"I werkt for it, mon," replied Little.

"What type of work?" he asked.

"Why dya wonna no, mon?"

"Where did you get the briefcase?"

He didn't know that Caple had spotted it on the floor of his cab in the front passenger seat.

"'I 'aint talkin'," said Little, ready to get out of the car.

Downes leaned over the seat, grabbed him by the collar of his shirt, and said, "Look, you little fucker, you either tell me how you got the money and where you got the case from or I'm gonna kick the crap out of you and then haul your sorry ass down to the police station. You understand?"

"Yeah, mon," said Little, shaking in his boots.

"He mean' it, Freddie," confirmed Caple.

Little was scared to death. He told them how he had been approached by a stranger who had offered him one thousand dollars to pick up George McLoud at his condo and drive him to the fitness club, where somebody would meet them. He was then to drive a van with the three of them—a short distance. It would take no more than one hour, the stranger had told him. He didn't know that they were going to shoot him, he said, and when Downes asked him who these guys were, he said he didn't know, other than he thought they were from Antigua.

Caple got the briefcase from Little's cab and told him that he should go to the police and turn himself in, but not until he had heard back from them.

They went back to the hotel to find Judy Smythe packing for her trip back to Florida. The three of them acted like they had found some lost treasure and couldn't wait to see what McLoud had been carrying around with him.

The case was locked and they knew that if they broke the lock, they could be faced with a tampering-with-evidence charge and possibly be kicked off the island. Caple had a Swiss Army knife, which he used to pry open the lock and force the case open without damaging the lock.

They hit the jackpot.

The first thing Smythe picked up was about five thousand dollars in cash, McLoud's passport, and a bunch of bank statements for a savings account at Barclays Bank in St. Kitts, clipped together, in the name of George McLoud. The most recent statement was for the month ending September 1989 and showed a balance of three hundred and fifty thousand dollars. There was no withdrawal activity, just deposits in even amounts, from five thousand to thirty thousand dollars, with no noticeable pattern.

"Looks like Mista George was skimmin'," Downes said, in a joking but serious way.

They found forged immigration forms showing that Syed Singh had entered the country on several occasions. There was a copy of the infamous numbered account showing Downes's forged signature as managing director and the fax receipts to international newspapers, including the Delhi Times and the London Observer. The activity in the account coincided with dates that Syed Singh had supposedly entered the country.

There were copies of numbered accounts reflecting balances of hundreds of thousands of dollars and copies of incoming and outgoing wires reflecting millions.

Much to their amazement, there was a diary of sorts showing money being washed through First Investors bearing the names of customers, bank affiliations, telephone numbers, mailing addresses, and wiring instructions. There were specific accounts of drug deals—huge shipments from Colombia and who the investors were.

By the time they had looked at everything, everyone was shaking, since they had just found the mother lode of incriminating evidence inside the briefcase of a dead man.

Monday, December 18, 1989

Three p.m.:
Judy Smythe returned to West Palm Beach to face Kevin Black, her boss, explain her extended leave of absence, and provide him with a report on her investigation. She had been torn between staying in St. Kitts and providing him with all the reasons why she should have stayed or returning immediately in hopes that he would agree to allow her to return.

Black was a reasonable guy. He'd been with the Palm Beach Journal eight or nine years and had risen up the ranks to assistant editor in charge of investigative reporting. Downes had met him on a couple of occasions. He lived in Wellington and their kids were on the same soccer team. Black was a very thorough and ethical journalist, with several accolades for his work uncovering and reporting on issues that subsequently captured national attention.

On the flight back to Florida, Smythe had finished a detailed report containing references to conversations that she had on tape and a timeline of all the activity that had taken place in the six days of her being in St. Kitts.

She rented a small car at Palm Beach International Airport, in anticipation of returning within a day or two, and drove directly to her office. The newspaper offices were buzzing to meet deadlines for the following day's paper.

"Well, Ms. Smythe, welcome back," said Black after she'd acknowledged a number of "welcome backs" from colleagues and supporting staff members.

Black had never referred to her as "Ms. Smythe" before, and she wondered if that was an indication of his being a little miffed with her. "Thanks. Nice to be back, I think," she said.

They both walked back to his office and he closed the door. Black was usually jovial, hid the pressure of the job very well, and made time for small talk with his reporters and staff. But this time was different; he was upset like she had not seen before. "Judy, what's goin' on?" he asked.

"Well, a lot is going on. Look, I'm sorry I've been gone for so long, but I have a big story here. I have an article for you," placing the document on his desk.

"Judy, to be honest with you, I'm not interested in seeing your article right now. I need some explanation of this," he demanded, placing a FedEx package in front of her.

With an inquiring frown on her face, Smythe reached into the envelope and was shocked to see several pictures of her and Downes having dinner together, in intimate positions outside the hotel, and then the ball breaker: having sex in her room.

Smythe turned several shades of red with anger and embarrassment. "Where did you get these from, Kevin?"

"Does it matter? Do you deny that this is you and Terry?"

"Who, who sent them? When did you get them? Where did they come from...where?" she asked, with tears flowing and nervously stuttering her words.

"You need to tell me what's goin' on, Judy."

"I have an article right here for you."

"I'm talking about these pictures."

"Can't you see that we're being set up, that they know we're on to their game, that they want us out of there? Jesus Christ, Kevin, our lives were being threatened if we didn't leave the island 'immediately!' So what if Terry and I got it on. I'm single and he's divorced from his wife. We shared a room to save money."

"That's not the issue!" barked Black.

"We're single, Kevin," said Smythe, this time screaming at him. "Why can't you just read what I have and judge me on my work?" she asked, standing up and walking toward the door.

"You know that's not the point. If we publish a report that's detrimental to island residents, they will bring this up, and our credibility will be shattered."

"But shouldn't this at least tell you that somebody's going to the extreme of installing a hidden camera in our room and that we're on to something?"

"You just don't get it, do you? I'm not about to publish an article and have the credibility of my staff and this newspaper questioned. What else will these guys have on you?" said Black.

"What else could they have? Kevin, I need to know where we go from here. I have an awful lot of work to do," said Smythe with one hand on the doorknob.

"I need some time to think about this. I will read your piece, but I can't guarantee that we'll support it."

"Fine. You know how to reach me," Smythe dropped the report on Black's desk and stormed out of his office, slamming the door behind her. She passed by a bunch of people, who had suspected a problem, and headed to the elevator, visibly shaken.

She spent the next couple of hours riding around Palm Beach, wondering what she should do before calling Downes.

Downes couldn't believe what she was telling him. While they were talking, he kept checking around the room searching for a camera.

He wasn't that surprised; a little embarrassed, maybe, but not surprised. Someone on the island behind those photos knew that the only way to avoid being disclosed would be by either getting rid of or somehow discrediting them. Looking back, sleeping with Smythe had probably not been the wisest thing to do, he thought, but it had been worth it, and those pictures wouldn't deter them from achieving their objectives.

Downes found a small camera hidden in the frame of a bland, watercolor picture facing the bed, placed there by the hotel manager on the instruction of Dennis Fisk.

This latest episode threw another twist into the scheme of things.

Smythe decided that she would go to her condo, pay some bills, try to relax, and make a few phone calls. She hadn't made up her mind on when she would return to St. Kitts, but abandoning the project was never in her mind.

Downes had told Smythe about a former senior loan officer at First Community Bank who headed up the lending division while he was there and suggested that she try to contact him to see if he'd be willing to discuss the bank, and Bruce Stanier, with her.

John Clemonds had worked for Detroit Fidelity Bank for a number of years as a commercial lending officer before joining First Community in 1979. His situation and circumstances were not unlike Downes's in that he had been attracted to bigger opportunities and a change of scenery. West Palm Beach was hard to resist, especially when one lived in Detroit in the bitter-cold months of November through March.

Clemonds had developed a good relationship with the directors of First Community and handled all of their personal borrowings, but the anxiety that those directors and Stanier had put him through caused him a heart attack and he'd decided that he was not going to take the crap any longer. Before he could secure another job, Stanier (Jim North) fired him.

He knew where all the 'bones were buried' and was told by North, when he left, that he "should exercise discretion if ever asked questions about the bank and/or its directors."

Clemonds and Downes had gotten along great while working at the bank. After Downes was fired, Clemonds called to assure him that this had been the best thing that could have happened to him, since the longevity of his life had just increased. They had lunch shortly after Downes left the bank and reminisced about some of the crazy and illegal stuff that Stanier did.

Clemonds was very cordial and gracious when Smythe called and, without hesitation, agreed to meet with her after she explained her mission. He knew of her from the articles she had written in the Palm Beach Journal and had no problem with being quoted.

Downes finally reached Jim North after he had posed as an interested, prospective buyer of one of North's townhouses and told the secretary that North's name had been given him by a mutual friend. After waiting a few minutes, North picked up the phone: "Hello."

"Hi Jim, this is Terry Downes. Remember me?"

"Yeah, what do you want?" asked a surprised Jim North.

"You know what I want. How about talking to me?"

"You've got to be kidding me. No, and don't call here again," North hung up the phone.

Downes hadn't really wanted to talk to the sonofabitch; he just needed him to know he was out there watching his moves. Besides, Devine had probably told North of his conversation with him at the bar in St. Kitts.

Tuesday, December 19, 1989

Ten a.m.:

John Clemonds was only too pleased to talk with Judy Smythe about Stanier and his minions; he had no problem in burning those bridges. They met at a coffee shop in West Palm Beach the day after she got back from St. Kitts.

Having retired early due to his health, all Clemonds did those days was play golf daily, something he was able to do since he had remarried into a lot of money. Clemonds had brought with him copies of some documents that, he thought, could help Smythe in her investigation.

They sat in a booth at the far end of the coffee shop so that they had a clear view of who was arriving. Both ordered coffee and exchanged a little small talk, mostly about Downes and how he had gotten shafted at First Community. "He was too good and too honest. I think Stanier was afraid that Terry would take the side of the regulators and help bring him down," Clemonds said.

"John, could we talk about the questionable deals that Stanier was involved in?"

"Sure, but let me show you what I have here, and then I'll be able to remember each deal."

At that, he opened a brown accordion-type file and placed on the table a bunch of memos titled "FCB Loan Committee Agenda"—and the date of each—together with the minutes of each meeting.

"I have copies of the agendas and minutes for the meetings of the eighteen months prior to my leaving the bank till a couple of months ago. I have copies of the non-interest-bearing notes that each of the directors was required to sign for capitalizing First Community Savings and Loan Association, which was clearly illegal. This led to Terry being fired when he refused to sign. Also, I have copies of letters to certain directors stating that their lines of credit would be approved on the condition that they made contributions to Style's campaign funds."

Smythe couldn't wait to get into them. She was beginning to forget about her meeting with Kevin Black. "How often did the loan committee meet?" she asked.

"A standing date was the third Thursday of each month plus whenever there was an emergency, in which case it could be anytime. As long as a quorum was present and Stanier wanted to push a credit through, he could arrange a telephone meeting. But we still compiled minutes and thus noted that the meeting had been held via telephone."

Smythe picked up the first agenda:
– First Community Bank: Executive Loan Committee Meeting September 20, 1989, 8:30 a.m.:
Bruce Stanier, Chairman
John Clemonds
Ben Gilbert
Dr. Clem Samson
Allen Gluckstem
Roy Hayes
Fred Weigel
James North
David Pfoutz

– Agenda Items: Minutes of previous meeting:
$500,000 Construction Loan—Jupiter Medical Clinic
$2.4 million Land Development—Boynton Partners
$15,000 Employee Auto Loan—George DeBay
$165,000 Single-Family Mortgage—Feeney
$250,000 Personal Line of Credit—John Garry (lawyer)
– Status of loan-loss reserve, charge-offs, and past dues. Please confirm your attendance prior to September 17.
Thank you.
Sheryl Mitchell, secretary

"Write-ups of each loan request on the agenda were handed out during the meeting. Stanier and/or I would give our opinions.

Questions were asked or comments made and a vote taken. Sheryl would sit at the back of the room and take the minutes," Clemonds explained.

"Were there any dissenting votes?"

"Sure, but never on loans that Stanier was bringing to the committee. Nobody would question his deals. The minutes would simply show how the members had voted, if there had been any declining vote, otherwise it was 'unanimously approved' or with conditions."

"So, could you point to those minutes—those you recall had problems?" she asked.

"Sure. We can go through each one, if you like."

Clemonds and Smythe sat for two hours going through his recollection of credit decisions at the committee meetings, and Smythe making copious notes. Clemonds zeroed in on a couple of large loans (over one million) that Stanier had approved without even going to the loan committee, one in particular to Ed Devine which was subsequently charged off. He also provided her with a copy of the note and the accounting entry that removed the loan from the asset ledger to the reserve for bad debts.

No payments had been made on the loan, and when he confronted Stanier, the explanation he got was that Devine had been involved in a deal with North and assured that "we will be paid from that deal." When the loan was made, there was no credit history or meaningful collateral securing it. Clemonds suspected that Stanier was involved in some illegal scheme but stopped short of saying "drug trafficking."

"See this loan," he said, pointing to the $2.4 million to Boynton Partners. "This loan was one of Stanier's. It was supposed to be a ninety-day bridge loan to a couple of guys who were buying some property to build a strip shopping center in Boynton Beach. When he presented the loan to the committee, he said that the bank would charge fifteen percent per month and collect a fee of two hundred thousand dollars at the maturity date."

"But Stanier said that the borrower was a personal friend of his," Clemonds continued, "and needed the money that day, so he, Stanier, would take responsibility for it. The loan department made the check out to Stephen Bartholomay, who happened to be the president of Funding Inc., Stanier's company. There were no loan documents, no note, no closing, nothing. Every time I asked Bruce about it, he told me that it was to be paid off in a week and not to worry. To my knowledge, the loan has not been paid, and there has never been a shopping center built where it was supposed to be."

"The insider loans, to directors, that is," Clemonds went on, "were a joke. I don't think any of those guys would qualify for the lines of credit they were getting at any other bank. Stanier would approve them solely based on what he could get out of the deals.

"One of my pet peeves with Stanier was, he would instruct us to rewrite past-due loans so as to make them current. He would just be delaying the inevitable, but it was his way of covering up the delinquency rate when the examiners came in," Clemonds finally paused.

Smythe was amazed that Clemonds had gone out on such a limb and provided documentation to support his suspicions.

"Employees, especially officers," Clemonds picked up from where he had left off, "were required to make political contributions to either Douglas Styles's campaign or somebody in Tallahassee who Stanier favored. Periodically, Stanier would get a list of employee contributors so that he could track who was giving what. If your name didn't appear on the list, you would hear about it or your raise would be delayed until you contributed. I know: I was one of them," he smiled.

"What can you tell me about his relationship with Styles?" asked Smythe

"Other than the fact that they were lovers?"

Smythe smiled, "Yes...and that, too."

"Well, the one thing about Bruce was that he never flaunted the fact that he was gay. At least I never saw it. But when he was around Styles, he was giddy. Styles owed him a lot, and the money he had made in real estate was attributable both to Stanier's finding the deals and to First Community for financing them.

"Also, Stanier would demand from his customers that a point be charged for their political contributions. The way that worked was to charge the customer an extra point and the bank would send the money to Stanier's favorite politician, usually Styles. Of course, this would only work when the borrower was desperate for his loan and couldn't get it elsewhere.

"The other deal that I was talking about—not going to the loan committee—was the one for 1.2 million. It was for a tract of land that Stanier and Styles had purchased from the two Canadian guys that you mentioned. They formed a company to buy the land and borrow the money. The loan was paid off from Funding Inc., so go figure."

"John, what do you think was going on?"

"Jim North was the connection with Ed Devine, who in turn was the middleman with Tim Ford and Don Draper. There was money floating all over the place—big money. I have no proof that they were directly involved in drug deals; after all, big money was being made in flipping development projects, too. The only thing I do know is that big money, and sometimes cash money, was allocated to Landmark Properties owned by Funding Inc. Stanier and North were the principals in Landmark."

Clemonds handed over the folder with the full set of documents and promised total support in Smythe and Downes's endeavors. He also offered to contact other former employees who would corroborate his comments.

Tuesday, December 19, 1989

One p.m.:

Smythe returned to her condo on Flagler Drive in West Palm Beach, where she hoped to relax and gather her thoughts. She needed to go through the folder that John Clemonds had given her, to see if there was anything that would help connect the dots, and then make a few calls to see if she could get more interviews.

Her place was on the twenty-fifth floor of a high-rise condo overlooking the Intracoastal Waterway and the Atlantic Ocean. It had a beautiful view, and a little balcony allowed her to take advantage of the ocean breeze while enjoying the scenery of one of the greatest spots in South Florida.

There were eight messages left for her on her phone: one of them from Downes, six unimportant ones, and the last one from Kevin Black asking her to return the call. After taking a shower and relaxing with a glass of iced tea, Smythe called her office and asked for Kevin Black: "Kevin, it's Judy returning your call."

"Hi Judy, can you stop by the office?" asked Black.

"I need you to tell me what's going on, Kevin," she observed, impatiently.

"Well, we've decided to suspend you without pay for thirty days," he said.

"Okay," she said, not knowing whether to accept the punishment and say nothing or say, "Fuck you, I quit."

"And during this time, we want you to stay away from St. Kitts."

"Fuck you, I quit!" she screamed and slammed down the phone.

The next two hours, she spent with her head in a pillow sobbing her eyes out, after which she called Downes in his room: "Terry, I lost my job."

"They fired you?!"

"No, I quit after Kevin told me I was on an unpaid leave of absence for thirty days and then added that I must stay away from St. Kitts."

"Good. Then I think you did the right thing."

"Now what?" she asked.

"Can you afford not to get a paycheck for a while?"

"For a little while. I have some money in savings. As long as I don't have to sell off any assets, I'll be okay."

"When can you get back down here?"

"I would like to get a few things done while I'm here. I need to see if I can meet with Styles and Stanier. I had a great conversation with John Clemonds and have a bunch of stuff that he gave me. I would also like to meet with Janice Radico, and John said he could arrange for me to meet with some former employees of First Community."

"Great! Well, we are onto something here," he said, then chose to cut the conversation, realizing that the phones could be tapped. "Judy, I don't know if there's enough connectivity here on the island, but try me on my cell phone," he asked.

They discussed her conversation with Clemonds and how convinced she now was of Stanier's involvement in some major drug deals in St. Kitts. She would have evidence and testimony to prove it.

"Judy, we need to do some real leg work to substantiate some of our suspicions, so I need you down here as soon as you can, okay?" asked Downes.

"Okay. I'll call you later."

CHAPTER 28

Sophie Albrightson had returned to work on Monday, December 18, terrified of what might be facing her. Henry Blackstone was aware that she had been talking to Terry Downes and Judy Smythe, but didn't know or suspect that she had also been working with them.

Ever since she first started at the bank, Blackstone had found her to be exceptionally loyal and hardworking, but very shy. He also knew that she didn't know a whole lot about the types of transactions the bank was handling, certainly not like Doreen or even Jasmine.

Albrightson arrived at the office, after being dropped off by Rufus Caple, only to find that all the remaining furniture and cabinets had been moved, just dirt and garbage left behind on the floor but otherwise bare space. She immediately went to Blackstone's offices, where she knew the books and records had been relocated.

Blackstone was reorganizing his office space and had a couple of workers installing a security system and extra locks on the doors. He could handle the extra furniture and people easily, since he always had way too much space for his small practice.

Blackstone greeted her with a "good morning," then with everybody together he said how sorry he was to hear about George McLoud's death and stressed that everybody should cooperate with the police whenever they visited. He also said that if anybody could shed any light on what had happened, to please let him know.

He then asked Albrightson to visit with him in his chambers. He closed the door and said, "Sophie, I understand that you have been talking to Terry Downes and his friend."

"Yes, I have had some conversation," she said, nervously.

"Would you mind telling me what you talked about?"

"No. Terry told me that Mr. George had forged his name on a numbered account and he wanted to know why he would do that. He asked me about what we do, and I told him I didn't know and that he should talk to you," she said.

"Good. Please don't talk to him anymore and let me know the next time he asks to talk to you, okay?"

Judy Smythe tried contacting Bruce Stanier at his office in North Palm Beach but couldn't get past his secretary. She asked if he was out of town and told that he was at his home in Boynton Beach.

Smythe had kept Stanier's mobile number from her previous contacts with him and decided to give it a shot. On the ninth or tenth ring, Stanier answered his phone: "Hello."

"Mr. Stanier?"

"Yes."

"Hi, this is Judy Smythe with the Palm Beach Journal"

"Oh, Hi Judy."

"I am writing a follow-up article on First Community Bank and was wondering if I could have a few minutes of your time."

Stanier had gained a lot of respect for Smythe after the last article she had written on the bank, primarily because it had been very complimentary. As a result, Stanier had been able to use it to generate business and shareholder interest.

"Well, I'll be in the office next week. Why don't you call my secretary and set up an appointment?" said Stanier.

"I myself will be out of town next week. Is there any way I could chat with you this week? I'm up against a deadline and would really appreciate it."

Thinking that he could use some positive press at that point, Stanier was only too pleased to cater to Smythe—at her convenience. "Can you, then, come to my house this afternoon?" he asked.

"Perfect, thank you. I'll be there around five," she said.

Smythe went to Douglas Styles's office in West Palm Beach and was told he was in Washington and wouldn't be returning for another three weeks. She met with Janice Radico but didn't get any more information than she already knew. It was difficult to get a hold of anybody as a result of the upcoming holidays.

John Clemonds called her and asked if she would like to spend a few minutes with Sheryl Mitchell, who had been Stanier's secretary when Downes was there but had left the bank to have her first baby about a year before he left.

That should be interesting, Smythe thought, and thanked Clemonds for setting up the meeting.

They met at the same place, the small coffee shop in West Palm Beach. It was two on Wednesday afternoon and the place was empty when Smythe got there.

Clemonds and Mitchell arrived together and went right over to the booth where Smythe was doodling on a notepad.

"Hi Judy, I'm Sheryl."

"Hi Sheryl, thanks for doing this."

"No problem. Anything I can do to put this guy in jail," said Mitchell.

Smythe turned to look at Clemonds and Clemonds looked at her. That was a rather harsh indictment, she thought, and was interested in what Mitchell would have to say. "How long did you work for Stanier, Sheryl?" she asked.

"About six years."

"As his secretary?"

"No, the first year or so I was a bookkeeper and then was asked if I'd like to be his secretary. He put me through a trial period, and I guess I did okay."

"Look, Sheryl, it's very important that you understand that all I'm looking for are the facts. I'm not interested in conjecture or what other people have said or what you think happened, okay?"

"I understand," said Mitchell.

"Could you briefly explain what your job description was?"

"Yes. I handled all of his appointments; took dictation, but most of the time he used a dictaphone; I took the minutes of all the board, executive and other committee meetings; filing; placed calls for him; made travel arrangements for him and his guests; and general clerical work. Sometimes he would ask me to change the minutes of loan committee meetings, after they had been approved," said Mitchell.

"I never knew that," said Clemonds.

"Yes, the changes were made to how the committee members voted. Sometimes he would add personal comments which I know he hadn't made during the meetings," she said.

"What else?" asked Smythe.

"I handled a lot of personal stuff at his house, like dealing with the maids and gardeners. I followed through on all the outstanding items due from the management staff and kept track of wires coming in pertaining to his companies, 'Funding Inc.,' 'BWS Nursery,' and 'North Palm Insurance Company,'" said Mitchell.

"What do you mean, you kept track of wires?" asked Smythe.

"When Bruce was expecting wires, he would ask me to check and make sure they had come in. Their accounts were with other banks, not First Community."

"How much were the wires for?"

"Many were for over one hundred thousand dollars. I would say between twenty thousand and one hundred fifty thousand dollars."

"And how often would these wires come in?"

"Two or three times a month to either of the companies."

"Did he ever say what the money was for?"

"No."

"John, what type of company was, or is, Funding Inc.?" asked Smythe.

"It was meant to be a consumer-finance company, but ended up as a subprime lender. I've always thought it was a front for some other deals, though," said Clemonds. "Stanier would refer loans to them whenever he thought the bank shouldn't handle them because of the credit. The insurance company is an agency, Stanier was also lobbying to allow banks to own insurance companies, and BWS Nursery was a wholesale plant and flower grower in Boynton Beach. He also had a company called Data Services, which did all the check processing for First Community, but I think he closed it down after he was indicted on fraud charges."

"Can we get any bank statements for these companies?"

"I don't have anything," said Mitchell.

"That may be tough. Let me see what I can do," said Clemonds.

Mitchell had known all along that Stanier was involved in something illegal but was afraid to say anything lest she lose her job. She had also suspected North of being a part of whatever was going on, as well as the guys who ran Funding Inc.. She had overheard phone calls and was often told never to repeat things that she heard in the office.

"Who were his friends? Who did he hang out with?" probed Smythe.

"Well, you know he is gay, right?"

"Yes, I'd heard that."

"Well, believe it or not, most of his friends were employees of the bank," Mitchell said. "When I was working at the bank, there were a lot of gay guys. It was like a little clique, and they would talk about parties they had. Bruce would often ask me to send stuff in the inter-office mail to his friends and it was always the same group."

"What kind of stuff?" asked Smythe.

"All kinds of weird stuff, like magazine articles with pictures of male models, copies of articles from gay magazines...stuff like that."

"What else?"

"Bruce would often take his vacations everywhere around the world, and I would make the arrangements for him and one of his friends—boyfriends. Douglas Styles was a very good friend of Bruce's, and Douglas would introduce him to some of his friends in Washington."

"Anybody in particular?" Smythe was curious.

"No, not really. I'm not familiar with names in politics, so the names wouldn't mean much to me. I know he was friendly with the insurance commissioner in Tallahassee, who he introduced me to, and the guy acted like he was gay."

"Jay Stoddard is his name," interrupted Clemonds. "Stanier sent a lot of money to him because he was lobbying for changes in the law which would allow banks to own insurance companies and Stanier owned one."

"How about any Indian names?" asked Smythe.

"I remember a loan made to an Indian named person, an apparent friend of Jim North. I can't remember his name. The Professor' had some Indian friends."

"Who?" asked Smythe, almost jumping out of her seat.

"The Professor. I don't know his name. All I know is that he is a wealthy guy who lives in Canada, and I overheard Stanier and Styles talking about the 'crazy professor and his Indian friend,'" Mitchell said.

"Unbelievable," Smythe shook her head. "Do you have any documents, phone messages, anything with their names on them?"

"'I'll take a look at home. I didn't take much with me when I left; just some books and personal stuff, but I'll take a look."

"Great. Thanks, Sheryl."

"Oh, there's still one thing that I was going to run by you. My husband just got laid off from his job and asked me if I wouldn't mind going back to work. I always liked the people at First Community, even though I despised Stanier, and I left on good terms. Would it help if I tried to get a job there? I'd rather not work for Stanier, but I could find out what's going on. Would that help?" asked Mitchell.

"Sure, but please don't do it on my accord," said Smythe.

They shook hands and Smythe expressed her gratitude to Clemonds and Mitchell for their assistance.

CHAPTER 29

Stanier's place was unique—more like a museum than a home. The off-the-beaten-track, 7,500-square-foot, relatively new home had been built by contractors who owed him either money or a favor. With five bedrooms, seven bathrooms, a huge dining room, and a spectacular kitchen, the home was built with the best materials and most modern appliances.

One would think that a wealthy family of ten lived in the house. The artwork and antiques were rare and ornate, and the indoor shrubbery and ferns were selective and meticulous. Had Stanier not been in banking, he would have been in the interior-design business.

Smythe arrived at exactly five p.m. to find Stanier working on the shrubbery outside his front door. "Hello, Mr. Stanier. Thanks for seeing me on such short notice," she said.

"No problem, Judy. Let's go inside. Make yourself comfortable. I just need to wash up a little," he said.

Smythe sat in the living room, in awe of the artifacts and the antique furniture. Stanier appeared very relaxed and offered her a tour of his home after she complimented him on his taste in interior design.

He was a very gracious host and made sure that she felt comfortable. A young butler type appeared with wine and cheese.

"So, what kind of article are you writing this time, Judy?" asked Stanier, bearing his usual sneaky grin.

"An update on the one I wrote a couple of years ago."

"Okay. I hope you'll be as complimentary as you were before."

Smythe smiled and jumped right into the tough questions: "To what do you attribute the decline in the bank's earnings over the past two years?"

With the grin gone and an expression of seriousness appearing on his face, Stanier replied, "For the past two years, we have been required to write off a lot more in bad loans than what we reserved for. The bank regulators have been exceptionally critical of us—why, I don't know. Majority of the loans that they have made us charge off will be collected. I know these people, and the bank needs to provide them more money to help them out rather than leaving them high and dry. The FDIC is really giving us a hard time and the guy in charge doesn't like us. I think it all stems from the indictment in '78."

"You mean that the regulators are punishing you for losing the charges against you from 1978?" asked Smythe.

"Absolutely," replied Stanier.

"Can I quote you?"

"Sure you can."

"In reviewing your 10K and your annual report for last year, the bank's net interest margin and fee income were off substantially from previous years. Can you comment?" she asked.

The net interest margin is the difference between interest income that the bank earns on its assets and interest expense, which is what the bank pays on its liabilities. This margin was considered the lifeline of a commercial bank. Fee income is from a multitude of non-interest income services and had been, historically, high at First Community due to it being primarily a real-estate lender and the related fees it collected.

"The net interest margin is lower because of the relatively high number of non-earning assets and the higher interest that we are paying for our money," Stanier explained. "Fee income is down because the public-accounting people are making us amortize the loan fees over a three-year period rather than letting us take the money into income when we close the loan, which is what we've been doing for years. Since we generate a lot of fee income, the accounting pronouncements force us to take one-third," he further explained.

He had an answer for everything.

"What about your management? You hired Terry Downes as vice chairman in '81 and then let him go after eighteen months. What have you done to replace him and what are you doing to build depth in your management?"

"First of all, Downes wasn't a good fit for us. He came from a big Northeast bank and wanted to run our bank the same way. Didn't work. We are not your typical Northeast bank. As to a replacement, we hired a new president from a bank in Michigan, but he couldn't take the pressure: had a heart attack and quit. This is a high-pressure situation, but I don't think management is a problem. Like I said, if the regulators would cut us some slack, we would be fine," replied Stanier.

"Mr. Stanier, how do you respond to the questions raised concerning your own companies and the possible conflict of interest with the bank?"

Stanier was taken off guard and immediately asked, "Who is saying that?"

"I can't disclose my sources, but I've talked to several people who are close to the bank and they all say that you should not be using the bank to line your own pockets or those of your companies, and that you should disclose the inter-company transactions. I have also heard that you give preferential treatment, credit-wise, to friends and directors, and that if any of the big loans become delinquent in their payments of over ninety days, you instruct your loan officers to re-write the loans to cover up their delinquency status," Smythe sounded very confident as she spoke. She didn't pull any punches and looked Stanier squarely in the eyes, waiting for his response.

"Judy, who have you been talking to? This is absurd! First of all, my companies are my companies. They are not public companies and do not fall under the supervision of any government agency. Whatever intercompany relationship exists is always in the best interest of the bank. I am not required to disclose anything, since the public accounting firm has determined that the transactions are not material.

"As to rewriting delinquent loans, of course we do, but again, it's always within the best interest of the bank in terms of collectability. And regarding your statement about preferential treatment, I'm guilty. I always take care of my friends and good customers, but not to the detriment of the bank."

"Why did you fire your public accounting firm last year—one of the Big Eight?"

"We had a disagreement on the accounting treatment of our merged banks," replied Stanier, frowning.

"Isn't it true that you offered the managing partner of the firm extra money, if they agreed to the way you wanted your financial statements to appear?"

"Absolutely not! That's absurd!" said Stanier, with anger in his voice.

"Will you fire the current one if they don't allow you to account for loan fees the way you want them, or has that deal been made?" she asked.

"The public accounting firm that we select is evaluated by our CFO and ratified by the board. It's not just my decision," replied Stanier.

Yeah, right! thought Smythe.

Stanier was getting angrier and wanted to terminate the conversation, but before this happened, Smythe said, "Mr. Stanier, I am not out to write a disparaging article about you and First Community without the facts, but I have a responsibility to address these issues. The bank monitor and stock quotations indicate that all is not well at your bank, and my sources have given me their opinion. When the bank was doing well, I commented accordingly."

"Well, you are relying too much on your sources and your sources are wrong."

"I also analyze your financial statements, and recently they have shown a substantial decline in net income, clearly reflected in the bank's stock price. The market is not as bullish on First Community as it used to be," she said.

Stanier had no response and was becoming very irritable with the interview.

"Okay, before I leave, I need to ask you about the rumors that have been floating around Tallahassee. People are saying that you have favorite politicians and you make contributions from loan closings, whereby in order for some customers to get a loan, they must contribute money to a campaign fund. I've also been told that you very strongly suggest that your officers in the bank make contributions."

"What?! Judy, that's enough. Unless you tell me where this shit is coming from, I need to stop this interview," shouted Stanier.

"That's enough, Judy. I must ask you to leave."

"Okay, but one last thing: How well did you know Donovan Draper and Tim Ford, and do you have an interest in the townhouse project in St. Kitts?"

"Enough. I must ask you to leave."

Sophie Albrightson was very cautious in whatever she said and did. Henry Blackstone was keeping tabs on her and told Doreen to tell her only the things she needed to know. He had both her and Rufus Caple followed to see if they were in contact with either Judy Smythe or Terry Downes.

Smythe had called Downes and said that she had some good stuff from her conversations, especially info on Bruce Stanier, and was anxious to get back to St. Kitts. She had already made reservations for a flight on Thursday the 21st and would be arriving that evening from San Juan, but asked that he not pick her up at the airport. She would catch a cab.

The flight was on time and Smythe deplaned the American Eagle Jet Prop 50-seater, along with about thirty other passengers, at nine p.m. She walked into a reasonably quiet immigration area and, when it was her turn, she approached the officer and presented her passport and immigration form.

"Where are you coming from?" asked the lady, dressed in a very official uniform, first looking at Smythe's face then at the picture on her passport.

"West Palm Beach, via San Juan."

"What is the purpose of your visit?"

"Business."

"What kind of business?"

"I am a newspaper reporter."

"How long will you be staying?"

"One week."

"And where will you be staying?"

"At the Ocean Terrace Hotel."

"Thank you, Ms. Smythe. Please take a seat in that office over there," she said, pointing to a corner space barely big enough for two people. "Someone will be with you in a minute."

"Is there something wrong?" she asked, waiting to retrieve her passport.

"Just take a seat, Ms. Smythe. Someone will be with you in a minute, and we will give you back your passport when you have met with the supervisor."

After waiting more than forty minutes and everyone else having left the building, an elderly gentleman in street clothes approached her, introduced himself as the supervisor of immigration and naturalization, and apologized for making her wait. "Miss Smythe, I'm sorry to inform you that your entrance into St. Kitts has been denied."

"What? Why? What's wrong?" asked Smythe, appearing alarmed.

"It appears that you are on the 'do-not-allow-re-entry list' due to problems that surfaced while you were here last week."

"What kind of problems?"

"I'm sorry, Miss Smythe."

"Do I have any recourse? Can I appeal this to anyone?"

"I'm afraid not tonight, and I am authorized to tell you that you are to leave on the next available departing flight," said the officer.

"When is that and where to?"

"There is a flight leaving in thirty-five minutes to Antigua. I have made arrangements for you to be on that flight."

"And what if I say I'm not going?" she asked, defiantly.

"Well, then we will place you under arrest and you will be sent to jail until the magistrate decides what to do with you. I would sincerely recommend the option I'm giving you," said the supervisor.

"If there were problems while I was here, don't you think that I should have been made aware of what they are?" asked Smythe, about ready to explode.

"I'm sorry, Miss Smythe."

"Where did this decision come from?"

"I'm very sorry. I have your baggage outside, and here is your passport and your ticket. I will walk you to the gate. Of course, there is no charge."

It was obvious that these trumped-up assertions had come from either Henry Blackstone or Dennis Fisk. They had gotten the word from the hotel that she was coming back on that flight, so they made sure she wouldn't be allowed in the country. Now all they had to do was get rid of Downes.

Smythe called him from the gate—the supervisor sitting next to her, making sure that she got on the airplane. She was beside herself, exhausted, and mad as hell.

Downes told her that this just added another notch and suggested that she get a room and relax. He would follow through in the morning and see if he could get her back in the country. He would go to the prime minister, if he had to.

Downes spent the next several hours working on his presentation to the government on the financing plan for the hotel project that the prime minister had been so impressed with.

The next morning, he made arrangements to meet with a local solicitor, Isabelle Clarke, who, after his giving her a five-hundred-dollar retainer, promised that she would get to the bottom of why Smythe was being denied entry into St. Kitts. Clarke told him that, while she was an avid supporter of Prime Minister Randolph, Henry Blackstone and Dennis Fisk were not on her list of favorites but that the person he must be really careful of was Walter Jones.

Clarke knew that Jones' law practice was a scam. He was never at his office and she knew of no clients whom he represented. She suspected that he was involved in some scheme, otherwise how could he afford to live that good? she had asked herself time and again.

She had known Walter Jones since he was born and knew his brother-in-law, Chief of Police MacCallister Crutchen. Until the past few years, neither one of them had much money.

Clarke was sixty-four years old and had practiced family law in St. Kitts and Anguilla for the past thirty years. She stayed out of politics as much as she could, but supported the principles of the PDM Party, not necessarily its members.

When Downes asked her about the violence and the recent murder of McLoud, she simply said, very sternly, "It had to be from outside influences. I know everybody in politics in St. Kitts and Nevis, and I don't think anybody here is capable of committing these acts of violence."

Isabelle Clarke was one of those people who, after the first few minutes of conversation, gave the feeling that she could be trusted.

Her office was very plain and functional. The only thing of notice was an official Certificate of Independence from Britain and photographs of her and Kendall Rudolph with the Queen of England.

After talking to her, Downes concluded that he wouldn't want to face her in court.

CHAPTER 30

Friday, December 22, 1989

It was after midnight when Smythe arrived in Antigua, a fifty-minute flight from St. Kitts. She was one of three people on the flight, and there were four people in immigration and customs to process them. She caught a cab to the Regency Hotel and Casino, after it had been suggested by a cab driver who appeared to have been waiting for her. Tired, frustrated, and generally pissed off, she entered her room, placed her luggage on the bed, and noticed the message light on her phone blinking.

Concluding that it was probably the front desk, she picked up the phone and dialed the retrieve-message number: "Miss Smythe, please dial room number 414—very important," was the message in an undetectable accent.

Wondering who that could possibly be and who would know where she was staying, Smythe reluctantly dialed number 414, not knowing it was the presidential suite.

"Miss Smythe, thank you for calling," said a voice with a Russian accent.

"Who is this and what do you want?" she asked, in an annoying tone of voice.

"Could we meet in the lobby, say in fifteen minutes?"

"No! Who are you?"

"No cause for alarm, Miss Smythe. I would like to review some business details with you regarding your work in St. Kitts."

"Who are you?" she asked again, sounding very alarmed.

"I will explain when I see you. Please, there is no need to worry."

"Then I'll meet you in the morning."

"Please, Miss Smythe, this can't wait. It is imperative that we talk now."

As an investigative reporter, Smythe was used to strange and possibly dangerous situations, it was an occupational hazard. She knew that she wouldn't sleep, thinking of who this could be and what was so important that this guy needed to speak with her right away.

She caught the elevator down to the lobby and walked directly to the front desk and motioned for the concierge, "Could you help me, please? I'm supposed to meet a gentleman here who I've never met before. Could you keep an eye on us and make sure that everything is okay?" she said, slipping the concierge a twenty.

"Yes, of course, ma'am," said the concierge, with a sneaky smile on his face.

"Miss Smythe?" asked the gentleman in khaki shorts, a New York Yankees T-shirt, and baseball cap.

"Yes," she said, with much concern.

"Can we sit over here? May I get you something to drink?"

"No, thank you." They both took a seat in the lobby of the hotel in view of guests coming and going, even though it was after one a.m., and in plain view of the concierge.

"Miss Smythe, my name is Victor Poslov and I represent a number of investors in Russia. We have some holdings here in Antigua, including this hotel, and other countries in the Caribbean, and we want to expand our investments to include St. Kitts."

"Okay," said Smythe, wondering what this was all about.

"So, I understand that you are a newspaper reporter and that you are in St. Kitts writing an article for your newspaper," said Poslov.

"Not anymore. They won't let me in the country."

"Ah, well, I'm sorry about that. I wanted to talk to you, but not in St. Kitts."

Smythe looked at him in horror: "So, it was you who prevented me from getting in? What else have you made happen in St. Kitts?"

Poslov smiled. "Let's put it this way: we have a lot of money and a lot of influence in St. Kitts. We will be building the hotel and casino in Frigate Bay, since we have recently purchased the property that, I understand, your partner was trying to buy."

"This sounds like a shakedown to me."

"Be that as it may, Miss Smythe, the bottom line is that we want you and your friend out of St. Kitts. We are prepared to pay you for your inconvenience, but we would like this to happen right away, with both of you returning to West Palm Beach. You are aware of Mr. McLoud's demise."

Smythe just stared at him, shaking with fear and anger.

The Izmaylovskaya gang had been around for a number of years and had its hands in narcotics trafficking, illegal arms deals, infiltration of legitimate businesses, murder-for-hire, prostitution, slavery, and extortion. It operated out of Moscow and had a presence in New York, Miami, London, Paris, Tel Aviv, and Toronto. The gang was headed by Semion Gasuchavik, considered by the FBI the world's most dangerous gangster.

The gang members saw the geography of the Caribbean as an advantage in dealing massive shipments of drugs from the South American cartels with worldwide distribution. They prided themselves in being able to recruit politicians, police commanders, and anyone else who could assist in their criminal activities.

They had already established a very lucrative business, running heroin from the Tamil Nadu region in India into Europe and the U.S.

In 1988, twelve months before the Russians pulled out of Afghanistan, General Milov Skersky and some of his soldiers captured two members of the Taliban who operated a small workshop that converted poppy seeds to opium. Instead of killing them, they decided to work out a deal whereby, once the Russians had pulled out of Afghanistan, they would use them to farm opium and find the necessary labs to convert it to heroin. In the meantime, they would be afforded some protection from the Russian Army until there was some resolution to the war. The general had bet on the Russians' pulling out, but it took twelve months of manipulating his own army to maintain the contacts he had found.

General Skersky had aspirations of involvement in organized crime, especially in the notorious Izmaylovskaya gang. He took his idea to Simeon Gasuchavik, whom he had met when arms were being diverted from the Russian Army to the Russian Mafia, and soon became a bona fide member.

It was easy to be involved with the Russian mob, but just like any other organized crime, it was impossible to get out.

Opium was produced from the seeds of the poppy grown in the Afghanistan hills and transported by donkeys into the Helmand Province in the southern part of the country, where it was processed into heroin. The Russians exchanged weapons, usually small arms, for the heroin, which was transported into Karachi, Pakistan, loaded into containers hidden amongst fabrics, and transported to several points in Europe. The Russians never had problems transporting the drugs, since the politicians in both Afghanistan and Pakistan were paid off and had become a part of the lucrative operation.

Sri Lanka's Liberation of the Tigers of Elam (LTTE) had a need for weapons and munitions and was able to negotiate deals with the Russians, after Sastari had informed its leader that providing them weapons in exchange for drugs had become too risky.

Before long, Skersky was coordinating buyers of heroin in Europe for drugs purchased from the LTTE.

Under the supervision of Victor Poslov, who ran the U.S. and Caribbean operations, they had already invested millions of dollars in Antiguan real estate and had recently purchased the Regency Hotel and Casino. A thriving prostitution ring had already been established and was well known that drugs were dealt directly from the hotel.

Poslov knew Dennis Fisk very well; in fact, he had paid Fisk a substantial amount of money in gaining favors from the government. He had recently closed the deal for the purchase of the land that Downes was negotiating for the hotel project in Frigate Bay, but had not informed anyone in government of the transaction. Poslov didn't need any financing, and construction was to begin within sixty days.

Walter Jones was Poslov's main contact in St. Kitts. Jones had never had a choice of whether or not he should work for the Russian.

The bottom line was, the Izmaylovskaya gang, under the leadership of Semion Gasuchavik and the direction of Victor Poslov, was already established in St. Kitts, especially after Poslov's assignment to Walter Jones in arranging the killing of George McLoud. After the two had met, Poslov wanted to make sure that Jim North got control of the bank.

Judy Smythe didn't know whether to cave in to Poslov and assure him that she and Downes would return to Florida or just tell him to go to hell. She opted for the former and said that she needed a day or so to reach Downes and convince him to leave St. Kitts.

"As I said, Miss Smythe, I will certainly make it worth your while and as soon as I have been assured of you and your colleague's departure, I will make arrangements to pay you fifty thousand dollars. Of course, if we find out later that you have published any article concerning your investigation of matters in St. Kitts, you and your partner will suffer the consequences. And please do not contact the authorities; we have that covered as well."

"Okay," said Smythe, trembling uncontrollably.

"You have until four o'clock tomorrow afternoon, at which time I expect you to call me in room 414 and tell me that plane reservations have been made. I expect the two of you to have arrived in Miami no later than four p.m. of the following day. Agreed?"

"Agreed."

"Wise choice, Miss Smythe. I wish you well. Oh, and by the way, the pictures of you and your partner are very nice. I'm sure that your editor enjoyed seeing them."

Smythe blew him off when he extended his hand. She made her way to the elevator, uncontrollably shaking with fright and anger. She reached into her purse to turn off the recorder as she fumbled to open the door to her room where she immediately placed a call.

"Terry, we have a problem," she said, in a strange and nervous tone.

"What's up?" asked Downes.

She described her frightening conversation with Poslov, the option she had taken, and told him that it had been he who had arranged the killing of McLoud, as well as paid off somebody in the immigration office to deny her entrance into St. Kitts, and who had sent the pictures to Kevin Black. She also told him that the entire conversation had been taped.

"Fuck 'im. I'm not leaving here because of a threat by some stranger who doesn't like us being here. He can kiss my ass."

"So, where do we go from here, Terry?"

"I've got to get you back here. Can you check and see if there's a flight to Nevis. They have a tiny immigration desk there, and I doubt that they have been tipped off. Once you get to Nevis, you are in the country and you don't have to go through immigration in St Kitts."

"I don't think there is a flight to Nevis, but I'll check."

"Then you have to charter a plane—which would probably be best, anyway—and hope that Poslov hasn't got to the immigration people in Nevis yet."

"Okay. I can do that, but then what?"

"Then we need to find a place in Nevis, in which case I will meet you there, or arrange to get you in here somehow. Let me think about it."

"Okay. It's almost three. I will check on flights, first-thing in the morning. You let me know what's going on; we have until four tomorrow afternoon."

Downes hung up and called Rufus Caple's cell phone. He never had his phone off, but it took a while for him to answer; it was three in the morning. It seemed like the phone was ringing for five minutes before Caple finally answered.

"Rufus?" he asked. "Rufus, are you there?"

"Yeh, mon," he answered, not knowing who it was, where he was, or for that matter who he was.

"Rufus, talk to me."

"Yeh, mon."

"Rufus," he screamed, "this is Terry!"

"Okay, mon."

"Rufus, get your ass over to the hotel right away. I'll meet you outside the lobby."

"Uh, okay, mon."

Downes wasn't sure Caple knew who he was or where to go. He just hoped he'd be there.

Smythe didn't sleep at all. She had flipped through the tiny yellow pages book that covered three or four countries looking for charter flights. Windwood Charters offered flights to anywhere within four hundred miles of Antigua, and she could charter a four-seater Piper Cub to Nevis for five hundred dollars.

Rufus Caple arrived at the hotel within five minutes of Down's call to him. He explained the predicament that he was in and went straight into arranging mode. "No problem, mon. Tell me when she will arrive, an' I'll git Rudolph to pick 'er up. Ya might be betta stayin' in Nevis, mon," he said.

"No, I need to be here, but maybe Judy should stay there for a while."

Smythe made a reservation for that Friday, December 22, on a charter flight from St. Johns, Antigua, to Nevis—flight time: one hour and forty minutes. The departure time was set at eight a.m. and she called Downes to confirm her arrival at 9:40. He asked her to be careful and try to hide her identity until she got to Nevis.

Smythe decided that she would not check out of the hotel but call them later...maybe. She reserved a cab, carried just one piece of luggage, and asked the cab driver to meet her at the rear of the hotel so as not to have anybody suspect that she was checking out. She wore her sunglasses, a large straw hat, and looked like a normal tourist.

At the airport, she went straight to the charter counter and was checked in by the very pilot who was taking her to Nevis. He requested her passport and credit card. As he was processing the payment, she had a favor to ask: "Is it possible that my identity be kept private? I would rather not have anybody know that I'm leaving Antigua for Nevis," she spoke, nervously.

Smythe didn't know if any carrier had been tipped off about the possibility of her leaving Antigua.

"No problem here," said the pilot, accepting the fifty-dollar tip. The flight was uneventful, and she was pretty sure that nobody had noticed that she was leaving the country.

She arrived in Nevis at the indicated hour, the single-engine plane landing on the shortest airstrip known to man. The plane was greeted by the only employee of the FBO, who asked the pilot if he was staying or if he was "turning and returning."

The employee grabbed Smythe's luggage and took it inside, where a customs immigration person greeted her. She looked at her passport, looked at her, and asked that she remove her sunglasses. She stamped her passport, kept the immigration form, and said, "Welcome to Nevis, Miss Smythe. Have a nice stay."

Outside the tiny terminal, with the Atlantic Ocean surf gently spraying over the narrow road, a cab driver with forty years experience in Nevis, waited for Smythe. He greeted her with a broad smile and said, "Dun worry 'bout a ting. You're in God's 'ans in Nevis."

She called Downes to tell him that she had arrived well and needed to know the plan.

"Judy, I think you should stay there for a day or so, but there is a boat that leaves the Four Seasons Resort four or five times a day.

"Okay, but please be careful. When this guy finds out that I've reneged on his deal, he'll be really pissed and want us dead."

"Don't worry. I'll be okay."

The cabbie took Smythe to his home, as requested by Rufus, a delightful little two-bedroom house two minutes from the airport, where he lived with his wife of thirty-five years.

Smythe felt comfortable and safe, so much so that she slept through until the following morning, Saturday, December 23.

CHAPTER 31

Downes was very grateful for Rufus Caple's help in arranging Judy's stay in Nevis, since they both knew that things had to start happening now, and it was important for them to be together. Before Caple left, he had mentioned that Downes should contact Sophie Albrightson. She had something important to tell him but didn't want to go to the hotel, since she thought she was being watched.

Albrightson had located a copy of a wire receipt dated November 5, 1989, from a bank in India for ten million dollars. There had been a mix-up in the swift code on the wire and she had overheard Doreen contact the bank in India since the funds were delayed. Blackstone had asked Doreen to call the bank and inquire on the whereabouts of the funds. Albrightson found the notes that Doreen had made from her telephone conversation. This was what they had been looking for, and Downes asked her to get a copy to him through Caple.

The notes were very clear:

$10 million: Orig. Sri Lanka, swift 1000098756
Bank of India: Nov 20

Albrightson also saw the instructions on the disposition of the funds:

40: BCCI Cayman
30: Excelsior Liechtenstein

30: Quantum, Jersey

900: Russian Bank

It appeared that small arms had been purchased from a Russian supplier, and the money received from India. The payment had been wired from First Investors to a Russian bank and commissions distributed accordingly.

Albrightson also mentioned that Blackstone had a lot on his mind and that she thought there was somebody threatening him. "There was a man here yesterday who I've never seen before and when he left, Mr. Blackstone was very upset," she said.

Later in the day, Downes called Dennis Fisk and was able to get through to him without any problem, probably because his secretary thought it was someone else. "Dennis, it's Terry Downes." He was sure that, by his tone of voice, Fisk was surprised.

"I was told that you had left St. Kitts," said Fisk.

"Oh really, Dennis? Who told you that?"

"I...I...I can't remember," Fisk stuttered.

"Dennis, why didn't you tell me that you'd closed the deal on the property with somebody else?"

"Who told you that?"

"I can't remember. Have you told the prime minister yet?"

"That's a private matter, Terry," said Fisk.

"Of course it is."

"Did you know that I met with the prime minister and that he asked me to compile a proposal for financing the project?" asked Downes.

"No, but we needed to move on with this right away. The developer needs no financing."

"You mean he made it worth your while, right, Dennis? Look, I know who these guys are and that you're involved with some pretty bad people. Watch your back," Downes said and, uncharacteristically, hung up.

His next call was to the prime minister's office, where he left a message with his secretary, Mrs. Stallworth, to tell Dr. Rudolph that it was his understanding—which had also been confirmed with Dennis Fisk—that the Frigate Bay property had been purchased by a Russian developer. Downes asked Stallworth to tell the prime minister that his proposal for financing had been fully completed and whether he still should forward it to him.

The secretary promised to convey the message.

It was after four p.m. on Saturday, December 23, the deadline that Poslov had given Judy Smythe to provide assurance that she and Downes were returning to Florida. He was pacing in his luxurious digs at the Regency Hotel planning his next move or, better still, who would carry out his next move.

Poslov placed a call to Walter Jones, asked to check Downes's whereabouts, and to please make sure that the hit left no traces. He simply couldn't afford to have things go wrong as they had with McLoud's murder.

Jones respectfully declined and told Poslov that he didn't want anything to do with another killing.

He had made the contact for McLoud to be killed, as instructed by Poslov and had hired a couple of goons from Antigua, who were supposed to make the hit and dump the body out at sea after meeting with Poslov. The ruffians had decided, instead, that they could just as well kill McLoud and get rid of the body by dumping it in the Great Salt Pond. It was easier than taking McLoud's body to the pier, hauling it in the boat, and running the risk of somebody seeing them.

The Great Salt Pond was a desolate area and they were convinced that nobody would find it. They hadn't figured, however, that McLoud was too heavy to be lugged to the pond and even if they had gotten him there, the water was very shallow. Sooner or later, the body would have been found.

Poslov was not used to so much stupidity and, as soon as things had calmed down, they would be punished.

As to Smythe, Poslov wanted her found and returned to Antigua right away. He surmised that she would probably be in Nevis. Jones told him to look for somebody else to find her and that, from that point on, he wanted nothing to do with him.

Dennis Fisk was very concerned and wondered if the one-hundred-thousand-dollar cash paid him by Poslov for the upfront fee for the property had been worth it. He could handle the p.m. and the cabinet members, but to think that it had been he who had introduced St. Kitts to the Russian mob, first with the deep-water port with Contec and now with the hotel, was unforgivable.

Poslov had been a degenerate 'confidence man' in Moscow in the early 1960s before he was recruited by the Izmaylovskaya gang as a hit man in their murder-for-hire program. He made his way up through the ranks and immigrated to the U.S. in 1985 intent on penetrating the banking and finance business, in anticipation of the ultimate demise of the USSR, as predicted by their leader, Semion Gasuchavik.

Within two years, he had invested money—all laundered from the sale of drugs and many other illicit activities—in a number of struggling U.S. companies, one of which was the Kalahari Corporation in San Jose, California.

When Kalahari was rumored to be filing for Chapter 11, AEI Investments came to the rescue as a white knight and placed an initial infusion of five hundred million dollars, with a promise of one billion more over two years for fifty-one percent of the company. AEI Investments was a U.K. equity fund owned by a number of Russian companies, all controlled by Izmaylovskaya.

Grabowski remained CEO of Kalahari and Poslov Chairman of the Board. The Russians' involvement in Kalahari was to use the company as a legitimate entity in the negotiation of worldwide deals and fronts for illegal weapons, drugs, counterfeiting, slavery, and any other trade where big money could be made.

This was by far Izmaylovskaya's biggest investment in the U.S., one they had to manage professionally and carefully in order not to leave any trail or suspicion of illegal activity.

In order to facilitate and maintain the credibility of their operation, they needed a U.S. and offshore banking network to help launder their money with credible and knowledgeable people running the companies.

Poslov had met Stanier at a bank reception in Wellington, Florida, a few years earlier. His take on Stanier was that he was an easy pick and the bank an excellent candidate for an acquisition or investment. He purchased ten thousand shares in First Community Bank at seven dollars per share, for starters.

Poslov met Jim North through Stanier and both were impressed that he had purchased shares in the bank. They referred to him as the "dumb Russian" who had more money than common sense.

They had no idea.

Poslov knew everything that was going on in St. Kitts. He sat back and waited for the right time to strike. In the meantime, he invested money in Antigua and methodically gained a foothold in the political process, to the point where he (the Russian mob) controlled most of what was happening on the island.

In order to legitimize or at least give the impression of legitimate business operations, Poslov regularly donated money to charities and sponsored civic programs in Antigua. At the same time, he managed to have local politicians, lawyers, and law enforcement in his pocket.

To be on the safe side, Downes made arrangements for Rufus Caple to have one of his buddies pick Smythe up in Nevis and bring her to the main island. He figured that, by now, Poslov's goons were looking for her and felt it best that she avoid public transportation. The boat shuttle usually took thirty minutes for the trip from the Four Seasons Hotel in Nevis to Basseterre, but Caple and his buddy had a small fishing boat that could barely hold three people and it was getting close to Christmas Eve.

The sea waters were dark and choppy and it took them three hours to make the trip. Smythe got to the hotel around 12:30 a.m. on Sunday the 24th, exhausted and scared. Downes wished her a Merry Christmas Eve's Day and she fell asleep in his arms. This would be their fortress for the next whenever.

They awoke at five a.m. on Monday, Christmas Day, and spent the next several hours bringing each other up to date and making sure they understood the importance of not answering the door unless they were sure of who was on the other side. They didn't think they had much to worry about on Christmas Day.

Services available at the hotel would be limited since there were few people working. They were able to get coffee and toast and ordered a hot meal in advance for later in the day. St. Kitts celebrated Boxing

Day on the day after Christmas, so all business and government offices were closed till Wednesday the 27th.

They spent the time making phone calls—Downes a couple of hours talking to his kids while they opened the gifts that he had left for them. Everybody seemed to be in good spirits, and he promised to be home for New Year's and have a special gift for them.

Wednesday December 27, 1989

Mrs. Stallworth called and asked Downes if he had a minute to talk to the prime minister.

"Mr. Downes, I received your message. I'm sorry I wasn't available when you called," said Dr. Rudolph, with his usual classy apology for not promptly getting back to his callers.

"That's okay, Dr. Rudolph. It's Christmas, after all. Thanks for calling me back."

"I am flabbergasted and very disappointed at the property's having been sold without my being duly advised. Of course Mr. Fisk does not require approval from government to handle the selling of the property, but common courtesy would dictate that he first discuss it with the cabinet. After all, we would like to know who our partner is going to be before we sign the deal."

"Exactly, and you won't like who your partner is."

"Who is it?" he asked.

"I don't know the corporate name, but the guy behind it is Victor Poslov, a reputed Russian mobster who is also involved with several projects in Antigua."

"Oh my! How do you know this?"

"Let me just say that my partner, Judy Smythe, met with Poslov in Antigua and he told her. Judy was denied entrance into St. Kitts a few days ago and forced to take a flight to Antigua. She had no choice. When she arrived, she had a visitor who proceeded to inform her of his business plans in St. Kitts. She was also given an ultimatum—she and I—to 'leave St. Kitts and arrive in West Palm Beach latest by four p.m. on Sunday, the 24th, or face the consequences.' Simultaneously, sir,

Poslov, in as many words, admitted to ordering the killing of George McLoud."

"What?"

"Dr. Rudolph, I have more and would like to meet with you, but we're afraid to leave our hotel room."

"Both of you are there?" he asked.

"Yes, Judy traveled to Nevis and then to Basseterre to avoid immigration at the airport."

"Let me call you back."

Dr. Rudolph was astounded. Downes hadn't meant to unload so much on him. Actually, all he had wanted to know was whether or not he should submit his proposal, as well as tell the prime minister about the property.

The prime minister made two calls: the first to Dennis Fisk, requesting his presence in his office immediately; the second to Clive Townsend from Scotland Yard, who had not yet returned from the UK.

"Dennis, I have known you and worked with you for a long time, and while we haven't agreed on everything, I have never known you to work around me," said an angry Dr. Rudolph.

"What do you mean?"" asked Fisk.

"The property, Dennis. The property!"

"Yes, I closed a deal between a U.K. company and the owner. I was paid fifty thousand dollars and will be distributing the fee accordingly."

"First, you know that I've been talking to Terry Downes about the project and he was planning to make a presentation to the cabinet. Second, why didn't you advise me before closing it? And third, this man Poslov: do you know who he is?" asked a most angry Dr. Rudolph.

"I thought I had clearance to broker the deal, without the cabinet's or your approval," said Fisk.

"Where's the courtesy, Dennis? You know we talk about everything before decisions are made," said the prime minister, with his voice elevated a couple of octaves.

Fisk placed his head in his hands, "I wanted to close it, Ken. I'm fed up with its lingering on. Victor Poslov is president of AEI in London. They have experience in hotel management and casino operations. They own the Wharf in Antigua," Fisk tried to reason.

"Poslov is a Russian mobster deeply involved in international crime. I don't want him in St. Kitts and I will block any attempt to get him approved to build here. Do you understand me?" screamed the prime minister, with no mention of McLoud's murder.

"Now, please leave and let me know when you've informed him of our decision, as well as refunded his fifty thousand dollars."

CHAPTER 32

Dr. Rudolph spent the next hour thinking about his conversation with Downes, concluding that there was a major problem developing in St. Kitts, and thinking that he should pay Downes a personal visit.

Downes received a call from Mrs. Stallworth asking if the prime minister could meet with him that night, for he had been very concerned. Downes and Smythe were surprised to hear that the prime minister was coming to visit them at the hotel and quickly cleaned the place up, throwing dirty clothes and stuff in the closet.

The prime minister entered through the hotel's back door and climbed the stairwell to avoid being seen.

Downes opened the door and let him in as soon as he heard the knock. "Welcome, sir. Sorry it couldn't have been in a more comfortable place," he said. "Prime Minister Rudolph, please meet Judy Smythe, my partner. Judy."

Smythe had called room service and had some drinks and snacks served. The three of them discussed the entire quagmire, repeating a lot of what Downes had already told him, starting with the initial meeting he had with Donovan Draper and Tim Ford and finishing with the last conversation he had with Dr. Rudolph. The PM interrupted several times for clarification of certain things. They presented the documents and taped conversations they had gathered over the previous several days, including the one Smythe had with Poslov.

Dr. Rudolph listened intently. "This is incredible," the prime minister shook his head. "I think we need more help here. We should make a request to Scotland Yard and maybe alert the FBI. What do you both think?"

"We are going to continue our work here, but it would be nice if we could get some protection. Obviously our work is not police-related, but we will cooperate fully with law enforcement," said Smythe.

Downes got a call from Isabelle Clarke saying that she had received the official manifest from American Airlines in Miami regarding the passengers' names on flight 102 departing St. Kitts on December 4, and there had been no George McLoud traveling that day. Moreover, the immigration department could not find any documentation that showed Judy Smythe's being denied entry on December 22 nor had there been any record of her being on the flight to Antigua.

Why didn't that surprise them?

Thursday, December 28, 1989

Nine-thirty a.m.:

Henry Blackstone connected with Ernie Mueller to keep him abreast of Poslov's activities, how he had been muscling his way into business activities in St. Kitts, and that his group had purchased the hotel property. He told him of Downes's presence on the island and the fact that he thought he was investigating money made from illegal activities which flowed through First Investors. "I was visited by the man running the townhouse project in Frigate Bay for the banker today," said Blackstone, careful not to use any names.

"This is not his first visit," Blackstone went on. "He first told me of his banking experience and how he could bring in a lot of business and manage the bank. I told him that we were not looking for business. Today he was more aggressive; in fact, he said he represented a very influential group of people and that if he couldn't be involved, there would be consequences."

"What's his, or their, motivation?" asked Mueller.

"They are involved in the same activities we are, but very, very aggressively. They have a much broader market share and offer many different types of products. They have already made friends in government."

"Okay, let me think about this and review with my partners. What about the witch hunt—anything new?" asked Mueller.

"No, they're just searching. They have nothing."

"And McLoud, anything there?" asked Mueller.

"Not that I'm aware of," replied Blackstone.

At the same time of Blackstone's call to Mueller, in his office in North Palm Beach, Stanier pondered how to get more involved in the huge deals about which he had heard from Jim North and decided to extend an olive branch to the 'dumb Russian':

"Victor, this is Bruce Stanier."

"What a pleasant surprise, Bruce. How are you?"

"I'm fine. How are things in Antigua?"

"Good, very good."

"Listen, I have a business proposition for you. When will you be back in South Florida?" asked Stanier.

"I am scheduled to be back this coming Monday, but if your proposition is a good one, I'll come back tonight," replied Poslov, with his screeching laugh.

Poslov had purchased a condo in Palm Beach Polo, not too far from Draper's old place, at the suggestion of Grabowski, his partner in Kalahari Corp. Ever since he had taken a position in First Community Bank's stock, he often wondered how he could get more involved, as it had been a part of Simeon Gasuchavik's long-term plan to get control of a U.S. commercial bank.

"I want to extend an invitation to you to join our board," said Stanier, with a slight effeminate giggle.

"Roy, I'm flattered. Thank you. I accept…I mean, subject to a little due diligence. I've never served on a bank board before. I would like to know what my responsibilities are and, of course, my liabilities."

"Okay, great. Can you bring a résumé with you and plan on spending a little time with a few friends and fellow directors while you're here, in order to get you comfortable with your decision?" asked Stanier, bubbling over with excitement.

Stanier's decision to invite Poslov to a seat on his board had been predicted by those familiar with Wellington, Palm Beach Polo, and the Kalahari Corporation. Stanier had built a branch in Wellington, in anticipation of its getting the banking relationship with Kalahari. To this point, he had been unsuccessful due to Grabowski's claim that First Community was not a big-enough bank for Kalahari. With all its ties to the community, Kalahari could bring millions of deposit dollars to SunFirst.

What Stanier didn't know, and hadn't figured into his plans, was the switch in loyalty of Jim North to Poslov. Even Downes had figured North would sell his mother for a few bucks.

Poslov met with Stanier and Dr. Clem Samson for lunch at the City Club in North Palm Beach, at which time they talked up the bank as the largest independent bank in the Southeast and one of the highest-earning banks in Florida. They also spoke of the solid position they held in the community, the success of their growth strategy, the quality of the banks services, and their loyal employees. They talked in a most persuasive manner, which really didn't matter.

Poslov had already made up his mind. He was in awe of the antiques and art that Stanier had collected and placed in and around his bank in North Palm Beach, especially the Remington statues scattered around the lobby as well as the Indian watercolor prints hanging every ten feet or so. It was a legitimate interest.

Before he left, Poslov graciously accepted the board seat and assured Stanier of the deposit accounts from Kalahari. Stanier didn't even have to ask.

CHAPTER 33

The Prime Minister respectfully requested additional assistance from Scotland Yard as a result of continued instances of murder, extortion, and fraud in St. Kitts. His request was heard and a commitment made to send another inspector not only to support Clive Townsend but also to increase the scope of their investigation.

Rudolph also contacted the head of the FBI and advised him of the situation. He was promised an agent to be sent to St. Kitts. This was great news for Downes, since he had this briefcase full of papers, which could blow things in a wide-open manner, and he simply didn't know what to do with it.

They definitely couldn't trust local law enforcement or the government officials or lawyers, and Clive Townsend would probably consider the information outside the scope of his investigation.

Rudolph summoned two constables to accompany them, in the event that they needed to leave the hotel. One of them remained outside their room twenty-four/seven.

The body of George McLoud had been returned to Toronto in the care of his sister, who had planned on visiting St. Kitts to see if she could get some answers. She sure as hell couldn't get any from the police over the phone and she didn't know how to hire a lawyer in St. Kitts—not that she had the money.

Mueller, Sastari, and Khallehki continued to worry over Kumar's election. They were also wondering how this would affect their preparations for an increase in business, as a result of the pending Gulf War. Khallehki had already closed a number of illegal sales through various groups in the Arab region and Sastari had received hundreds of millions in "parked" money from a number of countries, many of which in the Western hemisphere.

Thursday, December 28, 1989

Ten a.m.:

Dennis Fisk contacted Victor Poslov at his condo in Palm Beach Polo to give him the bad news: "Victor, this is Dennis. I have some bad news for you," he said, very nervously.

"What is it?" asked Poslov.

"It appears that Dr. Rudolph will not allow the construction of the hotel to go forward and he has instructed me to return the initial fees to you," Fisk fretted.

"What?"

"I'm sorry, Victor, but somebody has informed him of your apparent ties to Russian organized crime, and he will not allow you to do business in St. Kitts."

"I will call back," said Poslov, slamming down the phone.

Ten-thirty a.m.:

It was a very cold December morning in Mississauga, Ontario—not a cloud in the sky and hardly any wind. At Ernie Mueller's house, it was quiet. The Indian troupe had left and all that had remained was Mueller's Bentley parked out front with the engine running and the chauffeur sitting patiently inside, reading a newspaper and drinking a cup of hot coffee.

Mueller had requested that the driver be ready to take him into the city for a meeting with one of his lawyers, in preparation for a deposition he was to give earlier the following week. One of his companies was being sued for sexual harassment and the ex-employee's lawyer had issued Mueller a subpoena for him to be deposed.

What a waste of time, he thought, as he hurried through a quick breakfast prepared by one of the maids. Mueller's wife was out of town with some of her relatives and his kids were staying with some of their friends.

It was hunting season in Mississauga and it was quite common to see hunters appear from the woods with their catch, usually rabbits strung over their shoulders or a whitetail deer, if they were lucky.

About a half-mile away in the dense wooded area of their local community, there was a lone hunter dressed in camouflage gear and carrying a high-powered rifle equipped with a powerful scope. He had positioned himself in a cluster of dead leaves and brush, just waiting for a target.

His weapon was pointed directly at the front porch of Ernie Mueller's house. He had been there the day before for six hours, and now two hours waiting patiently for Ernie Mueller to appear at his front door. Today he was confident that it would be over, since Mueller's chauffeur was waiting for him inside the Bentley with the engine running.

The assassin was a murder-for-hire type, frequently recruited for assignments such as this. In the event that he were seen, which was never, there would be no connection back to the Russians; it simply would be the sniper's problem to deal with.

The large front door opened and Mueller appeared in a business suit and black overcoat. The shooter knew he would have only one shot, since Mueller would probably waste no time in getting in his car. The driver got out to open the door as a shot rang out. Mueller spun around and slumped to the ground. The noise spooked thousands of birds, but that was nothing unusual in the woods during hunting season.

A missile-sized bullet had hit him in the head and literally exploded on impact. Mueller didn't know what had hit him.

The chauffeur was horrified at the sight of blood, tissue, and brains splattered over the door and walls of the entrance. He crouched beside the Bentley, wondering what the hell had just happened.

The assassin got up from his little nest and casually made his way to the Jeep Cherokee parked about a mile away. A plane ticket and itinerary was left on the driver's seat: Moscow–London–Toronto–St. Kitts–Antigua–Miami–London–Moscow. Just another day at the office, except nobody had noticed his presence there.

News of Mueller's killing didn't take long to hit the media. Within hours, the surrounding area was infested with law enforcement and crime-scene investigators. However, the news took a couple of days to reach those who cared in St. Kitts.

Fisk was shocked and really concerned, as were Blackstone and Walter Jones. Jim North laughed about it and Ed Devine couldn't care less, although neither had any idea who had killed Mueller. For all they knew, it could have been an accident—a stray bullet from a hunter's gun.

Dennis Fisk wondered, however, if his recent conversation with Poslov had anything to do with it. Blackstone was still immensely loyal to Mueller and had no idea that Fisk had been more in Poslov's than in Mueller's camp.

CHAPTER 34

First Community Bank had not been doing well and the year-end earnings report had shown a loss of over five million dollars.

Once again, Stanier had threatened to fire the bank's CFO if he didn't adhere to his demands of reporting loan fees at the time of closing, rather than amortize them over the average life of the loan. Over fifteen million in loan fees had been collected for the year and, had Stanier's demands prevailed, the bank would have shown a slight profit for the year.

For the previous eight years, the regulatory agencies had problems with Stanier. It had all started with the twenty-seven-count indictment against him when he owned a data-processing company called Data Inc. The feds had charged him with several counts of bank fraud, mail fraud, and corruption, and much to the chagrin of the agencies, he had been found not guilty on all charges. The prosecutor's office had done a very poor job, they thought, and as far as the FDIC had been concerned, Stanier not only should have been kicked out of banking but also served time in prison.

Stanier continued to make a mockery of the FDIC and claim that they were a bunch of incompetent fools. Of course, Stanier was irate about the constant battles and the unusual frequency of their examinations. His lawyers were spending an inordinate amount of time and money defending Stanier's position on all regulatory matters.

On Tuesday, January 2, 1990, he received a call from the lead examiner's office in Atlanta, Georgia, telling him that he and his supervisor—who happened to be the FDIC's assistant director and a gentleman from the Florida State Department of Banking—would like to meet him at his office at ten a.m. on Monday, January 8.

Stanier agreed to the date and time and hung up. He began to get irritable and pace around his office. He placed a call to Bob Sales, but Sales's secretary called back soon after apologizing that her boss was sick and wouldn't be in the office. Stanier slammed down the phone, certain that Sales had asked her to lie.

After trying to reach Jim North—who was in in St. Kitts—and Senator Styles—who was tied up in a meeting—Stanier threw the telephone the other side of the room and swiped his desk with his forearm, sending papers, files, pens, and a full cup of coffee flying across the room. He stormed out of his office past a startled secretary and out of the lobby's front door. He got in his car and squealed tires as he left for the Lake Worth branch.

"Bruce, what on earth is wrong?" asked Larry Lewis, the manager of the Lake Worth branch and a personal friend.

"I got a call...a meeting...can't get hold of anybody, Sales is sick, this is fuckin' bullshit," said Stanier, not making any sense of what he was saying, sweating like a pig, and almost falling over Lewis's chair.

Customers waiting in the lobby and employees heard Stanier's rage and looked toward Lewis to calm him down. Stanier was like a little Hitler when things really upset him or didn't go his way. It was actually comical to see, and instances of his temper tantrums were often discussed and joked about amongst the employees.

Lewis politely escorted Stanier to his office, where he allowed him to calm down and gain some composure. Stanier explained what had happened and the fact that he hadn't been able to reach anybody.

Lewis called Sales's office and told his secretary, "If Mr. Sales is alive, then Mr. Stanier needs to talk to him." He placed the same call to Styles's office. He had no luck reaching North.

Stanier straightened his tie, stroked his hair into place, and brushed down his coat, indicating that he was fine. "Collins, the head of the FDIC will be here next Monday with the state's banking commissioner, and I suspect that they will try to levy fines against us," he said, rage still permeating his whole body.

"For what? That's crazy!" said Lewis, who was basically oblivious to what was going on.

They called Charles Garry, an attorney who represented the bank from time to time, who agreed to meet with Stanier at three that afternoon. Sales called back—he wasn't sick but on the golf course—and said he could make the meeting.

Styles called, hysterical that something had happened to Bruce. "Bruce, what's wrong?" the Congressman sounded distraught.

"We're okay, Doug,. I just needed to talk this morning, but we have it under control. Call me tonight."

"Are you sure?"

"I'm sure," Stanier reassured him and hung up.

Stanier, Sales, and Garry commiserated over the meeting with the FDIC and the state's banking authority scheduled for the following Monday in Stanier's office. Sales suggested that the meeting be held in his office in Palm Beach, which they all thought was a good idea. Stanier, then, buzzed his secretary and asked that she notify Atlanta of the change.

"Bruce, you really need to get along with these people. You can't keep fuckin' with 'em, because they will, and they have, made your life miserable," said Garry.

"What can we expect from them on Monday?" asked Sales. "Obviously it's not going to be a slap on the wrist again, if they're going to bring in the big guns."

"They could present us a more formal list of corrective action, with time frames for completion; they could issue a cease-and-desist order; they could tell us that they are placing a moratorium on expansion; they could do a number of things," said Stanier.

They discussed some of the more salient problems and discussed the corrective action outlined in previous examination reports.

"Is the board aware of these examinations and responses?" asked Garry.

"No, not really," replied Stanier.

"That may be a problem."

"We discussed some of the loan issues in the board meetings, but the examination reports per se were not presented," he said.

"Good morning, I'm Bob Sales, counsel for First Community Bank. This is Charles Garry, co-counsel, and, of course, I think you know Bruce Stanier, chairman of the bank."

"Good morning, I'm Ken Stuart, lead examiner, FDIC. This is Nate Collins, Assistant Director of the Atlanta Region of the FDIC, and this is Herbert Stangle, from the State Banking Division of the State Comptroller's office."

"Please have a seat. Sorry for the change of location, but I thought this was a more comfortable and private place," said Sales.

"That's okay, Mr. Sales. I don't think this will take long," said Stuart. "Mr. Stanier, I regret to inform you that the FDIC and the Florida State Banking Division are removing you as Chairman of the Board of Directors and Chief Executive Officer of First Community Bank, effective immediately."

The room was quiet—not a move, not a sound. None of them expected this. Finally, Sales said, "Well, that's a shocker."

In cases like these, the regulatory staff had been trained to talk only when a question was asked. Stanier's complexion had changed from a tanned, healthy look to being very strained and flush, the veins noticeably protruding from his neck.

"Who do you suggest will run the bank?" asked Sales.

"We will allow your board to appoint a chairman and we will place someone in the bank as president and CEO," replied Collins.

The issues outlined in the examination report, together with the bank's capital ratio after the stipulated adjustment, were enough to shut the bank down, which Stuart said he was prepared to do if things didn't improve.

"I have an agreement that I would like you to sign before you leave, Mr. Stanier, and we would appreciate your surrendering the keys, passwords, etc."

"Do you mean that Mr. Stanier cannot go back into his bank?" Sales was livid.

"That's exactly what we mean, Mr. Sales," said Collins.

Sales reviewed the short, formal agreement and passed it to Garry before showing it to Stanier.

"Do we have any recourse, any appeal to this action?" asked Garry.

"Sure. Mr. Stanier can apply for reinstatement, but I wouldn't waste my time," replied Collins.

Stanier refused to sign the agreement and said that they would have to physically remove him.

"We are prepared to do that, Mr. Stanier," said Collins, authoritatively. He then turned to the lawyer, "Mr. Sales, I'm sure you are aware of the regulations that give the FDIC and the State of Florida the authority to take this action. If you like, I can leave a copy with you."

"That won't be necessary."

"Thank you. Mr. Stanier is not allowed back into the bank. We can make arrangements for him to receive his personal belongings," said Stuart. "I will be working at the bank for the next several days, but would prefer that you make an announcement to the employees, Mr. Sales."

"This is ridiculous," said Sales. "Bruce Stanier has spent his entire life at this bank, and thus should be allowed some dignity and not kicked out on his ass."

It was difficult to understand what Stanier was talking about after they left—something about a conspiracy—but he signed the agreement, for which the regulators were thankful.

A notice of an emergency shareholders' meeting was typed by Sales's secretary. The bylaws stipulated that they had to be given ten days' notice of such a meeting:

"To the Shareholders of First Community Bank,

Notice is hereby given of an emergency meeting of the Shareholders of First Community Bank on January 22, 1990, at ten a.m. at the

Hilton Hotel, Hillsborough Boulevard and I-95, Deerfield Beach, Florida. The purpose of the meeting is to appoint a new Chairman of the Board of Directors.

Sincerely,

Robert A. Sales, General Counsel, First Community Bank and Trust"

Stanier and Garry read and approved the notice.

Inasmuch as most employees were shareholders, as part of the ESOP plan, they would be notified of the emergency meeting. With Stanier being out of the office, they thought it best to advise everybody of the news. Sales drafted a letter to be signed by Stanier:

"Dear shareholders, employees, and friends of First Community Bank,

Effective immediately, I am resigning my position as Chairman of the Board and Chief Executive Officer of First Community Bank.

As you are aware, the bank's earnings performance has not been good over the past two or three years and, together with personal investments and interests that have taken up so much of my time, I believe it's time for a change in the leadership of the bank.

I remain very confident about the future of First Community and believe that, with this change, the bank will better achieve its financial objectives.

I would like to thank you for your support, hard work, and dedication over the years, and I wish you all future success.

I remain, yours truly,

Bruce W. Stanier

Stanier just couldn't believe what had happened. After the regulators left, he, Sales, and Garry sat in the conference room of Sales's law office trying to come to grips with it all and attempting to plan a course of action.

"I'm convinced that certain board members were behind this," a teary-eyed Stanier lamented. "I need some time to figure this out."

Sales knew this wasn't the case, but rather Stanier's aggressively marketing the bank and ignoring bank regulations. However, Sales wasn't about to disagree with him since he had his eyes on the chairman's position.

"Bob, would you take on the position of acting chairman and let me know if this is something you could take on permanently? You are the only person I can trust," asked Stanier.

"Of course, Bruce. I would be happy to," replied Sales.

Stanier owned forty percent of the outstanding shares of common stock of First Community Bank, so he knew that, with his friends and loyal business associates, he would easily control the votes at the meeting.

In the meantime, he refused calls from directors and officers of the bank. He was humiliated, embarrassed, and most of all, paranoid, for he didn't know who to trust.

When North got the news, he was elated. He called Stanier to tell him that it was a bunch of bullshit, that the bank couldn't survive without him, and agreed that certain board members must have thrown him under the bus.

North also told Stanier that Victor Poslov had talked about his interest in buying a large stake in the bank, if the deal was right, and he should contact him to see if a deal could be made.

Terry Downes and Judy Smythe concluded that Victor Poslov was behind the murder of Ernie Mueller. He had the most to gain and, from where they sat, was the only one who needed him dead.

Mueller had been on a collision course with Poslov, in that Poslov wanted an offshore bank to launder the money from a multitude of international deals. It was something he had promised Gasuchavik he would take care of, and St. Kitts was the ideal theater of operations, considering that everything had already been in place there.

CHAPTER 35

Sitting on the dirty sofa with the temperature around ninety degrees and the stench of cheap perfume and Indian cooking, Victor Poslov waited impatiently for his turn to see the godman, Chandrasastari Murkarji.

There were eight other people waiting in the living room of apartment 43F to see His Holiness, one of whom introduced himself as a state senator from North Carolina. As a rule, Poslov didn't wait for anybody, let alone in a dingy condo under such extreme conditions.

It had taken a while for Sastari to agree to see Poslov. Only after he had found out that Poslov had probably been behind Mueller's killing that the meeting was arranged. Poslov had insisted on the meeting after learning from McLoud who the players were in the St. Kitts connection.

Growing angrier by the minute, Poslov removed his suit jacket, loosened his tie, and wiped the perspiration from his neck and forehead. He couldn't believe that Sastari would keep him waiting and couldn't imagine anybody waiting to see him who would have something more important to address.

After waiting almost three hours in the most uncomfortable conditions, the little man approached him and said, "His Holiness will see you now."

THE ST. KITTS CONNECTION

Leading back to the bedroom/meeting room, the little man knocked on the door and asked Poslov to enter. Sastari was sitting with Babbi standing at his side and greeted Poslov with his usual "Namaste."

"Mr. Poslov, so nice to meet you," said Sastari, without introducing Babbi. "What is it that I can do for you?"

Poslov did not expect this type of meeting. It took him a few minutes to gather his thoughts and words. "Mr. Sastari," he said, rather awkwardly, "I have come here today to talk about a possible solution to your problem in St. Kitts and discuss a plan between us that could prove very beneficial for both of us."

"What is the problem you refer to?" asked Sastari.

"The unfortunate deaths of Ernie Mueller and George McLoud and the disruption of your business in St. Kitts."

Both Sastari and Babbi sat in silence with fire in their eyes. "Proceed," said Sastari.

"I am infinitely aware of your operation in St. Kitts, the type of products you buy and sell, the names of your colleagues, the activity in First Investors, the transactions, and the assistance you are afforded by members of the governments in both India and St. Kitts. In fact, I have recently placed an order with your contacts for two thousand Kalashnikov AK 47s for my friends in Sri Lanka. Everything went smoothly, and my friends were very pleased."

Sastari continued his glare, without a movement or change in expression.

"I am not here to make threats, Mr. Sastari, but it would make sense for you to work with me. I represent an international conglomerate based in London, with operations in most Western countries. We have interests in the financial-services industry, manufacturing, real estate, and other very lucrative enterprises. We are involved in the same type of business that you and Mr. Khallehki have been so successful in, and I am here to offer my assistance in resurrecting your business in St. Kitts."

Again, silence from the holy man and his valued assistant. Finally, Sastari stood and said, "Mr. Poslov, thank you for visiting with me today but I'm afraid that, at this time, your assistance in whatever you believe our problems are is not needed."

"Mr. Sastari, please, I am not giving you a choice. I want control of the bank in St.Kitts. I have a person, a banker, ready to take over the operation. I inquired about the purchase of the bank, but I don't need to own it; I just need to control it for now. I have the infrastructure in place to transport the products and I have the politicians' interest in St. Kitts. I am building a hotel on the island and plan to expand my business there. I already own and operate legitimate businesses in Antigua, and St. Kitts fits perfectly into our long-range plans."

Again, no response.

"But the real reason I'm here is to talk about the support of our mutual friends in Sri Lanka, the Tamil Tigers."

It was like Poslov had hit both of them with a two by four. Poslov knew that Sastari was a sympathizer of the LTTE and saved his comments until last. Sensing that he had touched a nerve, Poslov talked about his commitment to help the Tigers and the amount of resources they needed to keep fighting their cause.

A smile appeared on Sastari's face as he sat back in his chair: "Please tell me how you propose working with us, Mr. Poslov."

Poslov explained that he wanted his Caribbean base of operations in St. Kitts. It was a sovereign country perfectly located between South and North America for the drop-off of shipments of product. "The bank is perfect for the transfer and laundering of money, and you have the right people on the island who uphold the privacy laws and shield the bank from outside influences," said Poslov.

Poslov further revealed much about the history of how he and his partners had supported the LTTE and the valuable contacts he had developed in Afghanistan and Pakistan, which allowed the "product" to be transported from the poppy growers to the refining labs and then to his beloved friends in India's Tamil Nadu and in Sri Lanka without interference.

He also discussed the shipping of "product" from northern Sri Lanka to destinations in Europe and North America. Poslov never used the word heroin—he never had to.

"As my partners," he went on with his sneaky chuckle, "I will reveal all my secrets to you. You and Mr. Khallehki will not only resurrect your business but also increase your volume without any added risk. And, of course, we can assist our friends in Sri Lanka."

"I would like to discuss the concept with my partners and then arrange another meeting with you, Mr. Poslov," said Sastari.

"Very well. I'm staying in New York for a few days. Can I hear from you by the end of the day tomorrow?" asked Poslov, handing Sastari a business card that read 'AEI Ltd., Victor Poslov, President' and included his cell number.

Stanier contacted Poslov on his cell phone at his suite at the Helmsley Palace, at Lexington and 42nd Street, to tell him of the recent FDIC decision and to follow through on Jim North's suggestion that he contact him.

Poslov had already heard the news from his new confidant.

"Victor, I'm afraid I have some disturbing news for you," said Stanier.

"What's wrong, Bruce?"

"I have resigned as chairman and CEO of First Community Bank," he said.

"You have what?"

"That's right, I've resigned."

After a long pause, Poslov said, "Can you tell me what's going on?" sounding legitimately unaware.

"Yes. The FDIC, the agency that insures deposits of the bank, has been pressuring me for the past several years to resign. They've had a 'hard-on' for me ever since I was found innocent of the charges filed against me in 1978."

"So, they are forcing you to resign?"

"In essence, yes. They maintain that the bank is undercapitalized. In their examination reports, they have insisted that a ton of loans be charged off. I have adamantly disagreed, but they have the final say. If we do what they want, our loan-loss reserve will be wiped out, whereupon they would insist that we replenish the reserve from our capital. This would result in our capital ratio coming up short. So the bottom line is, the bank needs more capital. I was visited by the regulators a couple of days ago and they were firm in their decision. I am convinced that there are certain board members who have been talking to them about the collectability of some of our loans in order to force me out," said Stanier, in a panicky tone.

"Why would they do that, Bruce?"

"I think jealousy."

"So, how much capital would be needed?" asked Poslov.

"Probably fifty million."

"Hmm...interesting."

"Is that something that you may have an interest in, Victor?"

"Probably not. If my friends and I invested that much money, we would have to have control," said Poslov.

"Would it be worth talking about? We have scheduled an emergency shareholders' meeting for next week, at which time I am nominating Bob Sales chairman. Although Bob is a close friend and someone I can trust, my options are still open, in the event that a capital infusion could be worked out."

"Okay. I can be there in a couple of days. I'll call you back after I've made arrangements," said Poslov, playing a little hard to get.

Stanier had felt that, in his short time of knowing Poslov, the Russian shouldn't have been perceived as dumb but as a possible great addition to the board. He felt as though he could trust Poslov, and with everything that he was involved in, he could open other doors to some very lucrative ventures. Poslov snapped the cover of his cell phone, leaned over to his girlfriend and partner, and said, "We are almost there. There is no doubt that the Indian guys will do what I say and the fool Stanier won't have any choice."

Arma Lozo was strictly business: "How will you control the bank in St. Kitts if you don't own it?" she asked.

"North will be the managing director and I will get McLoud's shares first, then get the rest later. I think the government holds most of the shares now. All it takes on these islands is money."

Poslov had met Arma Lozo as soon as she had finished her testimony with the grand jury and he had followed her throughout the ordeal. He knew of her at the time that she coordinated all of Draper's deals in Mexico. As soon as that had dried up, she became available to Poslov, as long as her deal was right.

Lozo was a savvy lady and had always put her business way in front of her emotions. She had made a lot of money working with Draper and Ford, and the one thing that impressed Poslov was that she had never divulged information to the authorities, despite their original offer of immunity and later threats of prosecution.

Although she was able to arrange purchases out of Guadalajara, Mexico, her main connections were in South America. She knew all the lieutenants in the Calli cartel. She had a home in Cartagena, Colombia; one in Carmel, California; and a plush condo on the Thames, in London. Her cut in any deal was always paid in cash, which she deposited in a Swiss bank. Her contribution to the cause was invaluable and her involvement was transparent.

Arma Lozo didn't mind being the girlfriend of whomever she could make a deal with and always carried a loaded Barretta in her Gucci purse, which she wouldn't hesitate to use if the circumstances warranted.

CHAPTER 36

Judy Smythe was intrigued by the transaction that Sophie Albrightson had come across, as a result of a screwed-up wire from India, and decided to investigate further. "Terry, would you look at this?" she said, excitedly. "The wire originated from the National Bank of Ceylon PLC and the funds were sent to the Bank of India for credit to an account called Excelsior (2)."

"That's the name on the piece of paper we found in the box," Downes reminded her.

"Wait, there's more," Smythe interrupted. "The money was wired from the Bank of India to Carib Bank with credit to the First Trust/Excelsior (2) account—the same name. On the same day it was wired out, the money was received by First Investors. Guess where?"

"We know where the one hundred thousand dollars went," said Downes.

"Yes, but nine hundred thousand went to Vneshtorgbank, Moscow."

"To the credit of...?" he asked.

"Izmash Arms, the manufacturer of the Kalashnikov weapons, better known as the AK 47."

"Unbelievable," said Downes.

"I also found out that there is a group of terrorists in Sri Lanka that has recently attacked government offices and kidnapped and killed a number of their government members," she added.

Downes and Smythe were visited by Clive Townsend, Chief Constable Crutchen, and Alberto Gomez, Special Agent—FBI, Miami, and were informed that there had been an expanded investigation to include conspiracies to traffic narcotics and illegal weapons, as well as the ongoing investigation of murder.

Gomez was a friendly type with plenty of experience investigating crimes in the U.S. and with relevant international connections. He made it clear that, if (and when) there was sufficient evidence, he would have total cooperation from the government of St. Kitts as far as extradition was concerned.

Downes opened up a little more about what they had uncovered and what they suspected was going on, since there appeared to be a concerted effort to prosecute those involved. Downes showed them transactions, the contents of the box, the tapes of conversations, and reviewed with them their suspicions. Crutchen never said a word but both Townsend and Gomez were amazed and determined to help bring the bad guys to justice.

Downes decided, at that time, not to turn over the briefcase. He suspected that Crutchen was somehow involved with drug trafficking, and thus he was nervous about the St. Kitts' Chief of Police becoming aware of everything.

Babbi called Poslov to tell him that His Holiness would see him at the end of the day at his condo.

"Please tell Mr. Sastari that he is to meet me at my suite in the Helmsley Palace at six p.m., and that I will not wait," said a very defiant Victor Poslov.

Babbi tried to explain that His Holiness did not meet people at their convenience, but there was nobody on the line. Poslov had already hung up.

At 6:10 p.m., Poslov had already left his suite when the front desk called announcing that four gentlemen were in the lobby requesting to see him. Arma Lozo gave the okay for them to come up to the room.

"Hello, I'm Arma," she said, extending her hand to the first gentleman.

"Where is Mr. Poslov?" asked Babbi.

"He had to leave and asked me to discuss matters on his behalf."

Babbi looked toward Sastari, who was standing back behind the others.

"Please come in," said Lozo.

As they entered, Babbi introduced Sastari, "It is my pleasure to introduce His Holiness Chandrasastari Murkarji."

Although all four were dressed in their cotton robes, Lozo assumed that two of them were bodyguards, for there had been no introductions made, and was sure that they were carrying weapons.

"Could you, please, tell us who you are and your relationship to Mr. Poslov?" asked Babbi.

"Yes, of course. I am Arma Lozo, Mr. Poslov's business partner. I negotiate all of his business in the Caribbean, and I will be the main contact in all transactions that we may become involved in," she replied.

Sastari was angry and humiliated from having had to catch a cab to the Helmsley Palace, by Poslov's absence, and above all from having to deal with a woman representing him. He thought that they should leave, but only for a second or two.

"Okay, let's get down to some business," said Lozo, retrieving a notepad and pencil from a stack on the conference-room table.

Sastari and Babbi took a seat at the table while the two bodyguards sat in lounge chairs facing them.

"What is it that you want?" asked Babbi.

"We want control of the offshore bank, First Investors," replied Lozo.

"What do you have to offer?"

"Nothing but heartache if you don't give it to us," she said, with a smile.

Sastari sat with his usual glare not saying a word.

"Let me put it this way: we want you to tell your contacts in St. Kitts—namely, Mr. Fisk and Mr. Blackstone—that Jim North will be managing director of First Investors Trust and they are to convey ownership, previously held by Mr. Mueller or Mr. McLoud, to him. You will have no problem with Mr. Fisk. We will take over all business stemming from South America. You can keep all of your current weapons business, but any new business is ours. So we need a list of your present customers and contacts. All business flows through First Investors, so we will be the custodian of your money."

Lozo paused and then added, "Are we clear?"

"I still don't see what we have to gain," said Babbi.

Lozo looked directly at Sastari and said, "Your colleague doesn't seem to get it, does he? We are taking over the operations of your business, Mr. Babbi!"

Sastari never said a word and motioned to Babbi that it was time to leave.

"We will be in touch," said Babbi.

"By nine o'clock tomorrow morning, Mr. Sastari, or our offer to work with you in the support of the LTTE will be off the table, and we will make arrangements to take over the bank and all of your business... without you," said Lozo, as Babbi motioned to the bodyguards that they were leaving.

There was no response as the four of them left the suite, obviously shaken by the words of a very powerful woman.

The assassin arrived in St. Kitts under the guise of a businessman and checked in at the Timothy Beach Resort. There was a large package awaiting him in his room, placed there by a co-conspirator who had given the concierge one hundred dollars and a threat "if this were told to anybody."

Included in the package was a 30/30 rifle equipped with a powerful scope, sound suppresser, and several rounds of ammunition. The rifle was broken down and fitted into a custom-made case. There was also a small amount of plastic explosives wrapped in brown paper and a triggering device with a sophisticated detonator attached.

Sastari and Babbi met with Khallehki to seek his advice on how they should proceed with Poslov and Lozo.

"They are a very ruthless group of people," said Babbi, after making inquiries into the Russians' businesses and reputation.

"At this point," said Khallehki, "I don't think we have a choice but to go along with them. Our business has fallen off dramatically since the election and will probably stay that way, until there is a new government in power which will allow us to continue. But I would like to know specifically what they want from us, other than controlling the bank."

"I think they will want us to provide arms for heroin," said Sastari. "And then they would probably want a share in the sale."

"Well, let's find out. But in the meantime, I think you should make plans to give them what they want: control of the bank," said Khallehki.

Khallehki was too shrewd a businessman to give something away simply because of a threat. But going along with them, for the time being, could at least help the cause in Sri Lanka. "I think we should direct our energy toward the Indian government and do what we can to force a confidence vote in parliament," he said. "And as far as the Russians are concerned, just make sure we keep records of everything that transpires in St. Kitts."

The reaction to Ernie Mueller's death was shock and disbelief. Even though the death had not yet been deemed a homicide or at least made official, Henry Blackstone couldn't help but think that his recent conversations with Jim North had something to do with it.

Blackstone had heard the news from Dennis Fisk. Jim North had been told to pass the word around of Mueller's murder and to call Fisk, and then he asked Fisk to call Blackstone.

Fisk almost collapsed when North conveyed him the news. North simply said that one of his friends in Florida had heard about it.

Blackstone tried, in vain, to reach Sastari and Khallehki. They were nowhere to be found.

Fisk was constantly looking over his shoulder, since he was sure that Poslov had Mueller killed as a result of the hotel deal going south. When Fisk told Poslov of his conversation with the prime minister, he assumed that Mueller had been behind the rejection.

CHAPTER 37

Judy Smythe received a call from John Clemonds asking if she had heard about Stanier. "Yes, I've heard that he resigned," she replied.

"More likely, he was told he had to resign. Stanier would never resign voluntarily," said Clemonds. "Anyway, I still have a few shares in First Community, so I'll be at the meeting on the 20th. I'll let you know what happens.

Everybody was shocked at the news of Stanier's departure. There were a few ladies who had worked at the bank during its entire existence and who had shed a few tears, but most employees were more concerned about their stock in the ESOP. Some had their entire savings invested, so they put up with Stanier's tempestuous behavior if it meant high stock values. The problem was that the share price had been declining in the past two years and had drastically fallen upon the news of Stanier's departure. Employees were getting very worried.

Then there were the officers of the bank, who were rejoicing at the news and couldn't wait to find out who the replacement would be.

Poslov, Sales, and Stanier met at Stanier's sprawling ranch in Boca Raton, where he had a nursery that encompassed three hundred acres of plants, shrubbery, and trees.

BWS Inc. was a premier plant wholesaler that had a major customer, First Community Bank. The bank leased plants for all of their branches and BWS Inc. had been given a lucrative contract to maintain all landscaping, inside and outside. It was also the recipient of other forms of income, not related to the nursery activities.

Stanier had built his home in the early eighties, a 7,500-square-foot ranch-style home designed and built with markers cashed in, mostly from his old loan customers. The appraised value of the property paled in comparison to the value of the antiques and artifacts that furnished the home, all purchased by First Community Bank.

"Bob, I have been talking to Victor about the possibility of him making a sizable investment in the bank and I thought it would be good if we meet and determine whether there is a deal to be made," said Stanier.

"What do you have in mind, Victor?" asked Sales, turning to Poslov.

"I'm open to anything reasonable," replied Poslov. "Bruce had suggested fifty million dollars, which would keep the regulators at bay," he added.

"Is that within your ability?" asked Sales.

"Sure. We would have AEI in the U.K. make the investment."

"Who owns AEI?" asked Sales.

"It's a public company, of which I am president and own about fifteen percent," replied Poslov.

"Would it pass scrutiny by our regulators?" asked Stanier.

"There's no reason why it shouldn't, but I'm not familiar with the standards that a prospective investor of this size has to meet," said Poslov. "I can provide audited financial statements. We have over three billion in assets and are debt free," he added, nonchalantly.

"What kind of deal would you want?" asked Stanier.

"What would you offer?"

"Well, I would propose that we issue another class of stock. A non-voting, preferred class, cumulative with conversion rights to the common stock pegged to the performance of the bank," said Stanier.

"What does that mean?" asked Poslov, scratching his head.

"That means the bank will issue another class of shares called preferred shares. They will be non-voting and will have conversion rights attached to them. This means that you will have the right to convert them to common shares, which are voting shares, at some future date. This will depend on the earnings of the bank. In other words, we will establish benchmarks and as they are met, you can convert the preferred shares to common," Sales explained.

"If we can get this done, in principle, by the time of our shareholders' meeting, it will help ease the tension amongst the shareholders and employees. They must be wondering if we will survive, especially with the number of bank failures the last few years," said Stanier.

"Whatever, we'll let the lawyers take care of it', said Poslov, not understanding the deal.

"Great. Don't forget that the FDIC is bringing in a CEO and we've yet to find out who that is," said Sales.

The three of them mulled over a letter of intent strong enough to convince the shareholders that the deal would be finalized and sent to the FDIC and the state.

Poslov called his people in Moscow and London to inform them of AEI's potential ownership in a U.S. commercial bank and requested immediate attention to the structure of the deal. He made sure that they contacted Bob Sales in order to expedite the paperwork.

The final item, and the most important, was the deal itself: how many shares were to be issued and for how much money, the conversion feature of the shares, and the benchmarks that had to be met in order to kick in the conversion rights.

St. Kitts is a Christian island, the majority of Kittitians Anglican—commonly known as Church of England—followed by the Roman Catholics, so Christmastime in Basseterre was always very festive and joyful. But the 1989–1990 holiday-season spirit was being dampened for a number of people as a result of the crime and fear of retribution by those who thought their newfound wealth was in jeopardy.

Judy Smythe and Terry Downes were in their room trying to determine whether they should pack up and go home and just let things sit for a while, when the room phone rang.

"Terry Downes?" said the unrecognizable voice.

"Who is this?" he answered, without giving his name.

"This is Sergeant Pete Sankowitz, from the Royal Canadian Mounted Police."

"Pete, what a surprise! Where are you?"

"Oh, about two floors below you."

"You are?"

"Yep. Do you have a few moments?"

"Sure. How about if I meet you in the lobby in ten minutes?"

Downes told Smythe about Pete Sankowitz, the deposition he had given in West Palm, and what a good guy he thought he was. They met in the lobby and he introduced her to Sankowitz. "So, what are you doing here, Pete?" Downes inquired.

"I'm investigating the murder of Ernie Mueller, which I'm sure you've heard about, and also following up on a couple of clues that tell us that George McLoud's murder may be connected. Since I was involved with the drug conspiracy that implicated First Trust and George McLoud, it made sense for me to follow up. So what about you?" he asked.

Downes explained the whole deal to him. Sankowitz was fascinated.

"This guy, Poslov: Do you think he may have something to do with Mueller's killing?" he asked.

"Yes, I think he ordered his killing and that of McLoud's," said Downes.

"Well, that's a different twist. My guys in Toronto are convinced it was by local guys and that I just wanted to come to St. Kitts to get out of the awful weather. And now that I heard about your stuff, I think that our answers are more likely to be found here. But there's only so much I can do here, of course. I would have to rely on Chief Constable Crutchen."

"Good luck with that, and be careful: we don't trust Crutchen. We believe he's very much involved in drug trafficking," said Downes.

"For that matter, we don't trust anybody," said Smythe.

They showed Sankowitz the extent to which Mueller had been involved in illegal arms deals and drug trafficking, and that he had been the guy whom Draper and Ford reported to.

"We were aware of his involvement with Draper, but we didn't have any material evidence. His name certainly didn't show up anywhere. I tried to interview him, but he had some pretty powerful lawyers and we just couldn't pin anything on him. The only thing we did know is that Draper was Mueller's lawyer when he owned some strip clubs in

Toronto. Has anybody talked to any of these characters, other than you?" asked Sankowitz.

"We're not aware of any conversations the police have had. The guys from Scotland Yard are gathering evidence, as is the guy from the FBI, but as I understand it, they are not allowed to talk to anybody without the presence of Crutchen."

Sophie Albrightson had called Smythe to say that there were two gentlemen from India wanting to talk to Henry Blackstone, and had also asked for Downes. They had shown their IDs as being from India's Central Bureau of Investigation (CBI).

"Okay, no problem. You can tell them where we're staying," Smythe told Albrightson.

The two CBI guys were full of themselves, and their conduct was overbearing. They demanded rather than asked, talked at them rather than to them, and told their opinions but never asked for theirs. They were conducting their ongoing investigation into the trumped-up charges against the new prime minister and other current problems working against the government, which, they believed, were originating from the same sources.

"Mr. Downes, it would be in your best interest to cooperate with us and reveal all the information you have gathered in your investigation," said one of the CBI agents, calling from Prime Minister Rudolphs' office.

"Let me just get something straight here," Downes said. "We don't work for you or with you. We are newspaper reporters and we've been here for ten days living in this room, scared to leave because of threats on our lives. We are not compelled to give you shit. Now, I suggest you go through the proper channels, which means the chief of police, and see if you can get what you need from them—and good luck with that," Downes hung up the phone.

They had no clue what they were looking for. Apparently they had had a contingency of federal police there several weeks prior, when the government had gotten word of the numbered account floating around, and they had left with nothing.

Albrightson had mentioned that MacCallister Crutchen was Walter Jones brother-in-law, which Downes had already heard from Isabelle Clarke, and that Rufus Caple had found out that Crutchen and a number of his constables had accepted payoffs in the form of cash and/or favors for turning a blind eye to drug activities. Caple had also been told by his contacts that Dennis Fisk and Walter Jones would often give instructions to Crutchen on the movement of drugs within the island.

Dennis Fisk was relentless in his attempt to get the prime minister to change his mind on the hotel deal, for he knew that Poslov was not going to go away considering that he had already closed on the property.

"We have this deal in the palm of our hands. Poslov can start building in sixty days, and we don't have to worry about financing. It will bring tax money into the treasury and create plenty of jobs. Our economy needs it, please," pleaded Fisk.

"I'm not getting into bed with the Russian Mafia, Dennis. They will bring nothing but crime and, God knows, we have plenty of that already," explained Rudolph.

"I don't see what the big deal is. The Mafia controls Las Vegas and Atlantic City, and both of their economies are booming. As long as we control them, I can assure you that their ties to organized crime will be transparent."

"No, we can't do it," Rudolph was adamant.

"Can you imagine the boost in tourism? We will be the vacation center of the Caribbean, you will be rewarded with another five-year term, and the Labour Party will fall apart. In fact, I would predict that the crime we are now experiencing will go away because our party will be so strong, nobody would want to hurt us. I can even get an additional one-hundred-thousand cash for you or your favorite charity," assured Fisk.

Rudolph sat back in his chair, paused for a moment, removed his glasses, and said, "Dennis, can we keep Poslov's name off the records and prevent him from making a big noise here?"

"Of course," said Fisk, starting to feel that he finally had gotten the PM's attention.

"What kind of arrangements have you made for ongoing government fees?" asked the prime minister.

"I will be bringing the package to the cabinet next week for their okay, but money seems to be no object with Poslov," replied Fisk, feeling that his boss was ready to give in.

"Okay, but I'm holding you accountable. I don't want any problems, understand?"

"Understood. And what about the fee,?" asked Fisk, trying to hold back a smile.

"Just bring me the cash. Please explain to him that the fee is for some unforeseen expense, and do not mention my name."

Fisk knew with whom he was dealing; all it took was a little more money. Everybody has their price, he thought.

Rudolph still had concern about Poslov, mainly based on the information he was getting back from Antigua. He couldn't afford to have even the speculation of organized crime in St. Kitts. The other thing he couldn't afford was to have the Labour Party gain a foothold to the extent that he could lose the election.

CHAPTER 38

Stan Vickers was sixty-three years old and the former president of First National Bank of Hudson, in Hudson, Florida, where he had spent his entire banking career. His father had founded the bank in 1924 and survived the Depression. Vickers had started as a teller and worked his way through every position. When his dad retired in 1970, he became president and CEO.

First National Bank of Hudson was a small community bank that complied with all regulations, had excellent performance ratios, and had become, over the years, a model community bank in the eyes of the FDIC.

So when Stan Vickers sold First National to Regions Bank in 1986, he looked to stay involved in the banking business. His reputation was so good that the FDIC and the state of Florida often called on him to take temporary assignments in troubled banks, where he could assist in loan workout situations.

Stan Vickers was an old-time community banker, as conservative as they came, and the FDIC—in its infinite wisdom—thought that he could manage the multi-billion-dollar financial quagmire that Stanier had created.

Vickers was dressed in a polyester sports coat and a short-sleeved shirt with a plastic pen holder in the shirt pocket for his first day on the job. His appearance told everybody that he was a dufus, and when he left the building at 4:30 every day, just to get back to his hotel room, it wasn't long before people stopped paying attention to him.

Vickers was just a caretaker for the FDIC, since they knew it was just a matter of time before they would step in and close the bank down.

There were over three hundred people at the Hilton Hotel in Deerfield Beach, Florida, for the special shareholders' meeting of First Community Bank. All were requested to sign their proxies upon entering the meeting.

In front of a podium standing to the right of a head table, Robert M. Sales as the acting chairman—the title had been bestowed on him by Stanier and approved by the FDIC—called the meeting to order. At that head table were all the board members. Stanier, looking as effervescent and as confident as ever, was seated in the front row with the shareholders, next to his friend Larry Lewis. Poslov sat at the end of the head table, next to Ben Gilbert.

Sales called the meeting to order: "Ladies and gentlemen, my name is Robert Sales. I am general counsel for First Community Bank and have been asked to serve as acting chairman until the shareholders have ratified a permanent replacement for Mr. Stanier"

"I hereby call this special meeting to order," he went on, "And the first and only item on the agenda is to hear nominations from the shareholders for the position of Chairman of the Board, as well as to vote and appoint someone accordingly. Could I hear nominations from the floor?"

"Mr. Acting Chairman, I would like to make a motion for the nomination of Victor Poslov as chairman of the board of First Community Bank," said Stanier, standing up with his finger pointing toward Poslov.

There was utter shock and amazement that Stanier would do this. Sales cupped his hand over the microphone and said to Stanier, "Bruce, what the hell is going on?"

"I second the motion," said Gilbert, sitting next to Poslov.

Stanier disregarded the question and said, "Bring the meeting to order. There is a motion and a second on the table."

"There is a motion, and a second, on the floor nominating Victor Poslov chairman of the board," said Sales, visibly shaken.

The FDIC's Ken Stuart, sitting in the back of the room, simply shook his head.

The buzzing continued for several minutes while Stanier, Poslov, and Gilbert sat patiently, waiting for everybody to calm down.

"Please, let's have some order," asked Sales for the third time. "We need to have some orderly discussion before a vote is taken," he shouted.

A microphone was set up in the middle of the room, which shareholders could use to ask any questions.

"Yes, I would like to know what qualifications Mr. Poslov has for this position, which other board members don't have," ventured one shareholder.

"Mr. Stanier, would you care to respond?" asked Sales.

"Yes, the board of directors is aware of Mr. Poslov's background, since we circulated a copy of his résumé when he joined the board last month. As you know, the bank is being required to charge off several million dollars in loan losses and, as a result, will leave the bank capital impaired. Mr. Poslov, through his company—AEI in the U.K.—has agreed, in principle, to invest an initial fifty million in the bank with the firm possibility of thirty million more in the near future for a twenty-five-percent interest in the bank. We have yet to work out the final details of the deal, but to show good intent AEI has escrowed the funds awaiting the final paperwork.

"This transaction, of course, must be ratified by the shareholders and approved by the regulatory agencies," Stanier proceeded. "As part of the deal, AEI has required that Mr. Poslov be named chairman of the board, which, again, must be approved by the FDIC. I would hasten to add that if we do not obtain this additional capital, the bank will be declared insolvent and closed down.

"I have strongly disagreed with the FDIC on their opinions regarding the collectability of the loans, but it appears that they have sought the opinions of certain officers and directors of the bank who have agreed to charge off the figure. So now you have a choice: appoint Mr. Poslov or face the wrath of the regulators," Stanier stopped.

"Is there any further discussion?" asked Sales.

The room went quiet.

"Are there any other nominations from the floor?" Sales continued.

"Is there any further discussion?" he insisted.

Nobody answered.

"All in favor of the nomination to appoint Mr. Poslov chairman of the board of directors of First Community Bank, please raise your hand and say aye."

Stanier, North, Lewis, and a group of Stanier's "friends," employees, and sycophants said aye and held up their hands, of which the secretary took note.

"All of those who say nay to the motion, please raise your hand."

Just a few shareholders responded, but obviously an insignificant number.

"Motion carried," said Sales. "Meeting adjourned."

Stanier walked over to Poslov and shook his hand, "Congratulations, Victor."

"Thank you, Bruce."

The crowd soon disappeared, leaving a few non-employee shareholders confused about the amount of charge-offs mentioned by Stanier.

"Bruce, we knew that the bank was going through some tough times, but fifty-seven millions, Jesus Christ!" said one shareholder.

Stanier ignored him. Sales approached Stanier, wanting an explanation, but he ignored him, too.

That evening, Poslov, North, and Styles were invited to Stanier's place for dinner, where they discussed the lucrative opportunities in the West Indies.

At nine a.m. on Monday, January 8, Downes received a call from Crutchen's office asking him to attend a meeting with him and Townsend, to discuss an update on the investigation of George McLoud's murder. The meeting was scheduled for eleven a.m.

Downes thought it decent of them to include him in a meeting with law enforcement, but he also wondered what their motive was. They were not inviting him because they needed to keep him in the loop, he thought. If the truth be known, they would all prefer that he and Judy Smythe leave...but not before they turned over everything that they had uncovered.

Downes concluded that they knew about the briefcase, even though he hadn't yet heard that they had talked to Freddie Little. If they asked, he would deny ever seeing it.

Smythe had scheduled a telephone call with John Clemonds and Sheryl Mitchell to discuss a few things that Mitchell had found in the short time she had been back at the bank, so she and Downes agreed that he should go to the meeting alone.

He requested that a police constable accompany him to the meeting and made sure that one remained outside their room.

Meanwhile, two Antigua gang members had been sitting in the parking lot, waiting to see him leave his hotel room. They entered the hotel from the rear and caught the service elevator to the fourth floor, where a large laundry cart had already been posted, waiting for them.

Smythe answered the door, not thinking it could be anyone else other than the guard. At once the two thugs rushed at her, one of them immediately placing a chloroform-substance soaked rag over her face. The other started gathering documents, tapes, and the briefcase and stuffing them in a large gym bag. Smythe was out cold as the laundry cart was retrieved from the hallway and used to transport her to a vehicle waiting at the service entrance.

The police headquarters was just ten minutes from the hotel, but on the way over Downes found it odd that neither the FBI nor the RCMP had been mentioned in the planned meeting. He decided to call Smythe from his cell phone. No answer.

He called Rufus Caple, who picked up the phone on the first ring. Downes told Caple he was concerned and asked him to go to the room and check it out. By this time, he had arrived at police headquarters in time for the meeting.

Smythe was carted down the service elevator, the police constable who had been on guard outside the room making sure that they weren't seen. After the "all clear" was given, the laundry cart was hoisted into the van in the loading dock and driven south to the makeshift pier, which was used for transporting the drugs.

Caple, expecting a problem, radioed some of his buddies to head to the pier, to the Great Salt Pond, and to the commercial docks, asking that they report back if they noticed a white minivan with anything looking suspicious.

As soon as Downes got out of the police car, he flagged down a cab and asked the driver to get him to the hotel as quickly as he could. He raced through the lobby and ran up the four flights of stairs to the room, where he found the door wide open.

He called Caple, who was on his way.

"She's gone," Downes screamed. He raced back down to the lobby and didn't even bother asking if they had seen Smythe. They wouldn't tell him shit, anyway.

Caple drove up outside the lobby and Downes jumped in the car, not knowing where to look first.

Freddie Little had heard the call for help from Caple and was already heading south on the new road. He had been hired to take a couple of passengers from the cruise ship for a tour of the Southern Point.

As he approached the pier, he saw the white minivan that had been used in the McLoud kidnapping and the two guys who had killed him, carrying something to a boat moored at the dock. He radioed Caple to tell him, while his passengers wondered what the hell was going on.

Poslov wanted Smythe delivered to his place at the Wharf. She had information that he needed. He felt that she would be good collateral before disposing of her.

"Rufus, 'tis Freddie. Dey here, mon, at da point gittin on a boat," shouted Little.

Downes grabbed the mike and shouted, "Freddie, don't let 'em leave!"

Little told his passengers to get out. The old Subaru reached fifty miles an hour across a sandy road, before becoming airborne and crashing into the thirty-foot yacht, completely demolishing the two-hundred-horsepower engines, with Little lying slumped over the wheel.

Downes and Caple got there just after it happened, followed by three other cabbies. The Antigua thugs were already in the water, trying to get away. Downes was able to get Smythe out of the cabin and Caple able to get Little out of the Subaru, just before the boat and the car exploded into flames.

Equipped with tire irons and wrenches, the cabbies pulled the two guys out of the water and held them, hoping they would have the opportunity to beat the crap out of them.

When Smythe became conscious again, she wondered what was happening. Freddie Little was in bad shape, carefully being loaded into a cab and taken to the hospital in Basseterre.

They left the pier with the two guys tied to a bulkhead, concluding that it would be a waste of time to call the police.

Smythe was still a little shaky but alert enough to say that she agreed with him and how indebted they were to Freddie Little and all of Caple's friends who had helped them.

Downes mustered enough courage to tell Smythe that they had taken all of their documents, notes, tapes, and the briefcase…and that it all had gone up in flames.

"A good reporter always makes copies of everything. Sophie has the originals, even the tapes. They took the copies," Smythe smiled as she spoke.

Back at the hotel, Downes called Pete Sankowitz and Alberto Gomez and asked them if they could stop over to the room.

"Pete, we don't know who to trust here. We figure that Crutchen is involved up to his ass and would think that many on the force are on the take. They would have to be, in order for the moving-dope system to work. They know where the storage points are, they must know who the runners are…. Hell, the cab drivers know! And Crutchen is Walter Jones' Brother-in-law."

They turned over all the documents that had been found in the briefcase and what Sophie Albrightson had found at the bank, together with the notes and the tapes of many conversations.

After feeling good that they had all the facts of their investigation, but not too confident that those responsible for the crimes would eventually be brought to justice, Downes and Smythe packed their gear and headed to the airport under the watchful eye of the FBI and the RCMP.

They said their goodbyes to Sophie Albrightson and Rufus Caple, feeling uncomfortable about their well-being and making sure that they came to visit in Florida when all this stuff had settled down.

Since Mueller's murder, there had been little going on at First Investors. Kumar's government continued to investigate corruption in defense procurement and illegal weapons trade. Henry Blackstone was maintaining a low profile, while constantly looking over his shoulder and wondering when the next shoe would fall.

Dennis Fisk was elated that he had been able to convince the prime minister to give Poslov the go-ahead to build the hotel and couldn't wait to tell him.

CHAPTER 39

It had been three months since Judy Smythe and Terry Downes had gotten back from St. Kitts. Smythe had become a freelance writer and doing pretty well, and had finished an article on the investigation that she and Downes had conducted in St. Kitts. They were literally waiting for the fall out, since they knew something had to happen.

They had contacted the FDIC for an interview concerning Stanier and First Community Bank, but were denied, as expected. They both felt that the FDIC had to know what was going on, so they were prepared to let it take its course.

Poslov had settled in as chairman of the board, although the capital infusion had not yet been finalized. Poslov had told Stanier that AEI was not interested in preferred, non-voting shares, but wanted a fifty-one-percent interest in the outstanding common shares of the bank for fifty million dollars and that the deal would be conditioned on AEI's recruiting a president and CEO.

At first Stanier balked, as did other members of the board, since the immediate effect of dilution of their ownership would be dramatic. They all knew that this was their only option, so the paperwork was sent to the FDIC for approval.

Poslov had no clue on how to go about managing the board or conducting a bank board's meeting and relied heavily on the president of the bank, Stan Vickers, who simply went through the motions. The bank was compelled to provide the FDIC and the state of Florida with monthly financial reports in addition to the daily call reports.

The morale of the employees was at an all-time low and the shareholders wondered whether to sell their shares and take huge losses or hold on to them, in hopes of a turnaround in the bank's condition.

Vickers was a complete waste of time and generally would not entertain questions from employees concerning the bank's well-being. He simply showed up at the office at nine a.m. and putzed around till 4:30 p.m., with an hour for lunch. Nobody knew what he did for his one-hundred-fifty-thousand-dollar base salary.

Stanier, although removed and prohibited from entering the bank, continued to get information from, and give advice to, his circle of friends. He even brokered loan requests and was in touch with most of his good customers. Nothing had really changed except Stanier's physical presence in the bank.

In Stanier's eyes, North continued to be a confidant—something he used to his advantage—since he, North, was in awe of Poslov as well as of his money and power. Poslov had promised North a lucrative opportunity in managing the new hotel in addition to running First Investors.

The Russian gang was starting to transform AEI into a big, legitimate international financial conglomerate.

Despite the initial infusion of capital and the promise of a lot more, the bank's adjusted capital ratio was, by regulation standards, still very low. There had not yet been material recoveries from loans which had been charged off. Two of the bank's senior officers had resigned and customer confidence was starting to deteriorate as a result of some recent bad press.

Questions were being raised regarding the qualifications and background of Victor Poslov, who had yet to put his motive to use for investing in the bank.

Henry Blackstone, upon pressure from Poslov, appointed Jim North managing director of First Investors. Blackstone was nervous about North and Poslov's involvement, even more so since Poslov had taken over all business relating to the bank. The Russian Mafia was well established in St. Kitts.

Arma Lozo had sent the prime minister a letter saying that she was a representative from AEI and wanted to show appreciation for the government's having allowed them to proceed with the Frigate Bay property by offering to build a new school in Basseterre, an offer that Rudolph couldn't refuse.

Poslov was building a huge illegal enterprise in St. Kitts, even though there was much skepticism at AEI concerning the brokering of weapons deals. This part of the business had been put on hold, as it looked to the future of the Indian government, something Sastari had been working on.

Kumar was becoming the lame duck in the Indian Parliament. Throughout the first six months of being in office, his only concern had been to stop the rampant corruption in the defense-procurement program and investigate those involved in illegal weapons trading. The rest of his time was devoted to finding those responsible for the smear campaign against him, since he knew that it was the same group that had been forcing a confidence vote in parliament.

On June 1, 1990, Ken Stuart and Nate Collins from the FDIC and Henry Flick from Florida State Banking showed up, unannounced, at Stanier's old office building of First Community, where Poslov and the senior loan officers were located. They were accompanied by Stan Vickers, with whom they had just had breakfast.

Poslov was not in his office; he seldom was. They asked for the CFO, the chief lending officer, or whoever else was in charge, with an obvious sense of urgency. Stan Vickers called Bob Sales and Charles Garry and left urgent messages. Employees who had noticed the regulators started to buzz and within minutes, word had passed around that something big was going down.

Stan Vickers stood on the side of Stuart, Collins, and Jones in Stanier's old office the moment that Rick Gerhardt, senior loan officer; John Ebers chief operations officer; and Mark Chadwick, chief financial officer, entered the room and closed the door.

After the introductions were made, Nate Collins said, "Gentlemen, I regret to inform you that the Federal Deposit Insurance Company and the Banking Department of the state of Florida are exercising their right in declaring First Community Bank insolvent, and we are closing its doors."

The three bankers simply stared at the regulators, shocked and confused. "What does this mean, Mr. Collins?" asked Chadwick, innocently.

"The bank will continue to serve its depositors but the bank will operate under FDIC control. What this means, in essence, is that the bank is closed for business. Employees will be paid for hours worked, together with accrued benefits. Customer deposits will be insured up to one hundred thousand dollars and loans will be worked out in accordance with their related loan agreements. We will handle the workouts and retain those employees who we think are needed and would be willing to work with us. We have a team of people from the state and the FDIC which will be assigned to branch offices and coordinated from here by Mr. Stuart. I will handle the press," said Collins, clearly in charge.

"What happens to our shares in the bank?" asked John Ebers, who had his life savings in the Employee Stock Ownership Plan.

"The bank is a Florida corporation and is in liquidation. The stockholder equity will be zero after it liquidates the assets, in order to pay off the liabilities, including insurance pay out to the depositors. So, Mr. James, I'm afraid that your shares in the bank are worthless, another financial institution would be interested in buying them, said Collins, unapologetically.

James put his head in his hands, "Now, what do I do? I'm sixty-three years old!"

A notice was placed on the bank's public entrances of all branches and the press notified. The FDIC and the state had a total of sixty bank examiners controlling First Community's assets, and they had arranged temporary employment for a number of the employees.

Stanier was busy 'putzing' around his plants on his farm in Boynton Beach when he got the news from Larry Lewis: "Bruce, they've closed the bank down."

"They've what?" screamed Stanier.

"They've shut us down. There's more fuckin' regulators than employees and they've shut the doors. We have customers banging on the doors demanding an explanation," screamed Lewis.

"Call Sales and Garry, tell them what's happened, and tell this guy Collins to call me," ordered Stanier, slamming down the phone.

When the message got to Nate Collins that Stanier wanted to talk to him he said, "I have nothing to talk to Bruce Stanier about except arranging to pick up the antiques in his home, which belong to the bank."

Stanier was completely devastated, seeing his personal net worth diminish, in three years, from one-hundred-plus million dollars to practically zero.

Stanier's problems, however, were just beginning.

Nine Months Later:

Judy Smythe had planned to talk to a major international magazine in hopes of publishing the story, but held off awaiting the conclusion of the criminal investigation under way in St. Kitts.

Stanier went into seclusion for a few weeks after the heartbreaking news of the fall of First Community, the largest bank failure in the state's history.

No legal team in the world could have helped; it was simply cut and dry. Bob Sales was laughing up his sleeve, even though he had a sizable investment in the bank, as had numerous other business people who had been either hurt or disregarded by Stanier. He soon found out how many friends in business he really had.

Poslov was livid and vowed to get his, or AEI's, investment back. His friendship with Stanier was over and in its place, the he-said-he-said war of lawyers words. Poslov claimed that Stanier had misrepresented the condition of the bank when he invested the money and Stanier claimed that, as chairman, he had access to all the information he had needed prior to finalizing the deal. Poslov sued Stanier and all the board members individually, the FDIC, and First Community Bank claiming unlawful wrongdoing of two hundred fifty million dollars.

Stanier couldn't have cared less.

CHAPTER 40

The three-thousand-ton freighter known as the "Bucket" had been a part of Contec's operation in the Caribbean for ten years. It enabled the company to compete in the large construction market, its projects becoming more frequent throughout the islands. The company manufactured cement at its plant in St. Thomas, and the freighter shipped the cement and other building supplies to the building sites in the various islands. The aggregate used in the manufacture of cement was either mined on properties that Contec owned on certain islands or, if needed be, hauled from South Florida via the Bucket.

Contec had big problems in the late eighties due to slow or nonpayment of invoices for work completed for big foreign contractors. The company was spread too thin, grew too rapidly, and leveraged too high with the banks. Contec was involved in litigation with a number of island companies, which were protected by their governments whenever payments for completed work were held up due to apparent local code violations. The end result was, Contec was strapped for working capital.

Dennis Fisk heard about Contec's problems during the bidding of the deep-water port in Basseterre and referred the owner, Herbert Ball, to Victor Poslov.

Contec had won the bid on the deep-water dock project after paying off Fisk, but needed working capital to start the work. Fisk, in protecting his bribe, contacted Poslov to see if he would infuse capital into the company, thereby assuring that the job would be completed on time and within budget. Poslov purchased a twenty-percent interest in Contec for ten million dollars, under the condition that he would have complete access and control over the Bucket for personal use. It would afford him more of a stronghold in St. Kitts, geographical presence on other islands, and access to his own transportation in the Caribbean basin.

The Bucket was a rusty, old freighter registered in Panama and captained by Les Marshal, who had been a loyal employee of Contec for twenty years. During that time, he and a crew of ten had sailed to every island in the Caribbean at least a dozen times.

Poslov had told Herbert Ball that, since he was spending more of his time in the Caribbean, he wanted to use the Bucket periodically to haul some personal items from island to island. Marshal had been told of Poslov's involvement with the company and was to provide him assistance in whatever he needed.

Poslov had met Marshal when the Bucket was moored in St. John's harbor delivering cement to a small Contec project in Antigua. At the time, he told marshal of a shipment that he wanted picked up outside of St. Kitts and delivered to a point twenty miles off the coast of Fort Lauderdale. At first Chadwick raised his eyes and said that it wasn't feasible, but after Poslov offered him one hundred thousand dollars cash for each load delivered and a promise of the re-routing of the boat risk-free, he agreed to try a run.

The Bucket had made three runs for Poslov's people. Each time the old boat had stopped at a navigational point twenty miles off the coast of St. Kitts, met by small fishing boats which off-loaded three thousand kilos of cocaine, proceeded to a point twenty miles off the coast of Fort Lauderdale, and off-loaded the drugs onto fast boats. The weather had to be close to perfect and the moon obscure.

The deals were easy and the crew of the Bucket, mostly Indonesians, ecstatic that they were able to earn over two months' additional pay for a couple of hours of work and keeping their mouths shut.

Poslov was fat and happy. He had control over First Investors, Dennis Fisk, Henry Blackstone, and to some degree, Prime Minister Rudolph in St. Kitts. He was building a hotel/casino that would assist in the laundering of the huge amounts of drug money from the South American cartels, and although his investment in First Community had gone south, he was planning on expanding his operations to include a commercial bank charter in Antigua.

His having an interest in a large construction company to which the hotel project would be given, as well as access to transportation for his primary interests, was reason enough not to complain.

Pete Sankowitz and Alberto Gomez had all the information and evidence to convince the St. Kitts government that Henry Blackstone and Dennis Fisk were involved in a major drug-trafficking conspiracy and that First Investors Trust Corporation Limited, under the direction of Ernie Mueller and management of George McLoud, was the company that had laundered several hundreds of millions of dollars, all proceeds of drug and illegal weapons sales.

Most, if not all, of this evidence had been provided by Terry Downes and Judy Smythe in their attempt to determine the reason for the phony account and to clear Downes's name in any wrongdoing.

A meeting was arranged with Prime Minister Rudolph and members of law enforcement and their supervisors, to review the evidence and determine a course of action. In order to maintain confidentiality, the meeting was held on board of the St. Kitts Coast Guard's cutter moored at the old factory pier in Bird Rock.

Clive Townsend made the introductions: among the participants were Pete Sankowitz and his supervisor from the RCMP, Alberto Gomez; Sankowitz's supervisor from the FBI in Miami; and Townsend's supervisor from Scotland Yard in London.

The meeting was, for the most part, contemptuous, with PM Rudolph refusing to accept the fact that Dennis Fisk and Henry Blackstone were so deeply involved. He understood Walter Jones' involvement but was bitterly disappointed when evidence pointed to Crutchen and members of the police force. Rudolph shouldn't have been surprised, since they had already presented him with irrefutable facts.

"Dr. Baste," said Gomez, "we have all the evidence we need to arrest and charge a number of people on the island with conspiracy to traffic narcotics, bank fraud, wire fraud, etc., but we need to get more evidence on Poslov and his gang.

"The Izmaylovskaya gang, in which Poslov is a lieutenant," Gomez continued, "is composed of international terrorists as well as sympathizers and supporters of the LTTE, a terrorist group in Sri Lanka responsible for thousands of killings. They need to be stopped. If we charge local people before getting Poslov, we will miss a golden opportunity to stop these people."

Rudolph was lost. He knew that he hadn't been exactly forthright over the past several weeks and was feeling pretty lousy in agreeing to let Poslov develop the Frigate Bay property for extra cash for himself. It was time, first, that he redeemed himself and, second, to call on people who could assist him in these trying times.

Sir Brian Ashe was the former Governor General of St. Kitts and a major supporter and contributor to Rudolph's campaign for prime minister. However, when he got elected, he kicked Ashe out of government claiming that his services were no longer needed. Ashe was the privy council's leader, that is, the head of the court of appeals. This caused a major rift between them, which led Ashe to change ranks in political parties and support the Labour Party.

The one thing that Rudolph knew about Ashe was that he was impeccably honest, devoted to his country, and could be relied on to help resolve the issues at hand. Rudolph also knew that he couldn't call on him because of past problems, so he contacted Isabelle Clarke to see if she would head up a task force and ask Ashe to join her in investigating the crimes and bring those responsible to justice.

It was important to Rudolph that his government take charge of the situation and have the support of foreign countries, rather than the reverse. Clarke would lead the task force and have Sir Brian assist as a legal and constitutional advisor.

The task force was formed and included Clarke, Ashe—who was only too pleased to assist his country—and two retired judges with impeccable credentials.

Sankowitz, Gomez, and Townsend were advisors to the task force and answered only to them. They had their private meetings on board the coast guard's ship moored in the old harbor.

Meanwhile, Stanier was shaking in his shoes when told that a federal grand jury was meeting to consider a whole bunch of criminal charges against him. But he had been here before and had beaten them, so he thought he could beat it again.

Both Downes and Smythe were subpoenaed to testify in the Stanier case, which they were only too glad to do. They provided the lead prosecutor with all the documents and evidence they had which was pertinent to the case.

The federal grand jury handed down a twenty-three-count indictment against Stanier for, among other things, bank fraud, wire fraud, and conspiracy to traffic narcotics. He retained a team of lawyers which owed him favors and which began to prepare his defense.

Under the leadership of Isabelle Clarke, the task force garnered all the incriminating evidence it needed to arrest the players in the St. Kitts Connection. However, the coordination efforts had to be perfect since there was a risk that some would travel to foreign countries, where extradition laws were nonexistent, to avoid prosecution.

On the morning of August 20, 1990, Henry Blackstone received a phone call from Mrs. Stallworth asking that he join the prime minister at a confidential luncheon meeting on board the coast guard's cutter in Bird Rock. Blackstone thought it unusual for the prime minister to have a meeting on board the ship, especially without notice, and questioned Mrs. Stallworth on the nature of the meeting.

"I think it's to do with a request from St. Barts to use the ship for a problem they're having, since their governor is here," said Mrs. Stallworth, embarrassed for having to lie but proud of herself for thinking of a plausible reason for the meeting.

Although Blackstone didn't quite understand why he was being asked to go to a meeting without any forewarning, he shrugged his shoulders and thought that at least it was a free lunch. Blackstone caught a cab to the old dock and made his way up the ship's ramp after passing through some rudimentary security check. A sailor showed him to the captain's quarters where the meeting was being held.

"Good morning, Henry," said Dr. Rudolph, with Isabelle Clarke and Sir Brian Ashe sitting at a small table—clean of any papers or the usual coffee, tea, or water.

"What's going on here?" asked Blackstone, surprised to see everybody.

"Have a seat, please," said a somber-looking Rudolph.

"Henry, we are placing you under arrest for narcotics trafficking, bank fraud, wire fraud, and other charges that will be assessed later," said Clarke.

Had he not been sitting, Blackstone would have collapsed. He clasped his head with both hands as tears began to stream down his face. No comments from the two prosecutors sitting at the table or the two retired judges who formed the special task force. After a few minutes, Blackstone looked up at Rudolph and said, "Ken, please tell me what's going on."

"You know what's going on, Henry," said an insensitive Isabelle Clarke. "You must have known that you couldn't get away with all the money laundering that's going on, your involvement with Ernie Mueller, and recently Victor Poslov. We have documented evidence and supporting testimonies, Henry."

"Please stand," requested Rudolph, as one of the ship's officers prepared to handcuff Blackstone. We will be holding you temporarily here on board until all arrests have been made, and then you'll be officially charged and arraigned," said Clarke.

"What about my family?" asked Blackstone.

"We hope that all have been arrested within the next twenty-four hours. Until then, there will be no information released on your whereabouts."

Jim North had arranged to catch a flight to San Juan on the morning of the big day and was in the real-estate office gathering papers to take back to Florida for a meeting with Bruce Stanier.

"I don't think you'll be traveling today, Jim," said Special Agent Zach Mason, with a stern look on his face.

"What do you mean? What's going on?" asked North.

"Well, I thought they would be here by now, but I guess there has been some delay."

"Who will be here? What are you talking about?"

"You're done, Jim. It's over," said Mason, showing him a badge.

North was shocked beyond belief. "I'm leavin'," he said, as Mason pushed him back.

North was no match for Mason, so when he made an attempt to retrieve a gun from the top drawer of his desk, Mason simply lifted the entire desk and pushed it forward, leaving North in a tangled mess with the desk on top of him. Hearing the commotion, North's secretary came running in and then ran out saying, "Oh my God!"

Mason reached down, pulled North from underneath the desk, and said, "You'd better be still or you're going to get hurt."

Zach Mason had been working undercover since Draper and Ford had first set foot in Wellington. He had worked for Bill Grabowski in San Jose, California, and the two had become close friends, as originally planned, when in fact he had been, all along, a special agent with the FBI investigating white-collar crimes and corruption in local governments. Mason was given an assignment to monitor activities in the Kalahari Corporation, when suspicion had first arisen that illegal payments and kickbacks were being made on government bids, and then expanded to include drug trafficking. At the time, his arrest was made in order to hide his real identity. He was released from custody after all other arrests had been made.

Sergeant Pete Sankowitz arrived at the sales office to see Mason hovering over Jim North and telling him that it was all over. "Jim North, I'm Pete Sankowitz, with the Royal Canadian Mounted Police. I'm a member of a task force that has been formed by the St. Kitts government, which has been given powers to make arrests in matters concerning crimes committed in the country. In this regard, I am arresting you and taking you into custody on charges of narcotics trafficking and bank fraud."

North said nothing, as Sankowitz handcuffed and led him to his vehicle for transportation to the coast guard's cutter.

Dennis Fisk was at the fitness club when Inspector Clive Townsend and his assistant arrived. Fisk was hitting on two young ladies who had just finished working out when he was rudely interrupted: "Mr. Fisk, do you have a moment?" asked Townsend, looking very official and out of place in his business suit.

"Later," said Fisk, blowing off Townsend's request.

"No, not later, Mr. Fisk. I would like to talk to you now, if you don't mind."

"What is it?" asked Fisk, seemingly irritated as the two ladies walked away.

"Is there a place where we could talk in private?"

"Nobody can hear us, Townsend. What is it?"

"Very well, Mr. Fisk. You're under arrest for narcotics trafficking and conspiracy to commit murder."

"What are you talking about? Are you a fool?" asked Fisk, with a nervous laugh. " I have not committed any crime; and you have no powers to make an arrest anyway."

"I beg to differ, Mr. Fisk. A, we have all the evidence that you did, indeed, commit a number of crimes, and I have a warrant for your arrest; and B, Mr Rudolph has formed a special task force to investigate and prosecute those who have committed crimes. The task force has given me the power to arrest you. Oh, and C, I'm not a fool, Mr. Fisk. Please handcuff the gentleman."

Madder than hell, Dennis Fisk was led to a waiting car and transported to the ship.

MacCallister Crutchen was in his office when Townsend and his assistant arrived at police headquarters. "Mac, I'm sorry to inform you that I'm here to arrest you on charges of conspiring to traffic drugs in St. Kitts," said Townsend.

They had established a good relationship over the past several months, but Townsend knew that Crutchen had some involvement, since major leads in the investigation had been stonewalled and it could only have been done at the top. Crutchen was not surprised. In fact, Townsend thought that he was relieved that he, Crutchen, had been looking over his shoulder all the time, especially after Walter Jones had disappeared.

"I have warrants for the arrest of four of your constables, Mac. Could you tell me where I can find them?" said Townsend, providing Crutchen with a list of names.

Crutchen gave the whereabouts of the constables and each was arrested, without incident, by that day's end.

CHAPTER 41

When Jai Kumar was elected prime minister of India on December 2, 1989, it came as a huge surprise not only to those who had illegally lobbied to prevent him from getting elected but also to those in government when Kumar proposed that Devi Lal be made prime minister in a dramatic meeting in the Central Hall of Parliament on December 1. Devi Lal, in turn, said that Kumar should be prime minister and refused the nomination.

From the day that Kumar was elected, the forces were against him. As a result of the pressure placed on him by the opposition party and his chief rival, Chandra Shekhar, leader of the socialist People's Party, he lost a confidence vote in parliament and was relegated to the opposition.

This was great news for the likes of Poslov and his associates, since it paved the way for a number of pending transactions brought to the table by Sastari. Kumar had vowed to investigate the corrupt defense contracts and illegal arms deals brokered in India. These investigations, although in their infant stages, came to a sudden halt.

This was also good news for Semion Gasuchavik, since his business plan had called for the further expansion of weapons deals with certain terrorist factions and in countries where he had predicted major defense expansion.

THE ST. KITTS CONNECTION

The news of the dissolution of Kumars' government and the announcement that Rajiv Gandhi was, once again, running for office was rejoiced by many. However, shortly into his campaign, it was feared that Gandhi would send Indian peacekeeping forces back into Sri Lanka. This move was considered to be against the Tamil liberation struggle and against everything that Sastari wanted in the region. Poslov was upset because he knew that it would affect his heroin supply.

Sastari couldn't believe that his friend and main contact in government would do this. As soon as Poslov heard it, he placed a call to Sastari.

"I will have His Holiness call you at his earliest convenience," said Babbi.

"Make it soon," replied Poslov, closing the cover of his cell phone.

Poslov was mad as hell. He sat back in his chair in his office at the Wharf Hotel in Antigua, wondering why Gandhi would make this statement in a campaign speech when everything seemed to be going according to plan.

"Ah, Mr. Sastari," said Poslov. "Tell me, what's going on with your friend in New Delhi?"

"You heard the news, Mr. Poslov?"

"Yes, and I'm not very happy about it."

Sastari was a man of very few words, unless he was preaching.

"We need to talk," Poslov continued. "I will be in New York tomorrow. I will come to your flat and, please, don't make me wait."

Sastari had developed a deep hatred for Poslov and regretted the day he had agreed to work with him. Sastari claimed to be a loyal friend of Gandhi's, but his true loyalty was to the LTTE, which wanted and demanded secession from Sri Lanka.

Sastari was not happy when the little man told him that Poslov had arrived. He had not given thought to a plan to offer the Russian.

"Well, Mr. Sastari, have you given any thought to solving the problem?" asked Poslov, getting right to the point and still wearing his shoes.

"I was hoping that we could discuss some options," said a nervous Sastari.

"What options are there? Do you want to construct another phony account in the bank?" said the sarcastic Russian, with his screeching laugh.

Sastari didn't answer.

"Are you willing to let Gandhi bring in the Indian peacekeeping forces into Sri Lanka and destroy everything that we've been supporting and making money from?"

Sastari just stared at him.

"Let me tell you what I want," said Poslov, standing up, picking up the small statue of Shiva, and walking over to the window. "I want you to contact your people in Tamil Nadu and offer them a deal for his assassination. Your contacts in New Delhi can provide the logistics of his campaign itinerary and pinpoint where and when this could take place. We would need someone to sacrifice their life, which is the only way to handle it. You agree?"

Sastari still didn't answer.

"Mr. Sastari, I want this done. You understand?"

No response.

"Good. Let me know how much money it will take. But I think the LTTE would be honored to take care of this project, as long as your contacts can provide the information.

"Good," an exasperated Poslov went on, since nothing that he said elicited the Indian's response. "Well, then this will be done, correct?"

Again, no comment from Sastari.

"We will have a very serious problem if it is not taken care of," said Poslov, needing some kind of acknowledgement.

"Mr. Shekhar will serve us well, Mr. Sastari," he said, as he opened the bedroom door to see his own way out.

Sastari called Khallehki in a fit of desperation and asked if he could meet right away. He and Babbi left together and climbed the stairwell to Khallehki's palace.

"You can fret all you want, but we would be better off with Shekhar in office. Maybe not good for the country, but certainly better for us. He may be a socialist, but a very flexible one, and he would be more likely to send India to war against Pakistan than Rajiv would. He definitely would not interrupt the civil war in Sri Lanka, which would support your friends, and we will continue to provide them weapons.

Mr. Poslov will be happy for the time being, but if things work the way I'm planning, his happiness will be short-lived," said Khallehki, looking out of his window over Central Park.

"What do you have planned, Omar?" asked Sastari.

"He is a ruthless gangster and has made ridiculous demands. For this, he will pay. But first you must follow through with this: contact Prabhakaran in Tamil Nadu and explain what has to happen. They will tell you that the best way is by suicide bomber, since—if everything is done correctly—there will be no trace. Rajiv has been very vocal about his fate and believes that his death is imminent, anyway, since there have been numerous attempts on his life."

Sastari glared at Khallehki, feeling at peace with the project at hand and thankful for the wisdom and understanding of his friend.

"I love Rajiv, as do the two of you," said Khallehki, trying to rationalize his opinion. "But he is not the leader that India needs, and none of us would be able to tell him to stand down from his political aspirations."

Special Agent Mason boarded the Bucket in St. Barts, together with several other agents and members of other law-enforcement agencies. Les Chadwick and his crew were placed under arrest as the vessel was commandeered and heading toward St. Kitts carrying four thousand kilos of cocaine.

At the drop-off point north of the old fort, the agents arrested the operators of two fishing vessels and unloaded the drugs. Agents took over the vessels and made their way to Antigua, where other arrests were to be made.

Agents swarmed the Wharf Hotel with arrest warrants for Poslov. Simultaneously, agents raided the Helmsley Palace's penthouse and his condo in Palm Beach Polo in search for the Russian mobster.

Poslov had received a call from Herbert Ball, while he and Arma Lozo were waiting in a first-class lounge at Kennedy Airport to board a flight to Aruba, asking why the Bucket was being diverted from her regular route and why he couldn't reach Les Chadwick.

Poslov and his partner were to attend a meeting with a representative from the Calli cartel, during which payment for a shipment would be arranged.

"Victor, could you tell me why the ship was in St. Kitts and now headed to Antigua?" asked Ball.

"I have no idea. I didn't give them instructions," replied Poslov.

"She's carrying a load of cement that's supposed to be delivered to San Juan."

"Don't worry, Mr. Ball. I will find out and call you."

"The deal was that your side trips would only be done if there was no delivery date set for the usual cargo. What kind of cargo are you delivering to Antigua?"

Before Poslov could answer, Herbert Ball said, "Victor, I want to meet the ship in San Juan. Why can't I reach Chadwick?" he asked.

The Bucket was headed for port in Antigua and then the authorities would direct it to San Juan, Puerto Rico. It was captained by the FBI and completing her roundup of drug traffickers before delivering her main cargo to San Juan.

There was no response from Poslov as he slowly closed the top of his cell phone. "What's wrong?" asked Lozo.

"I need to reach Chadwick right away."

"Why?"

"I can't get a hold of Fisk, Blackstone, or North, and now Ball is asking why the ship is on a course to Antigua, when she's supposed to be delivering cement in San Juan. He wants to meet the ship there. What the hell is going on?"

"Well, let's just wait a while until somebody calls you back from St. Kitts," said Lozo, as Poslov's cell phone was ringing.

"It was Ball," said Poslov, as a message was being left.

Poslov tried again to reach his contacts in St. Kitts. Frustrated beyond belief, he called the office number at the bank.

"First Investors, can I help you?" said Sophie Albrightson, with a federal agent at her side.

"Yes, could you tell me where I can reach Henry Blackstone?" asked Poslov.

"May I ask who is calling?" asked Albrightson, taking instructions from the agent.

"Victor Poslov."

"Oh, Mr. Poslov, Mr. Blackstone is at home, very sick. Is there anything I can help you with?"

"No," said Poslov, very rudely, and hung up, but not before Albrightson and the agent listening had caught what sounded like the beginning of a flight announcement. "Flight 64...."

"He's at an airport," said the agent, placing a call to the FBI office in New York.

Within minutes, the FBI, the New York Police Department, and airport security personnel were put on alert for a person fitting a specific description and possibly waiting in an airport lounge.

"Flight 64" was the last call for a United Airlines flight from Kennedy Airport to LAX. Los Angeles

Security personnel were positioned at the gate while Poslov's name was searched through the computer.

Collecting their carry-on luggage, Poslov and Lozo made their way to the gate of Aruban Airlines flight 102. Still perturbed and very anxious, they were the last to board the full airplane.

As the plane was taxiing to the main runway for takeoff, the captain received a call from the tower asking that he return to the gate immediately and that he notify passengers of a minor equipment malfunction, which would only take a few minutes to correct.

As the ramp pulled closer to the plane, three FBI agents positioned themselves, ready to board. "Mr. Poslov, we would like you to come with us," said a young agent, immediately identifying the Russian sitting in the first row.

"What's this all about?" said the Russian, in a state of panic.

"Just come with us, and we will explain."

"Mr. Victor Poslov, I'm Special Agent George Hausner, FBI. You are under arrest for murder, conspiracy to commit murder, narcotics trafficking, bank fraud, and mail fraud," he said, as Poslov was read his rights and handcuffed without incident.

Flight 102 was buttoned up and allowed to leave, with Arma Lozo sipping on a Beefeater martini, shocked at what had just taken place but never questioned by authorities. Once again, she had avoided being linked to a major international crime.

The arrest of Victor Poslov marked the beginning of intense negotiations between Antigua, St. Kitts, Canada, and the U.S. in jurisdiction and subsequent extradition. The Wharf Hotel in Antigua was closed by the local authorities, and the transfer of property ownership in St. Kitts was declared null and void.

On May 21, 1991, eight months after the arrest of Poslov, came the news of Gandhi's assassination. Both Khallehki and Sastari rejoiced at the news of Poslov's arrest, but had decided to let their plans for Gandhi's demise stand. The LTTE had already been contacted and a person selected and confirmed to take on the mission.

Indian agents swarmed the government offices in St. Kitts, demanding answers to questions concerning the brokering of illegal weapons activities and the ties to Sastari.

On September 1, 1991, Chandrasastari Murkarji was arrested by the Indian Central Bureau of Investigation at his home in New Delhi for conspiracy in the assassination of Rajiv Gandhi. He was held in custody for six months prior to one of the most publicized trials of the century in India.

Two and a half months earlier, on the morning of June 15, Downes received a subpoena from the U.S. Attorney's Office in Miami to appear for a deposition on July 10 relating to the numbered account and the assassination of Rajiv Gandhi. Present at the meeting was Adi Patel, chief investigator from the Central Bureau of Investigation.

Downes arrived at the U.S. Attorney's Office with Art Lavelle and began a four-hour interrogation of his involvement, his knowledge, and his opinions of the entire St. Kitts Connection. Not once did Lavelle object to any question and Downes all along felt completely at ease with the questions asked by the Assistant U.S. Attorney.

There was little tangible evidence supporting the prosecution's case against Sastari in the assassination of Gandhi, although it was clear that he had played an active role. He was ultimately found "not guilty" in an Indian court. Neither was there evidence that Sastari had been connected to drug trafficking or illegal weapons deals. Both he and Khallehki escaped prosecution and both presumably went about their normal business lives.

EPILOGUE

- Jacques "Ernie" Mueller: Murdered by an assassin's bullet, ordered by Victor Poslov.

- George McLoud: Murdered by off-island thugs, ordered by Victor Poslov.

- Bruce Stanier: Found guilty of bank fraud and conspiracy charges. Served seven years in federal prison.

- Congressman Douglas Styles: Not charged with any crime, but resigned from Congress after it was reported that he had made sexual advances toward male pages.

- Chandrasastari "Sastari" Murkarji: Tried for the assassination of Rajiv Gandhi—subsequently acquitted.

- Omar Khallehki: Presumably retired.

- Prime Minister Dr. Kendall Baste: Returned to his medical practice after losing election to the Labour Party.

– Deputy Prime Minister Dennis Fisk: Served five years in prison and kicked out of government, as a result of illegal activities. Presently in the entertainment-promotion business in St. Kitts

- Walter Jones: Dissappeared

– Henry Blackstone: Served five years in prison. Disbarred. Presently owns a food store in Nevis.

– Chief Constable MacCallister Crutchen: Tried and found guilty of drug trafficking. Served five years in prison.

– Rufus Caple and Sophie Albrightson: Got married and have two children. Caple has a fleet of twelve taxicabs in St. Kitts.

– Zach Mason: Retired from the FBI.

– Jim North: Served eight years in St. Kitts and five years in the U.S. for organized crime.

– Victor Poslov: Served fifteen years for bank fraud and narcotics trafficking. Abandoned the hotel/casino project in St. Kitts and disappeared from Antigua. Whereabouts unknown.

– Judy Smythe is a freelance journalist in West Palm Beach, Florida.

– Terry Downes is a businessman in West Palm Beach, Florida.

www.ingramcontent.com/pod-product-compliance
Lightning Source LLC
Chambersburg PA
CBHW020453030426
42337CB00011B/103